Unfinished business

Items should be returned on or before the last date shown below. Items not already requested by other borrowers may be renewed in person, in writing or by telephone. To renew, please quote the number on the barcode label. To renew online a PIN is required. This can be requested at your local library.
Renew online @ **www.dublincitypubliclibraries.ie**
Fines charged for overdue items will include postage incurred in recovery. Damage to or loss of items will be charged to the borrower.

Leabharlanna Poiblí Chathair Bhaile Átha Cliath
Dublin City Public Libraries

 Comhairle Cathrach
Bhaile Átha Cliath
Dublin City Council

Date Due	Date Due	Date Due
2 1 MAR 2019		

MANCHESTER
1824
Manchester University Press

Unfinished business

The politics of 'dissident' Irish republicanism

MARISA McGLINCHEY

Manchester University Press

Published by Manchester University Press
Altrincham Street, Manchester M1 7JA

www.manchesteruniversitypress.co.uk

British Library Cataloguing-in-Publication Data
A catalogue record for this book is available from the British Library

ISBN 978 0 7190 9697 6 hardback
ISBN 978 0 7190 9698 3 paperback

First published 2019

The publisher has no responsibility for the persistence or accuracy of URLs for any external or third-party internet websites referred to in this book, and does not guarantee that any content on such websites is, or will remain, accurate or appropriate.

Typeset in 10.5/12.5 Adobe Garamond by
Servis Filmsetting Ltd, Stockport, Cheshire
Printed in Great Britain by
Bell & Bain Ltd, Glasgow

For my Mum, Kathleen McGlinchey
and
In memory of my Granny, Margaret McGlinchey

Contents

List of figures

Preface

This book is the product of seven years' research, the majority of which was conducted after gaining my PhD in Irish Politics from Queen's University Belfast in 2010. The topic of my thesis was the decline of the Social Democratic and Labour Party in the post-Good Friday Agreement period. My interest in the SDLP stemmed from intellectual curiosity coupled with familial connections to the party. Throughout my childhood I overheard many political conversations regarding the SDLP and Irish nationalism in general, thus igniting a passion for the study of Irish politics which has remained with me to the present day. Upon completion of my PhD, I embarked formally upon research into Irish republicanism and particularly what is commonly referred to as 'dissident' republicanism. My intellectual curiosity on the topic has been present for as long as I can remember. The Irish republican hotbed of West Belfast provided me with a multitude of experiences growing up, including peeking around the door of our living room as a child to witness my mum opening the front door of our home to British soldiers who were undertaking house raids in the area. Other vivid memories include school friends of mine looking through the view-finder of British soldiers' guns while on our way to school; or walking along a path home from school thinking I was alone and hearing a rustling in the trees, only to look closer and realise there were British soldiers in the surrounding greenery. Or I vividly remember opening the front door to go to school and finding a British soldier lying in the grass of the front garden of our home holding a rifle.

I recall an incident from my childhood when I dragged a chair from our dining-room into the kitchen to climb up on it and see the men with balaclavas who were patrolling through the street, constantly turning as they walked and observing all around them, and I further recall my mum coming into the kitchen and panicking, quickly lifting me down and saying 'we're not supposed to stare at those men'. Then, at the age of twelve, while travelling home to Belfast after visiting family in Dublin with my mum, our CIÉ bus was hijacked by the IRA on Daisyhill Road in Newry in 1996. As we sat in the front seat of the bus, the first indication that something was amiss was the bus bumping up and down footpaths to avoid burnt-out vehicles scattered on the road. Then, from the grass at the side of the road, emerged balaclava-wearing armed men who pointed their guns at the driver and while walking up and down the aisle of the bus demanded that everyone get off quickly. During that period, disturbances were taking place throughout the North of Ireland as the tension over Orange marches at Drumcree heightened. The IRA was strategically using buses to block roads across the North in protest. As soon as we had exited the bus the vehicle was blown up in front of our eyes, thus blocking the road, after which we walked down Daisyhill Road behind the Dublin driver, who was carrying his metal money box – no doubt a peculiar sight to any members of the public observing. As I grew older I became increasingly curious for knowledge about the events which surrounded me.

In another vivid memory, I recall being in my West Belfast home at ten years of age when I heard an avalanche of gunshots being fired. When I inquired as to what this was I was informed that the IRA was ceasing military activity and the shots signalled this fact. In the following days I witnessed a cavalcade of cars, including black taxis with tricolours hanging out of their windows, driving up and down the Falls Road, beeping their horns as an atmosphere of celebration and jubilation prevailed.

Throughout this research I have been asked by interviewees, who were often suspicious of an academic's motives, what my interest is in this topic. When I look back at my life to date, living in a republican heartland, it would be more curious had I not developed an interest in this topic. I can recall childhood memories of Gerry Adams coming into our area and being hailed as a God, and I developed a particular interest in those former comrades of his party who are no longer supportive of the mainstream Sinn Féin Movement. Around me in West Belfast I saw seeds of discontent blooming and growing, and more recently in 2007 I attended a Sinn Féin public meeting in Clonard Monastery. This meeting was one of several being held across the North of Ireland where senior Sinn Féin politicians were urging acceptance of the Police Service of Northern Ireland, a pivotal point in the journey of Sinn Féin from a revolutionary movement to a constitutional party. During this meeting, which took place in the actual church of the Monastery, I witnessed heated exchanges as people at the back of the church shouted words like *traitor* to the Sinn Féin politicians standing on the actual altar. This highly emotive experience left me with even deeper curiosity about the more nuanced picture regarding Irish republicanism than was being presented in the mainstream. I thus embarked on a journey of research which has culminated in this book.

This highly complex and emotive topic is not an easy one to write about. However, I feel that this is an important body of oral history that was in danger of being lost. In fact, some interviewees who have occupied senior roles in the Republican Movement and who gave me hours of their time to tell their story have since died, namely Tony Catney (Belfast), Gerry McKerr (Lurgan) and

Brendan Madden (Galway). Several of the interviewees for this work, including Gerry McKerr and Brendan Madden, have never given another known interview to any other study.

I would like to thank my interviewees for staying with this research through turbulent waters.

Dr Marisa McGlinchey
Belfast
December 2017

Acknowledgements

I would like to sincerely thank all the interviewees, without whom this book would not have been possible, and in particular Des Dalton, Richard O'Rawe, Gerard Hodgins, Angela Nelson, Tommy Gorman, Pádraic MacCoitir, Tommy McKearney, Geraldine Taylor, Fergal Moore, Ciaran Cunningham, Martin Óg Meehan, Brian Leeson, Louise Minihan, Andy Martin, Francie Mackey, Josephine Hayden, Christy Burke, Joe Dillon, Barry McKerr, Eamon Cairns, Jim McIlmurry, Anthony Ryan, Tomas Ó Curraoin, Francie McGuigan, Kevin Hannaway, Billy McKee, Michael McCann, Nuala Perry, Albert Allen, Mickey McGonigle, Hugh Brady, Gary Donnelly, Dessie McCrystal, Tommy McCourt, John Donnelly, Jim McCrystal, Gregory Creaney, Martin Duffy, Lita Campbell, Pádraig Garvey, Pat Quirke, Maurice Dowling, Dan Hoban, Richard Behal, Phil O'Donoghue, Jim McDonald, Fra Halligan, Dee Fennell, Stephen Hyslop, Michael Maigheo, Cáit Trainor, Mandy Duffy, Paul Kells, Bobby Keane, Veronica Ryan, Dr Anthony McIntyre, Máire Óg Drumm, Ciaran Mulholland, Peig King, Paddy King, Danny Morrison and Jon Tonge.

In memory of interviewees Brendan Madden, Tony Catney and Gerry McKerr.

With special thanks to the prisoners in Maghaberry prison: Gabriel Mackle, Martin Corey, Willie Wong and Nathan Hastings. I wish to sincerely thank their families, who so generously gave up their visits for me to conduct my interviews.

I would like to give special thanks to Des Dalton for his invaluable support and encouragement. I am deeply grateful. I would also like to give sincere thanks to Professor Robert W. White for his great support and kindness 'as we travel the same road' – words he wrote to me when signing his book in Dublin. Further, I wish to express sincere thanks to Dr Anthony McIntyre for his support.

I thank Professor Mike Hardy, Professor Harris Beider and Professor Alp Ozerdem in the Centre for Trust, Peace and Social Relations at Coventry University for their continued support for this book.

Finally, I would like to thank Manchester University Press for their on-going support and commitment to this book.

Glossary

1916 Societies	Irish republican organisation formed in 2009. The membership includes individuals who are also members of other republican organisations. In 2012 the Societies launched their single-issue campaign 'One Ireland One Vote', which seeks an all-Ireland vote on Irish unity
32CSM	Thirty-two County Sovereignty Movement, formed 1997
A chairde	Friends
Amhrán na bhFiann	Irish national anthem
An Garda Síochána	Police force in the South of Ireland
An Phoblacht	Sinn Féin newspaper
Ard Chomhairle	Ruling executive
Ard Fheis (plural Ard Fheiseanna)	Annual conference
Blanket Protest	Protest by republican prisoners in the H-Blocks of Long Kesh prison (the Maze). The protest began in March 1976 after the removal of special category status (political status). Prisoners on the protest refused to wear prison-issue uniforms, instead wrapping themselves in the prison blankets. The Blanket Protest culminated in the Dirty Protest of 1978 and ultimately the Hunger Strikes of 1980 and 1981
Boston College Project	Also known as the 'Belfast Project'. Research project which began in 2001. Oral testimonies were collected from IRA and UVF members, among others, on the understanding that the interviews would be stored in Boston College and not released until after the interviewee's death. The PSNI initiated legal proceedings in 2011 to gain access to the tapes

Bunreacht na hÉireann	Irish constitution, 1937
CABHAIR	Republican Sinn Féin, Continuity IRA, Irish Republican Prisoners Dependant's Fund
CAIN	Conflict Archive on the Internet. Archive containing information and source material on politics in the North of Ireland from 1968 to the present
Cathaoirleach	Chairperson
Ciorcal	local branch
Cisteoirí	Treasurer
Clár	Agenda
Cogús	Republican Network for Unity, prisoners' group
Coiste Seasta	Standing committee responsible for the running of the organisation between Ard Chomhairle meetings
Continuity IRA (CIRA)	Shares an ideology with Republican Sinn Féin, formed 1986
CRJ	Community Restorative Justice
Cumann	Local branch (plural = cumainn)
Cumann na gCailíní	Girls' republican organisation (ages 8–16), formed 1930s
Cumann na mBan	Women's republican organisation, formed 1914
DAAD	Direct Action Against Drugs
DMP	Dublin Metropolitan Police, founded in 1786. Distinct from the RIC, it was an unarmed police force covering the area of Dublin (city and county) and Co. Wicklow. The 'G' Division of the DMP was responsible for gathering intelligence. Under the Police Forces Amalgamation Act 1925, the DMP became part of the Garda Síochána in April 1925
DUP	Democratic Unionist Party
Éire Nua	Federalist policy of Republican Sinn Féin
Éirígí	Republican group formed in 2006 (name means 'arise')
ESRC	Economic and Social Research Council
Féile	Festival
First Dáil Éireann	Comprised Sinn Féin candidates elected in 1918 who abstained from Westminster and established a Parliament in Dublin's Mansion House on 21 January 1919
GAA	Gaelic Athletic Association
GARC	Greater Ardoyne Residents' Collective
GFA	Good Friday Agreement
GPO	General Post Office, O'Connell Street, Dublin

Green Book	IRA training manual focusing on aims, objectives, security and resisting interrogation
Hooded men	The fourteen hooded men were interned in August 1971 and were subject to sensory deprivation interrogation techniques by the British army and RUC, including the use of white noise, sleep deprivation, food and drink deprivation, hooding, and were forced to stand in 'pressure positions' (including standing on their toes with only their fingertips against the walls)
Inghinidhe Na hÉireann	'Daughters of Ireland'. A nationalist movement founded by Maud Gonne and Constance Markievicz at Easter 1900. It led protests against the visit of Queen Victoria to Ireland in 1900 and was instrumental in preventing Dublin Corporation from delivering a 'Loyal Address'. It produced a magazine, *Bean na hÉireann* (*Women of Ireland*) from 1908. The movement was incorporated into Cumann na mBan in 1914
INLA	Irish National Liberation Army, formed 1974. Known as the military wing of the Irish Republican Socialist Party
IRA	Irish Republican Army
IRB	Irish Republican Brotherhood. Secret oath-bound society founded in 1858. It was responsible for the 1867 uprising and was instrumental in planning the 1916 Rising. Disbanded in 1924
IRPWA	Irish Republican Prisoners' Welfare Association
IRSP	Irish Republican Socialist Party
Leas-Chathaoirleach	Vice-chairperson
MI5	British intelligence and security agency
MLA	Member of the Legislative Assembly in the state of Northern Ireland
Na Fianna Éireann	Boys' republican organisation, formed 1909
New IRA	In 2012 RAAD, the REAL IRA and independents merged into the 'Irish Republican Army' which became known as the 'New IRA'
NICRA	Northern Ireland Civil Rights Association
Óglaigh na hÉireann (ONH)	Irish Republican Army
OIOV	One Ireland One Vote campaign by the 1916 Societies, established in 2012

Oireachtas	Irish Parliament
PIRA	Provisional IRA, formed 1969
Provisionals (Provos)	Provisional IRA. 'Provisionals' is also commonly used to refer to the wider 'Provisional' Sinn Féin Movement
PSNI	Police Service of Northern Ireland
RAAD	Republican Action Against Drugs
REAL IRA	Shares an ideology with the 32 County Sovereignty Movement, formed 1997
Republican Bulletin: Iris Na Poblachta	Paper produced by Republican Sinn Féin from 1987 to 1988
RIC	Royal Irish Constabulary. Founded in 1836. It was granted the title 'Royal' for its role in suppressing the IRB Rising of 1867. It was disbanded in 1922 as a result of the Anglo-Irish Treaty
RNU	Republican Network for Unity, formed 2007
Roes Three and Four	Wings in Maghaberry prison which house republican prisoners
RSF	Republican Sinn Féin, formed 1986
RSM	Republican Socialist Movement
RTÉ	Radio Telefís Éireann, TV station
RUC	Royal Ulster Constabulary
Rúnaí	Secretary
Saoirse	Republican Sinn Féin newspaper (meaning 'freedom')
Saoradh	Republican group, translates as 'liberation', formed 2016
SAS	Special Air Services. Special Forces Unit of the British army
SDLP	Social Democratic and Labour Party, formed 1970
Sinn Féin	Irish political party, translates as 'Ourselves alone'
Teachta Dála (TD)	Member of Dáil Éireann
The Disappeared	People who were killed and secretly buried by the Provisional IRA; typically after being accused of being an 'informer' or agent for the RUC or the British security services. The Independent Commission for the Location of Victims' remains was set up in 1999 with the purpose of obtaining information which may lead to the location of the remaining missing bodies
TUV	Traditional Unionist Voice. Political party in the North of Ireland. Formed in December 2007
UDR	Ulster Defence Regiment. An infantry regiment of the British army, 1970–92

Urlabhraí	Spokesperson
UUP	Ulster Unionist Party
UVF	Ulster Volunteer Force

Introduction

The present leadership of Sinn Féin – if they were out for an Irish Republic they failed. If they were out for civil rights they got it in 1973. So what the fucking hell was the other thirty years of war for?

Kevin Hannaway, interview with the author, Belfast, 24 July 2013

On the steps of Stormont

On 10 March 2009 Martin McGuinness, the deputy first minister of Northern Ireland and former Provisional IRA commander, stood on the steps of Stormont alongside the PSNI chief constable Hugh Orde and First Minister Peter Robinson to address the assembled press in the wake of the killing of PSNI constable Stephen Paul Carroll in Craigavon the previous night. The killing was claimed by the Continuity IRA (which shares an ideology with RSF) and took place days after the killing of two British soldiers, Mark Quinsey and Patrick Azimkar, at Massereene Barracks in Antrim, which was claimed by the REAL IRA (which shares an ideology with the 32CSM). During the press conference Martin McGuinness vehemently condemned the organisations which had carried out the attacks, stating 'these people, they are traitors to the island of Ireland. They have betrayed the political desires, hopes and aspirations of all of the people who live on this island.'[1] McGuinness's comments provoked a strong backlash from non-mainstream republicans, as was reflected in a statement from the 32CSM which read: 'the British Strategy has now reached its pinnacle with a Provisional Sinn Féin leader standing at Stormont, under the British flag, as a minister of the British crown, calling IRA volunteers "traitors" for continuing to resist British occupation.'[2]

McGuinness's comments were widely viewed as a watershed moment in Irish politics, with the *Irish News* heralding his statement as 'a De Valera moment'.[3] The press conference served as a visible testament to the vast and bitter gulf which exists between the Provisional and so-called 'dissident' worlds. It was a seminal moment in contemporary Irish politics in which Sinn Féin was forced (despite the party's continued republican rhetoric) to ultimately declare its position; the time had come for Sinn Féin to unequivocally demonstrate its allegiance to the state of Northern Ireland, including the institutions of the state such as the PSNI. In this respect Ed Moloney described McGuinness's comments as 'the Four Courts moment in the Northern Ireland peace-process'.[4] Moloney argued that 'the dilemma facing the leaders of Sinn Fein, Gerry Adams, Martin McGuinness and their colleagues is, in its essentials, exactly the same that Michael Collins faced some 87 years ago'.[5]

McGuinness's statement and the subsequent reaction from republicans evidenced a bitter divide within the contemporary republican world, the fault lines of which can be traced back to the late 1970s when republican comrades assumed opposing sides on fundamental ideological and strategic issues. As the fault lines deepened and became entrenched, former comrades became bitterly divided. The republican world has witnessed instances of 'staunch' republican families divided along 'mainstream' and so-called 'dissident' lines, reminiscent of the Irish Civil War period of the 1920s. A prominent example of such contemporary familial division was evidenced in an interview conducted by the author with Belfast radical republican Kevin Hannaway, a former adjutant-general in the Provisional IRA, one of the 'hooded men' and a first cousin of Sinn Féin President Gerry Adams. When referring to the connection, Hannaway quipped 'he is a cousin of mine, not the other way round'.[6] Similarly, in an interview, the late Tony Catney of the 1916 Societies in Belfast remarked 'you know that Gerry Kelly is my brother-in-law?'[7]

Close your eyes and it could be the Provos in the '80s

The 'traditional' Irish republican ideology and stance which are articulated by non-mainstream republicans could be mistaken for the message of the Provisional IRA and Sinn Féin in the 1970s and 1980s.[8] Statements released by so-called 'dissident' organisations, as well as political speeches given throughout the country at republican commemorations, are often synonymous with the language and message that were presented by the Provisional Sinn Féin Movement in the 1970–80s. When assembled at gravesides of 'fallen comrades' around Ireland, radical republicans are listening to the same message at the same gravesides as they did as members of the Provisional Movement in the 1970s and 1980s. Thus radical republicans such as Hannaway and Catney have asserted the continuity of their republicanism and have emphasised that it is 'Provisional Sinn Féin' which has altered its message and thus 'dissented'.

Sinn Féin as an organisation has transformed into a constitutional party which at times is required to reconcile its present identity with its past, as was demonstrated in May 2017 when the Northern leader of Sinn Féin (and deputy First Minister of Northern Ireland) Michelle O'Neill came under criticism from unionist commentators regarding a republican commemoration in Cappagh for the eight IRA men that were killed at Loughall in 1987. Responding to unionist criticism, O'Neill argued that there is 'no contradiction' in Sinn Féin's outreach to unionists while simultaneously commemorating IRA volunteers, and stated that republicans are 'proud of our freedom struggle'.[9] O'Neill continued: 'Let me be clear. I am an Irish republican. Make no mistake about it – I will always remember and commemorate our patriot dead – and each of our fallen comrades who gave their lives for Irish Freedom.'[10]

The mainstream Sinn Féin message has shifted from one which emphasised 'freedom' to one which emphasises 'equality'. Thus forms the pinnacle of the 'Provisional–Dissident' divide. At the heart of the competing narrative rests an emphasis from Sinn Féin on the altered structural conditions within the state of Northern Ireland. While organisationally disparate, 'dissident' republicans are united around their rejection of the significance of changed structural conditions within the North, and make a significant distinction between ideological Irish republicanism and a civil rights agenda which was paramount within the Provisional Sinn Féin message throughout the late 1980s and early 1990s. Sinn Féin's call for sovereignty in the form of a thirty-two-county Republic has become secondary to demands for equality. Sinn Féin has advanced the argument that equality 'within' the North of Ireland would form a stepping stone to Irish unity.[11] Radical republicans have rejected this narrative and have continued to assert their belief that altered structural conditions within the North of Ireland do not impact on republican ideology or activism. Radical republicans have labelled the altered conditions as 'reform' rather than 'radical change', locating such arguments within a narrative which rejects the 'normalisation' of the state of Northern Ireland.

Good Friday

Almost unanimously, radical republicans have asserted that the Good Friday Agreement does not significantly change anything for ideologically driven republicanism. However, the Good Friday Agreement *did* alter the conditions in which radical republicans are operating due to its enshrinement of 'parity of esteem', 'mutual veto' and 'segmental autonomy'.[12] Enshrined as a right is the ability to be formally recognised as 'British', 'Irish' or both. Formal recognition of both cultures, coupled with the principle of consent, has led the mainstream to question why radical republicans persist with their campaign, both violent and non-violent. In response, Bernadette Sands-McKevitt, a founder member of the 32CSM and sister of Hunger Striker Bobby Sands, famously stated 'Bobby did not die for cross-border bodies with executive powers. He did not die for nationalists to be equal British citizens within the Northern Ireland state.'[13] Radical republicans are united in their belief that Bobby Sands did not die for internal power-sharing in the state of Northern Ireland. They are also united in their opposition to the current political process. However, the radical republican family is fraught with division regarding strategy. Such fundamental division helps to explain why, despite calls for republican unity, the radical republican world remains so fragmented with little prospect of formal unity.

Principles versus tactics

A central plank in the contested narratives of Provisional and radical republicanism concerns the issue of what constitutes a tactic and what constitutes a principle. Central to the republican message is the assertion of 'principles' which must not be compromised regardless of a changed environment. Since the mid-1980s Provisional Sinn Féin has presented ideological shifts as 'tactical' and has argued that this does not compromise 'principle'. In contrast the radical republican narrative continues to warn about the 'slippery slope' to constitutionalism which inevitably befalls those who emphasise tactics to alter republican fundamentals. Debate which has raged around tactics versus principles has struck to the very heart of what it means to be a republican. The question of what constitutes fundamental principles is deeply contested between the Provisional and radical republican worlds; the most notable examples being Provisional Sinn Féin's ending of abstentionism in 1986 or acceptance of the Mitchell Principles in 1997 which removed the long-held position of Irish republicanism that the consent principle was tantamount to a 'unionist veto'.[14]

The mainstream message propagates the narrative that 'dissident' republicanism emerged (and is sustained) in opposition to the IRA ceasefires of the 1990s and the subsequent final decommissioning in 2005. However, a closer study finds that while the ending of the armed campaign (and subsequent decommissioning) is significant for a number of radical republicans it is secondary to their opposition to the Mitchell Principles and the Provisionals' acceptance of the consent principle. This fact is unsurprising given that acceptance of the consent principle removes the ideological rock upon which republicanism has rested. Sinn Féin's acceptance of the principle of consent greatly altered the political stage. Central to the Irish republican message is the assertion that the Irish people as a whole have not undertaken an act of self-determination since 1918. This argument has provided a major cornerstone in republican justification for the armed campaign. The consent principle undermines the ideological basis of republicanism regarding the 'unit' for 'self-determination'. Therefore Sinn Féin's acceptance of the consent principle was a major departure from republican ideology.

The long trajectory

So-called 'dissident' republicanism is located within the long trajectory of Irish republicanism stretching back to the Fenians of the 1860s and the United

Irishmen of 1798.[15] The location of radical republicans in the continuum of Irish republicanism is evident not just ideologically but also through the 'living link' of the people involved. For many interviewees their activism pre-dates the formation of the Provisionals in 1969, notable examples being Peig King in Dublin (originally from Tyrone), Paddy King in Dublin, Dan Hoban in Co. Mayo, Richard Behal in Killarney in Co. Kerry, Billy McKee in Belfast, Maurice Dowling in Tralee in Co. Kerry, Phil O'Donoghue in Kilkenny, Mickey McGonigle in Dungiven in Co. Derry, Tommy McCourt in Derry and Joe Dillon in Skerries in Co. Dublin, among others. The radical republican narrative rejects the word 'dissident' given that many activists have not altered their politics or ideology, but rather argues that the Provisional Movement has altered course and has moved away from radical republicanism.[16]

Given that non-mainstream republicans have not altered the republican beliefs which they have continually held, and given the 'living link' to the pre-peace process period (and in fact to the pre-1969 period), this study predominantly does not refer to 'dissidents' but rather uses terms such as 'non-mainstream' and 'radical republican' interchangeably. The terms 'Provisional Movement' and 'Provisionals' are used in an all-encompassing sense to refer to the mainstream, and Provisional Sinn Féin is largely referred to as 'Sinn Féin', as distinct from Republican Sinn Féin. Notably, Republican Sinn Féin reject the Provisionals' continued use of the name 'Sinn Féin', arguing that the individuals who stayed in the Ard Fheis in the Mansion House in Dublin in 1986 were the true 'dissidents'. RSF has argued that the ending of abstentionism regarding Leinster House signalled an ideological departure from the politics and constitution of Sinn Féin.

The contestation of language and terminology reflects the complex nature of the subject, and an understanding of the contested terminology contributes to our understanding of the nature and politics of the radical republican world. The word 'dissident' as propagated by the mainstream in the North and South of Ireland strikes fundamentally at the heart of republicanism, undermining the ideological continuity of the republican struggle. The word, as it is used in the mainstream, also contains a challenge to the legitimacy of radical republicans. The location of 'dissidents' within the long trajectory of Irish republicanism demonstrates the cyclical nature of the development of the movement. The central themes of contestation within contemporary radical republicanism – thus principles versus tactics, the 'slippery slope to constitutionalism', fears of 'sell-out', and the ethics and morality of an armed campaign in current conditions – have remained consistent throughout Irish history and have assumed importance during the 1916 Rising, the Irish Civil War and the IRA border campaign of the 1950s–60s, also known as Operation Harvest. Drawing on books such as Bell, White, Hopkinson, English and O'Brien (among others), this work reflects on significant debates which were taking place within the leadership of the Republican Movement around tactics, ceasefires and 'dump arms orders' at significant junctures in republican history. Notably, the same debates are arising in the internal narrative of radical republicanism today. Irish republican Dan Keating joined Na Fianna Éireann in 1918 and subsequently joined the IRA. Keating died in 2007 at the age of 105, having been patron of RSF from 2004 until his death.[17] Undoubtedly Keating witnessed the same aforementioned issues arising within republican debate at the various junctures from the Civil War in the 1920s to the present day.[18]

Electoral mandate

An issue which has repeatedly surfaced throughout republican history is the contesting of elections as relative to the 'slippery slope'. The contemporary Sinn Féin message is dominated by references to the party's electoral mandate in the North and South of Ireland. Since 2001 (when it eclipsed the SDLP) Sinn Féin has been the largest representative of the nationalist community in the North of Ireland. Sinn Féin is operating within a consociational power-sharing system where intra-ethnic out-bidding and electoral competition are more significant than inter-ethnic competition. Cross-community voting figures remain negligible.[19] Sinn Féin has successfully moderated its message to that of a constitutional political party while simultaneously emphasising its 'green' credentials in its appeal to the republican base.

A central component in the Sinn Féin critique of 'dissidents' is the latter's lack of an electoral mandate or public support. An indication of levels of support for 'dissidents' was first presented in the 2010 general election survey in the North of Ireland conducted by Professor Jonathan Tonge which was funded by the ESRC. The survey found that 14 per cent of those identifying as nationalists claimed 'sympathy for the reasons behind dissident republican violence'.[20] This finding was publicly rejected by Sinn Féin at the time. Crucially, radical republicans do not derive their mandate from the ballot box, nor do they seek their mandate from the electoral process. Therefore, through their own testimonies, the question of mandate (and from where it is derived) is examined; and 'dissidents' are located within the historically deterministic tradition of Irish republicanism.

Armed struggle

Radical republicanism is heterogeneous in nature. Radical republicans are divided regarding support for an armed struggle at present, with views spanning from outright support to outright condemnation. PSNI security figures demonstrate a sizeable amount of guns, ammunition and equipment which have been seized from radical republicans in the recent period, since 2015.[21] However, the armed campaign is sporadic and minimal at present. Based on primary interviews with spokespersons for the Continuity and REAL IRAs, as well as current prisoners who were arrested for offences including possession of firearms or explosives, this study examines the rationale behind continuing the armed campaign, given the fact that the Provisional IRA's sustained and high-level campaign did not achieve its objectives.

Based on first-hand testimonies with spokespersons for armed organisations, mainly in the North of Ireland, an insight is provided into who joins armed 'dissident' organisations and what they hope to achieve. Within the radical republican world there exists a nuanced spectrum of views on the armed campaign; debates are taking place between republicans regarding the utility of violence and whether there should be any republican prisoners in the current climate. The fact that the majority of interviewees fall into the 'non-condemnation' category regarding support for a current armed campaign is unsurprising given the history of Irish republicanism, which is largely reflective of this position. Reduction of 'dissident' republicanism to simply those who seek to continue the armed campaign provides a less than holistic view of radical republicans.

Peace-processing

The Irish peace process has been transported around the world as a model process; however, the issue of 'dissident' Irish republicanism is not one that will 'go away' and constitutes the 'unfinished business' of Irish republicanism. The dominant narrative on the Irish peace process largely fails to acknowledge the fact that there are current republican prisoners in Maghaberry and Hydebank prisons in the North of Ireland and in Portlaoise and Mountjoy prisons in the South of Ireland. This popular narrative fails to acknowledge that republicans who are opposed to the political process (and have been arrested in the post-Good Friday Agreement period) exist beyond this legislation, and in notable cases such as Martin Corey and Marian Price republicans have been imprisoned for up to four years without trial. Interviews with current republican prisoners in Maghaberry prison enable an assessment of the ideology and strategy of current republican prisoners.

Research of this nature relies on personal testimony and oral history as one cannot consult IRA council minutes or even Sinn Féin Ard Chomhairle minutes. While oral history has its critics, who may argue that interviewees may simply provide a false narrative for the purpose of the research, rigorous academic analysis has been conducted on the vast amount of material collected (alongside triangulation of sources), including extensive thematic coding across the interviews which spanned location, gender, age and organisation. This book adheres to a sentiment expressed by Richard English in *Armed Struggle: A History of the IRA*: '[T]his book is written in the belief that, whether one supports the IRA or not, it is important to understand what they have done, why and with what consequences – and to do so in terms of serious, detailed explanation rather than simple stereotype.'[22] Similar to works by English and White, this study seeks to delve into the psyche of radical republicanism through the actual voices of republican activists.

Notes

1 A. Fox, 'Widow of PSNI officer hails Martin McGuinness for denouncing "traitors"', *Irish News* (20 January 2017).

2 O. Bowcott, 'Hardliners vent their fury at Martin McGuinness', *The Guardian* (13 March 2009).

3 *Ibid.* The phrase 'De Valera moment' is making reference to De Valera signing the oath of allegiance to the British king in September 1927, which ended abstentionism and resulted in Fianna Fáil taking their seats in Leinster House. During the Civil War De Valera fought against the state; however, once in power he interned hundreds of former IRA comrades. See The Earl of Longford and T.P. O'Neill, *Eamon De Valera* (London, Arrow Books, 1974).

4 Ed Moloney, 'Now Sinn Fein MUST break with their old friends', *Mail Online* (16 March 2009). www.dailymail.co.uk/debate/article-1160647/ED-MOLONEY-Now-Sinn-Fein-MUST-break-old-friends.html. Accessed 1 November 2017.

5 *Ibid.* On 28 June 1922, following an ultimatum from the British government to take action against anti-treaty republicans who had occupied the Four Courts building in Dublin, the Pro-treaty Provisional government under Michael Collins used field guns borrowed from the British army to bombard the Four Courts. This marked the beginning of the Irish Civil War.

6 Kevin Hannaway, interview with the author, Belfast, 24 July 2013.

7 Tony Catney, interview with the author, Belfast, 14 September 2012.

8 Radical republicans frequently cite a BBC interview with Martin McGuinness in 1982 during which McGuinness stated 'at the end of the day, it will be the cutting edge of the IRA which will bring freedom'. This clip can be viewed on YouTube: www.youtube.com/watch?v=nzvpMlHuIrs. Accessed 4 July 2018.

9 D. McAleese, 'Michelle O'Neill tells republicans she is "proud of freedom struggle"', *Irish News* (1 May 2017).

10 *Ibid.*

11 See R. English, *Armed Struggle: The History of the IRA* (Oxford, Macmillan, 2012).

12 Good Friday Agreement, 10 April 1998.

13 S. Breen, 'Sister of hunger-striker denounces peace process as deception', *Irish Times* (8 January 1998); see also English, *Armed Struggle* (2012), p. 317; and T. Hennessey, *The Northern Ireland Peace Process: Ending the Troubles?* (Dublin, Gill &Macmillan, 2000), p. 112.

14 Northern Ireland Political Collection, Linenhall Library, Belfast, P3394, 'Papers and Correspondence from Gerry Adams and Sinn Féin to SDLP', 18 March 1988.

15 L. Ó Broin, *Revolutionary Underground: The Story of the Irish Republican Brotherhood 1858–1924* (Dublin, Gill &Macmillan, 1976), pp. 1–2.

16 S. Whiting, *Spoiling the Peace? The Threat of Dissident Republicans to Peace in*

Northern Ireland (Manchester, Manchester University Press, 2015); M. Frampton, *Legion of the Rearguard: Dissident Irish Republicanism* (Dublin, Irish Academic Press, 2011).

17 Patron is an honorary position within Republican Sinn Féin, bestowed on an individual who is a 'veteran of the republican cause' and who has given life-long service to the Republican Movement. The patrons of RSF are Tom Maguire (1987–93), George Harrison (1994–2004), Dan Keating (2005–7), Ruairí Ó Brádaigh (2009–13) and Peig King (2015– present).

18 See an interview with Dan Keating in *Saoirse: Irish Freedom*, No. 234 (October 2006).

19 See G. Murray and J. Tonge, *Sinn Féin and the SDLP: From Alienation to Participation in Northern Ireland* (London, C. Hurst & Co. Publishers Ltd, 2005).

20 J. Tonge, '"No-one likes us; we don't care": "dissident" Irish Republicans and mandates', *Political Quarterly* 83:2 (2012), p. 225.

21 PSNI, 'Police recorded security situation statistics'. www.psni.police.uk/ Accessed 28 July 2018.

22 English, *Armed Struggle* (2012), p. 338.

1

Who are the 'dissidents'? Motivations and aspirations: the drawing of the fault lines

I have no home like Martin McGuinness in Donegal, or Gerry Adams. I don't want to have a home like that. All I want is a free united Ireland and that's all the people who came before me wanted. But these people took gold and as I said at Ruairí Ó Brádaigh's funeral – Ruairí Ó Brádaigh took no gold.

Dan Hoban, Republican Sinn Féin (from Mayo), interview with the author, Dublin, 3 November 2013

When you look at the like of McGuinness and what he has done – McGuinness shaking hands with the Queen – you've donned the red of England, you're England's creature now.

Francie McGuigan, interview with the author, Belfast, 24 July 2013

I would say this is the most difficult time to be a republican, an Irish republican, in the history of republicanism.

Pádraic MacCoitir, éirígí, interview with the author, Belfast, 4 October 2012

There's no use recruiting young people into a movement if you don't educate them on why they are there and what the end result is.

Peig King, Republican Sinn Féin and Cumann na mBan, interview with the author, Dublin, 26 July 2016

Introduction

The dominant narrative on so-called 'dissident' republicanism has failed to adequately convey a thorough understanding of exactly who the 'dissidents' are and what their aims are. Drawing on qualitative in-depth interviews with radical republicans throughout Ireland, this chapter seeks to explore who joins 'dissident' organisations (both violent and non-violent), what their motivations are, and what they hope to achieve in the long and short term. Interviewees include the leadership of Republican Sinn Féin, the leadership of Cumann na mBan, Na Fianna Éireann members, the leadership of the Thirty-two County Sovereignty Movement, IRPWA members, 1916 Societies members, the leadership of éirígí, a senior member of the Republican Socialist Movement in Belfast, members of Republican Network for Unity, members of Saoradh, spokespersons for the REAL IRA and spokespersons for the Continuity IRA; as well as individuals who formerly held senior positions within the Provisional IRA both in the North and South of Ireland. Interviewees also include members of Republican Sinn Féin cumainn in Nottingham, Stafford and Birmingham. This chapter details interviews with a wide spectrum of active radical republicans – as stated by Paul Nolan, 'the most obvious source of information on the well springs of "dissident" republicans can be found in the accounts they themselves provide'.[1]

Through in-depth analysis of personal testimonies, it is possible to identify individual agency and elicit an understanding of what motivates radical republicans. This work draws on Social Movement Theory and the work of Donatella Della Porta which seeks to 'identify some common processes that are present … [M]echanisms should allow us to build general causal explanations.'[2] Della Porta has described a mechanism as 'a precise, abstract and action-based explanation which shows how the occurring of triggering events regularly generate the type of outcome to be explained'.[3] Through identifying 'common processes' this chapter will illustrate the significance of the following on the development of radical republicanism: family background; ideological changes in the mainstream Provisional Movement; a sense of betrayal by the mainstream Provisional leadership; and belief in the continuity of the struggle.[4]

Within the mainstream narrative, republican 'dissidents' have been described as 'former Provisionals who can't let go', spoiler groups,[5] vigilantes and criminals,[6] micro-groups,[7] 'traitors to Ireland'[8] and as 'ostensibly serving little purpose other than to annoy Sinn Féin by highlighting the party's U-turns and hypocrisies (from a political perspective)'.[9] On the formation of éirígí,[10] Horgan has commented 'like many dissidents before them, éirígí emerged due to the perceived failings of Sinn Féin'.[11] However, locating the emergence of radical republican groups as simply a reaction to Provisional Sinn Féin or the Provisional Movement fails to holistically understand the nature of such organisations. Many non-mainstream republicans maintain that the views which they presently hold are the same views that they have always held; similarly their activism is the same activism which they have always undertaken. Former members of the Provisional IRA or of Provisional Sinn Féin have argued that their political position remains consistent; in contrast Provisional Sinn Féin has altered *its* position and has thus 'dissented'.

Several interviewees were active in the Republican Movement prior to the formation of the Provisionals in 1969, thus dispelling the common narrative that 'dissidents' are 'Johnny-come-latelys'. Analysis of so-called 'dissidents' as simply ex-Provisionals is inaccurate and devoid of historical context. A failure to recognise this potent fact will inhibit an understanding of the motivations of such republicans in the contemporary period. Interviewees were drawn from the North and South of Ireland, were male and female, and represented a wide age spectrum from nineteen to ninety-three. It is notable that some narratives to date have predominantly focused on the North of Ireland, disregarding the significant fact that the leadership of RSF, the 32CSM and éirígí reside in Kildare, Kilkenny and Dublin respectively.

Regarding occupation, interviewees in the North and South include community workers, elected councillors, members of conflict resolution services, a retired psychiatric nurse, a farmer, a mature student at Trinity College Dublin, taxi drivers, a barrister and two solicitors, among many other professions; thus compounding the findings of an ESRC 2010 general election survey, conducted by Tonge and Evans, which commented on 'dissident sympathy' by stating 'most demographic and occupational categories fail to reach statistical significance'.[12] Based on the survey evidence, Tonge concluded that 'the (very limited) tendency towards dissidence is held by those making an ideological choice rather than one necessarily conditioned by structural factors'.[13] As stated by J. Bowyer Bell, 'in national movements the spectrum of individual rebels is apt to be sufficiently wide to include all types and professions. Even those who have something to lose if the cause succeeds – privilege or power – are often represented, certainly by their children.'[14]

Family connections: an insular world

Biographical information on the ninety interviewees for this work reveals a nuanced picture of radical republicanism and challenges the dominant narrative which suggests that radical republicans are 'lurking in the shadows'. In contrast, radical republicans are frequently integral and visible members of their communities. Numerous radical republicans come from long-standing republican families and, reminiscent of the Civil War period in the 1920s in Ireland, many traditional republican families have split along Provisional and radical republican lines.[15] As noted earlier, prominent contemporary examples include hooded man Kevin Hannaway, who is a cousin of the Sinn Féin President Gerry Adams. Another example is Tony Catney, who was a brother-in-law of Sinn Féin's Gerry Kelly. Des Dalton, the President of RSF, contested the council elections in Athy, Co. Kildare in 2004 and 2009. During the campaign his election posters could be viewed on lamp-posts alongside those of his brother, Mark Dalton, who was contesting the election for Fianna Fáil, leading their parents to state that they had a system where each parent would give a first and second preference to each brother. The republican world is an insular one and therefore such close familial links across the spectrum are unsurprising. During the course of the research, links often emerged between interviewees, one example being Cecilia Conway from Kildare, who is a member of RSF and Cumann na mBan. When the author mentioned radical republican Anthony McIntyre to Mrs Conway she replied 'that's my first cousin'.

Bob White's *Provisional Irish Republicans: An Oral and Interpretive History*

(1993) has illustrated the importance of family tradition in the Provisional republican world. Similarly, in *Clandestine Political Violence* (2013), Donatella Della Porta has emphasised the significant influence of family tradition on political activism. Throughout this study interviewees from republican families have recalled experiences of family members (including parents) being arrested for republican activity. They have also cited house raids as significant formative influences on the development of their republicanism. Kevin Hannaway in Belfast has recalled, 'my mother went into hysterics. I was a child and I remember holding her apron and squealing and the house had been demolished.'[16] Kevin Hannaway, an independent republican and one of the hooded men,[17] spoke of his father's involvement in republicanism and recalled an incident from his childhood when an elderly priest named Father Marcellus visited his classroom and asked the boys what they wanted to be when they grew up, to which Hannaway replied:

'I'm going to be an IRA man like my daddy' … He never really said anything and gave me a sweet like he did the other children but I remember the teacher saying to me 'tell your mother that I want to see her in the school tomorrow'.[18]

Another prominent Belfast republican, Billy McKee, has recalled formative childhood influences. McKee remembered his grandmother minding him as a child when his parents were at work, and stated:

I was playing with my wee tin soldiers with my grandmother and she sang old republican songs – Who fears to speak of '98, Kevin Barry, the wearing of the Green, and I was singing them with her … later on I started asking questions. We were only kids when these lads used to bring us round the parks, up to chestnut trees, and they were saying that's a chestnut and that's a birch tree and I said 'but where's the gallows tree?' And the older ones all busted out laughing. I thought the gallows tree where Kevin Barry was hung was one of them trees.[19]

As illustrated by McKee and Hannaway, family tradition has assumed a central characteristic throughout the history of Irish republicanism and in fact some republicans' records with the Special Branch began at their own christening, as was the case with Seán MacBride. Elizabeth Keane has cited the following Special Branch report on MacBride's christening:

Chief Commr, DMP informs Inspector General RIC that McBride [sic], accompanied by his mother arrived in Dublin on 30th … and returned home on 2nd instant. Most of their time was spent at Mrs McBride's, and on 1st they were present at the christening of 'Major' McBride's child. Like the wedding, the christening was a political event. The flag of Inghinidhe na hÉireann was prominently placed in the midst of John MacBride's guns and sword from the Boer War.[20]

Historical continuity emanating from family experience is rooted in the radical republican psyche, as demonstrated by RSF's Brendan Madden who, when discussing his own republican activity, stated 'a lot of my ancestors were killed fighting them going back as far as Cromwell'.[21] Stories which have been passed down from parents and grandparents have proven highly influential in the development of the majority of the interviewee's republicanism; interviewees often located *their* republicanism within a long trajectory of republican history dating through ancestors and contextualised in the wider republican struggle 'against occupation in Ireland'. A significant number of interviewees from the North and South of Ireland recalled selling republican newspapers as a child as well as attending republican commemorations with family members. Fra Halligan of the RSM in Belfast has stated:

> The republican socialist movement will always carry its support base from father to son to daughter. And it will be small but it will always be there. There will always be a core of support.[22]

Similarly, Dan Hoban of RSF has referred to the influence which his family had on the development of his politics. Hoban was born in Castlebar, which was a garrison town, and has made reference to his family home by stating:

> My mother's house was headquarters of the IRA in the Black and Tan war and my mother's two sisters were involved in Cumann na mBan. My mother made me very aware of all this when I was going to school.[23]

Hoban's father was also politically active, having been interned in Ballykinlar camp in Co. Down during the Black and Tan war. Hoban has stated 'he was first taken to Galway and his brothers – and their father was a judge in the Sinn Féin courts in 1918'.[24] Hoban also cited the influence which his school education had on the development of his politics, stating 'I had a Kerry man, a de la Salle brother whose people were IRA down in Kerry and he would give a history lesson once a week which I looked forward to and I also got it from there.'[25]

The research also elicited interviews with individuals who do not come from republican backgrounds but from Fianna Fáil or SDLP backgrounds, or have no familial background in politics but were drawn to radical republicanism through their own experiences. Many cited the Hunger Strikes of the 1980s as pivotal in the development of their republican politics.

Hunger Strikes: a formative period

It is certain that the Hunger Strikes of the early 1980s constituted a significant formative period for many republicans today. In 1980, during the first Hunger Strike in the H-Blocks of Long Kesh prison, republican prisoner Sean McKenna was within hours of dying. At that time the current President of RSF, Des Dalton, was nine years old and attending St Patrick's Christian Brothers school in Athy in Co. Kildare. As the pupils and parents attended a school concert that night the school's principal, Brother Kenny, asked those in attendance to rise from their seats to sing the national anthem Amhrán na bhFiann and 'to remember the young Irishmen who were at that very moment on Hunger Strike in a jail only one hundred miles away'. Dalton recalled, 'as the national anthem was played it had a profound effect on me'.[26]

The Hunger Strikes of 1980 and 1981 have proven not only a formative influence but are also bitterly contested, as evidenced in exchanges in the *Irish News* in 2005 and 2008 between Danny Morrison and radical republican Richard O'Rawe after the release of the latter's book *Blanketmen*. In *Blanketmen* (2005) and subsequently *Afterlives* (2010) O'Rawe claimed that the Provisional leadership have 'said one thing and done another', and this is most evident regarding the Hunger Strike of 1981 in which ten republican prisoners starved themselves to death after political status had been removed from the prisoners in 1976.[27] This 'holy grail' of Irish republicanism has formed a central plank in the message of Sinn Féin and republicanism in general; therefore O'Rawe's explosive claims regarding the 1981 Hunger Strike have struck to the core of the Provisional Sinn Féin narrative.

In his books O'Rawe has claimed that elements within the Sinn Féin leadership outside the prison were duplicitous with the prisoners regarding what was on offer from the British.[28] O'Rawe has suggested that the Provisional Sinn Féin leadership knowingly allowed the Hunger Strikers to die unnecessarily in order to boost the electoral fortunes of the party.[29] He has argued:

> Adams for definite and Morrison directed, negotiated directly with the British over our heads. Never showed us the statement from the Secretary of State for Northern Ireland, gave us a brief outline … Never told the Hunger Strikers anything of substance about any of this. They merely told them there was a contact with the British and for whatever reason they said they rejected the offer, after we accepted and consequently Joe McDonnell died.[30]

O'Rawe has cited David Beresford's *Ten Men Dead* as integral to his realisation, stating that he read the book after his release from prison. O'Rawe pored through the communications ('comms') in Beresford's book and has stated:

> I realised there was major major flaws in the line that Sinn Féin was putting out in the way they were telling people the Hunger Strike went … You try to put them to the back of your head because you don't want to think the worst.[31]

O'Rawe's narrative is vehemently contested by Danny Morrison and by Sinn Féin, who have rejected the argument that the leadership had a 'long strategy' in place. O'Rawe's revelations have proven central to the development of a narrative throughout the radical republican base which argues that the leadership of the Republican Movement, or a section within it, misled the base regarding the overall strategy of the leadership in relation to the direction in which the movement was progressing.

Perceptions of duplicity and resentment

Existing literature on radical republicanism has highlighted the significance of the various 'breaking points' from the Provisional movement for individuals now labelled 'dissidents'. So-called 'dissident' groups can be divided into RSF (1986) and the 32CSM (1997), and latterly groups which have been formed in the post-1998 period. While ideological breaking points are detailed, the mainstream narrative has largely neglected to incorporate the significance of 'resentment' and 'perceptions of deception and betrayal' towards Sinn Féin from former members of the wider Provisional Movement. This narrative of betrayal and duplicity forms a central plank in the radical republican message. As highlighted above, O'Rawe is a prominent example of an individual who departed Sinn Féin and the Provisional Movement (in 1985) due to the perceived 'duplicity' of the leadership, stating:

> I don't trust them. I don't think they are even genuine republicans ... all they were really doing was conditioning people. They are always conditioning people for their next move.[32]

The argument that 'Sinn Féin was saying one thing and doing another' was prominent throughout the interviews and was cited by 100 per cent of individuals (who are former members of the Provisional Movement or Sinn Féin) as a significant factor in their decision to leave Sinn Féin, and for some to subsequently join a radical republican organisation. O'Rawe's publications have struck an emotional chord with republicans and have contributed to a feeling that there was an overall 'plan' or 'mission' on the part of the Sinn Féin leadership which was not shared with the grassroots of the organisation.

Republican Sinn Féin

Accusations of duplicity on the part of the leadership also exist regarding the period preceding the Hunger Strikes of 1980 and 1981. Lita Campbell (originally from Cork) is a History and Literature graduate from Trinity College Dublin and is a prominent member of RSF and Cumann na mBan in Dublin. Campbell has been on the editorial committee of RSF's newspapers *Republican Bulletin: Iris Na Poblachta* and *Saoirse* since 1987 and has been a member of the Republican Movement since 1971. In 1980 she was a member of the committee for the first Hunger Strike in Long Kesh prison and recalled a feeling of being 'talked at'. Campbell has stated:

> They were saying 'oh dear what shall we do, they are going to go on Hunger Strike whether we like it or not' and it didn't make any sense to me because they were volunteers. So I said 'have you ordered them not to?'. The response was, 'oh they wouldn't do what they were told'. That was bullshit.[33]

Campbell has asserted her belief in O'Rawe's claims, based on her own experience within the Republican Movement, and has stated 'I don't think you could have saved the first four ... but I think the last six should never have died. I have never believed they should.'[34] Contemporary criticism of the Provisional Sinn Féin leadership has centred on a belief that the prisons were being 'used for a purpose'.[35] Similarly, Dan Hoban (a former senior member of the Provisional Movement), when discussing the period of the Hunger Strikes, has stated 'I do have a lot of queries as to how the men were let die and there was messages sent and messages that weren't sent – and were they sacrificed?'[36] It is apparent that O'Rawe's arguments have permeated throughout the radical republican base. Angela Nelson in Belfast, who was a member of Sinn Féin from 1970 until 3 July 2012, has commented on O'Rawe's arguments regarding the Hunger Strike and the position which has been propagated by some radical republicans that the Hunger Strikers were allowed to die unnecessarily to boost the electoral fortunes of Sinn Féin:

> It's monstrous to even deal with that. I can't emotionally deal with it and every time it comes into my head I close the door to it quite quickly because I lived through it. I knew many of the Hunger Strikers on a personal level who were friends of mine as was their families. I just can't cope with that, you know. But the older I get the more sceptical I have become. I think that those people in power whether they're elected or otherwise are capable of anything. And it is scary.[37]

The 1980s: the drawing of fault lines

Literature on so-called 'dissident republicanism' has often focused on the North of Ireland and on the post-Good Friday Agreement period, thus neglecting the fact that the fault lines of 'dissent' were actually drawn from the early 1980s. Robert W. White has traced 'dissent' back to the 1970s, stating that 'soon after their formation [Provisional Movement] there began a gradual change in the leadership of the Provisional Irish Republican Movement as the southern-based old guard were replaced by a northern-based mix of old guard and younger republicans'.[38] In the 1960s similar ideological conflict had occurred over the issue of entering Leinster House which culminated in the 1969/70 split and the emergence of the Provisionals and Officials. In 1966 Republican Sinn Féin member Pat Quirke was a member of the North Kerry executive of Sinn Féin which was expelled after their criticism of the then party leadership regarding reports of potentially entering Leinster House.

In *An Phoblacht* in February 1970 those expelled, who had by then thrown their support behind the emergent Provisional Movement, 'called on all true republicans to reject the idea of recognising either Leinster House or Stormont'.[39] The individuals in Kerry made reference to what they regarded as a 'rigged' 1970 Ard Fheis and stated '[I]t brings out into the open at last the deceit and treachery which has been going on in the Republican Movement for the past five years, we welcomed its revelation.'[40] The piece continues, 'have they so set their hearts on the kudos of the parliamentary way that the advantage to the cause of national unity and freedom is no longer considered?'[41] In total 250 members (13 cumainn) were expelled from Sinn Féin at that time over the issue. Pat Quirke went on to be a founding member of RSF in 1986.

A critical point was reached in 1982 at the Sinn Féin Ard Fheis during which Gerry Adams called for the removal of the policy of federalism from the Sinn Féin constitution.[42] The federalist policy was a key policy of Ruairí Ó Brádaigh and Dáithí Ó Conaill which called for the creation of four regional Parliaments in Ulster, Munster, Leinster and Connaught. White has stated that Adams argued against the federalist policy, fearing 'they would never escape loyalist domination – that the IRA might win the war but lose the peace for them in a loyalist-dominated federal state of Ulster'.[43] Significantly Adams won the debate and consequently at the 1983 Sinn Féin Ard Fheis Ruairí Ó Brádaigh resigned as president of Sinn Féin, citing 'a lack of support for his policies'.[44] At this stage Dáithí Ó Conaill also resigned as vice-president of Sinn Féin. The fault lines were drawn.

Describing himself as 'the first fallen soldier', Dan Hoban departed the Provisional Movement in the early 1980s prior to the 1986 split.[45] Hoban, who went on to become a leading member of RSF, has claimed that in the lead-up to the split:

> The Provos went around and they picked every man's brains … and all those who went from the Republican Movement to set up a political organisation that would be with the status quo – they didn't make the same mistake as the people in the past made. They sussed out everybody and they took control before they made their move.[46]

Hoban has recalled the 1979–80 period by stating:

> There was one occasion where I was sent into a situation where I wasn't going to come out of. They wanted me arrested and they sent me with a crowd of men into the camp and we got away, but it wasn't their intention that we would get away so then I was more or less court martialled – they would say 'you're not carrying out your job'. So what I said to them was well maybe I'm slipping or something but what you're putting up against me I don't dig.[47]

Further, Hoban has recalled that during that period he was asked his opinion of then Sinn Féin President Ruairí Ó Brádaigh. He has commented:

> Well I said to them, 'my opinion of Ruairí Ó Brádaigh is this. If I were going into battle in the morning', I said, 'he'd be the man I'd be with because', I said, 'I wouldn't be looking back over my shoulder to see was he coming after me because he would be two paces in front of me'. So the writing was on the wall for me after that.[48]

In fact in 1986, the emergence of RSF under Ruairí Ó Brádaigh signalled the beginning of what would come to be termed 'dissident republicanism' in the modern period. Among those who exited the Ard Fheis in 1986 behind Ó Brádaigh were Peig and Paddy King from Dublin.[49] Peig King first walked in Bodenstown (the burial site in Co. Kildare of Wolfe Tone, who was leader of the Society of United Irishmen) in 1942 as a member of Cumann na gCailíní and her first parade in Cumann na mBan uniform was in 1947. Peig is the present patron of RSF and is a senior figure in Cumann na mBan. Recalling the period leading to the 1986 split, Peig King has recalled visiting Dáithí Ó Conaill in prison in 1977 and telling him 'there's a take-over', to which Ó Conaill responded 'I want you and certain people to stay and the time will come when you will be needed'.[50] King proceeded, '[S]o I rounded up the Cumann na mBan women and I told them to stay.' Peig King has commented:

> It got to the stage in the early '80s where I wouldn't know if a meeting was on, neither would Lita Campbell because they felt, and they were right, that we would probably have given the game away on them. So they picked their personnel well.[51]

Referring to this period in the 1970s, Peig King has stated that the republican prisoners in the jails didn't know what to believe and has commented:

> Some of the boys in the jails, they didn't know who to believe. They were getting stories from different people and they were getting orders from different people and they came to realise that the orders that they were getting were from our famous friend Adams … They were not coming from the council … the prisoners didn't know because he was their liaison.[52]

Paddy King, a member of the Republican Movement since the 1950s (King was on the Gough Barracks raid in Armagh in 1954) has stated 'that was the disaster'.[53] In reference to the confusion of that period, Peig King has recalled that Cumann na mBan were instructed to disband and has stated that in 1986 'they told everybody down tools, you're dismissed. So a few of us at the top, we had a terrible job to convince people that it was more important to be there now.'[54] At this time it was publicly announced that Cumann na mBan were dismissed. Richard Behal in Kerry, who has been involved with the Republican Movement since the mid-1950s, has referred to this period by stating 'a coup d'etat was taking place within the IRA'.[55]

Resolution 162: the formation of Republican Sinn Féin

On 2 November 1986 at the Sinn Féin Ard Fheis, resolution 162 stated:

> That this ard-fheis drops its abstentionist attitude to Leinster House. Successful Sinn Féin parliamentary candidates in the 26-county elections:

a. Shall attend Leinster House as directed by the Ard Chomhairle.

b. Shall not draw their salaries for personal use. (Parliamentary representatives shall be paid a Sinn Féin organiser's subsidy, and the Leinster House salary shall be divided at the direction of the Ard Chomhairle to defray national and constituency expenses.)[56]

The resolution detailed how the Sinn Féin constitution would be amended to 'accommodate this change'. As Ruairí Ó Brádaigh prepared to make his speech Gerry Adams reached over to shake his hand. Ó Brádaigh took Adams's hand and then stated to the hall 'A chairde I'll shake hands with everyone and at every time, not just in front of the media.' The stage was set for a bitter battle over the issue of abstentionism – which would come to be known as the first breaking point in the emergence of what is commonly referred to as 'dissident republicanism'. Ó Brádaigh described the motion on the clár (and the consequent debating of it at the Ard Fheis) as 'totally out of order'. In his illuminating speech he stated:

> The discussion is totally out of order if this constitution of Sinn Féin means anything. Because it says there that no person who approves or supports candidates going into Leinster House, Stormont or Westminster shall be admitted to membership or allowed to retain membership, and yet on this floor we have plenty of resolutions proposing to go into Leinster House and indeed some of them proposing to go into Westminster and Stormont as well because they want to end abstentionism altogether …
>
> It says here [Sinn Féin constitution] the first allegiance of Irish men and Irish women is due to the sovereign Irish Republic proclaimed in 1916. It doesn't say that we go into Leinster House or Stormont or Westminster.
>
> We were told last night that we can agree to disagree on fundamentals, how in the name of heavens can we do that?
>
> I ask you to reject 162 and to accept 184, and, in God's name, don't let it come about that tomorrow, the next day or the day after, that Haughey, FitzGerald, Spring and those in London and Belfast who oppose us so much, can come out and say, 'Ah it took 65 years, but we have them at last.'
>
> Never, that's what I say to you – never.[57]

Martin McGuinness, then vice-president of Sinn Féin, spoke in favour of resolution 162 and stated:

> I can give a commitment on behalf of the leadership that we have absolutely no intention of going to Westminster or Stormont.
>
> Sadly the inference that the removal of abstentionism would lead to the demise of military opposition to British rule has indeed called into question the commitment of the IRA to pursue the struggle to a successful conclusion.
>
> I reject any such suggestion and I reject the notion that entering Leinster House would mean an end to Sinn Féin's unapologetic support for the right of the Irish people to oppose in arms the British forces of occupation.
>
> This Ard Fheis and you, the delegates, deserve to know the whole story of this

debate. In fact, what you're witnessing here is not a debate over one issue, but two – abstentionism and the leadership of the republican struggle.

The reality is that the former leadership of this movement has never been able to come to terms with this leadership's criticism of the disgraceful attitude adopted by them during the disastrous eighteen months' ceasefire in the mid-1970s.[58]

Dáithí Ó Conaill, who was at the Ard Fheis (but not as a party delegate), expressed his anger at the back of the hall, particularly at the last paragraph quoted above in McGuinness's speech, due to the fact that McGuinness was part of that 1975 leadership and had been involved in the talks of the mid-1970s. After a lengthy debate, motion 162 succeeded, with 429 in favour of dropping abstentionism and 161 opposed.[59] Consequently Ruairí Ó Brádaigh led a walkout from the Ard Fheis, and those who had departed reassembled at the West County Hotel in Chapelizod, County Dublin. As detailed by Robert W. White, the assembled group were asked by the press what their attitude was to Sinn Féin, to which they responded 'We are Sinn Féin.'[60] In the final years of Ó Brádaigh's life he commented on the 1986 Ard Fheis by stating 'it was as if I could see a whole lifetime's work being lost'.[61]

The emergence of RSF in 1986 has been significantly detailed in Robert W. White's *Ruairí Ó Brádaigh: The Life and Politics of an Irish Revolutionary*. The emergence of the organisation has also been described in Liam Clarke's *Broadening the Battlefield*,[62] Ed Moloney's *A Secret History of the IRA* and Bowyer Bell's *The IRA: 1968–2000*. Building on the aforementioned literature, this work seeks to provide an insight into the formation of RSF (and the currents at that time) through interviews with individuals who exited the Ard Fheis behind Ó Brádaigh and Dáithí Ó Conaill and who reassembled at the West County Hotel.[63] As Robert W. White has stated, 'by car, van and bus, the walkouts made the half hour trek to the West County Hotel in Dublin's suburbs … by six o'clock in the evening, 130 or so people – 'hard-liners' the BBC called them – were reassembled in a banquet room. Joining them were forty or so reporters.'[64] Those assembled set about reorganising and, as recalled in *Republican Bulletin: Iris Na Poblachta* in November 1986, 'The meeting adopted with minor amendments, a draft statement of their position. They were "unanimous in agreeing that as they upheld the fundamental principles of the Sinn Féin Constitution, they were Sinn Féin"'. The bulletin also detailed the adoption of the name Republican Sinn Féin and stated:

> The question of a name for the organisation was discussed. Various proposals were made. It was agreed that as a temporary measure, until such time as the country is reorganised, the name Republican Sinn Féin (in Irish Sinn Féin Poblachtach) would be used in order to facilitate the media and avoid confusion in the public mind.[65]

Among those assembled in the West County Hotel in 1986 was Geraldine Taylor from Belfast, former vice-president of RSF (2009–13).[66] Referring to that period, Taylor has commented:

I just walked away from it in 1986 when it was passed at an Ard Fheis by a small majority to recognise Leinster House. To me it went against the grains and the principles of the Republican Movement which I joined and that's why we now have Republican Sinn Féin.[67]

Taylor has referred to the period of the split as 'a difficult time' and has emphasised how isolated she was in Belfast:

Now when the split in '86 – I was here on my own [Belfast]. I went out and sold papers. I was part of a big mass organisation and I was left. People walked past me and all this craic and it was very very hard to take. Very hard to take. And for years it was terrible and we got a few people on board and we were selling our papers and there was manys a night I cried myself to sleep. So one night I was fighting with myself and I said what are you crying for? I said pull yourself together. Look at the men and women, boys and girls that's buried in Milltown Cemetery.[68]

The split in 1986 was an emotionally difficult time within the Republican Movement when former comrades and friends took opposing sides. When asked if he ever felt any personal bitterness about what happened in 1986 Ó Brádaigh commented, 'if I were to just sit in Roscommon dwelling on these things I might well drift into bitterness. But instead I remain active and continue writing, speaking and campaigning. I don't have the time for such thoughts.'[69] Messages of support for the newly formed RSF were recorded in the January–February 1987 edition of *Republican Bulletin: Iris Na Poblachta* from three prisoners in Long Kesh. Similarly, the March–April 1987 edition of the paper published a letter of support from John Hayes in Albany prison on the Isle of Wight.

At the time of the 1986 split, three Sinn Féin councillors left with Ó Brádaigh, namely Mickey McGonigle in Derry, Frank McCarry, in Ballycastle, Co. Antrim and Frank Glynn, a member of Galway County Council. McGonigle joined the Republican Clubs (the name used by Sinn Féin in the Six Counties during this period as it was a proscribed organisation) in 1965 and supported the Provisionals in 1969/70. He then went on to join the Provisional Movement and was the first Sinn Féin councillor elected to Limavady Council in 1984, topping the poll of fifteen councillors. In reference to 1986 McGonigle has simply stated 'when the Provos entered Leinster House I resigned.'[70] McGonigle has argued:

Republican Sinn Féin, the way I see us on the ground, we are what republicans were before this conflict started. True republicans. Before the Provos was formed there were just a few hard-line republicans here and there and that's the way it is at the present minute.[71]

McGonigle has referred to 1986 by stating:

They gave me wild stick. All I said, well now I'm not accepting Leinster House. Youse give me stick or not but you'll have to wait and see and down the line you'll be coming and telling me I was right. Well that's what's happened.[72]

Another interviewee who left with Ó Brádaigh in 1986 is Lita Campbell. Campbell referred to the period prior to the split by stating:

> Gerry Adams and company, when he came out of jail straight away he began to change the movement to his way of thinking and he did it by very underhand means and by using the IRA really, like ... 'it's what the army wants', you know. I just didn't believe him ... I couldn't have stayed with those people, because I knew they were going down the wrong road basically.[73]

Campbell, a senior member of the Republican Movement since 1970, and a member of Cumann na mBan since 1971, has recalled that when the split happened in 1986 it was seen as a priority to get a republican newspaper out immediately. Campbell has stated that a meeting took place shortly after the split to 'decide what we were going to do and we decided to get out a paper, a tabloid-sized paper and call it *Saoirse*.'[74] Ruairí Óg Ó Brádaigh was the editor and has assumed this position until the present day.

Tomás Ó Curraoin, who left with Ó Brádaigh during the 1986 split, has been an RSF councillor in Galway since 2009. He has recalled his family on both his mother's and father's sides as 'having taken part in the war against the Black and Tans in 1920'.[75] Ó Curraoin has identified his father's mother as a significant influence in the development of his republicanism and has recalled that when Feargal O'Hanlon and Seán South were killed in 1957 (at the time Tomás was ten years old) his granny had a saying in Irish 'that their mothers should be very proud of them'.[76] During the Hunger Strike period in the 1980s Ó Curraoin was active in Sinn Féin in London after immigrating to England, before returning to Ireland permanently in 1982. Commenting on the direction which the Provisional Movement has taken, Ó Curraoin has stated:

> It's amazing you know – all the lives that were ever lost and what happened in Loughall and the Hunger Strike and everything. If it were to achieve what they've got out of it by going into Leinster House – I feel very very sorry for the people who put their lives on the line right down through the years.[77]

Interviewees who joined RSF in more recent years (post-1990) have cited their belief in RSF as the true Republican Movement as a defining factor in their decision to join. Fergal Moore in Monaghan (a former vice-president), who was a member of Na Fianna Éireann, joined RSF in 1991. Moore has stated:

> I felt that Republican Sinn Féin are the only legitimate *Republican* Sinn Féin out there to be able to claim that name. Recognition of Leinster House –you know, I don't see how any republican could do that. So the only republican group is ourselves.[78]

Similarly, Pádraig Garvey (elected vice-president of RSF in 2017), who joined the organisation in 2000 in Carisheveen in Co. Kerry, has stated 'RSF have kept true to the mandate of the 1916 Rising itself and then after it the formation of the First Dáil and on through the treaty.'[79]

When asked about the 1986 split and whether the recognition of Leinster House mattered, a senior member of the 32CSM leadership in the South of Ireland has commented:

> Oh it was important all right. But what was important to us was there was a vast amount of equipment and if we could get our hands on it it would make an awful difference … I wasn't comfortable with it [recognition of Leinster House] but sometimes the end justifies the means. If we grabbed a hold of all of what was supposed to be around, it would put us in a stronger negotiating position. Let's put it that way.[80]

This unique insight provided by someone who was present in the Republican Movement prior to the formation of the Provisionals in 1969 offers an alternative and more nuanced picture of what happened in 1986, suggesting that there were strategic considerations by some of those who stayed with the Provisional Movement after 1986. However, this begs the question as to why such individuals did not subsequently join RSF. The mainstream portrayal of the 'dissident' world is often a simplistic one which does not fully acknowledge the complexities which are evident beneath the surface.

No criticism allowed

For many who stayed with the Provisional Movement throughout the ideological changes in the 1980s (who then departed in the more recent period) their criticism is directed at the nature of the Provisional organisation, and for some their criticism manifested during the later period such as the 1994 and 1997 PIRA ceasefires or the Good Friday Agreement. In fact several prominent radical republicans have described themselves as formerly critics within the Provisional Movement (prior to their departure) – a point largely absent from the existing narrative and which proves illuminating regarding the motivation of individuals who have departed the Provisional Movement in recent years (since the mid-1990s to present). Notable examples include Anthony McIntyre, Richard O'Rawe, Tommy McKearney, Gerard Hodgins and the late Tony Catney (all of whom have expressed criticism of the current armed campaign waged by republican groups). Current republican prisoner in Maghaberry, Nathan Hastings has argued 'even beyond the armed campaign there was room for a revolutionary alternative. They didn't have to go into Stormont etc.'[81]

A dominant theme throughout the radical republican criticism of the Provisional Movement (and a prominent reason for departure from the movement) surrounds the inability to express dissenting views regarding the direction in which the movement was proceeding. The Provisional Movement, including Sinn Féin, is notably authoritarian in nature, with little room for dissent from the leadership.[82] The way in which decisions were taken within the movement is a common thread throughout the radical republican discourse. Radical republicans make reference to the lack of debate within the Provisional Movement and many have cited it as the reason for their departure from Sinn Féin in recent years. Gary Donnelly in Derry, who became involved in republican politics at the age of eleven through selling *An Phoblacht*, was a member of the Provisional Movement until 1998. He has been with the 32CSM since 1998. Describing the Mitchell Principles as 'the final nail in the coffin', Donnelly has stated:

> Within the Provisional Movement there is no room for dissent. You speak out, you question decisions, you suddenly become a British agent, you become blackened, you become demonised, marginalised.[83]

The late Tony Catney, a prominent radical republican from Belfast and member of the 1916 Societies, departed from the Provisional Movement in October 2005. Catney, who was a member of the Provisional IRA, has stated that:

> In 2005 everybody, all IRA volunteers were instructed that as per the text of the IRA statement that IRA volunteers would be involved in nothing but political activity. Within that my role was as the Six County director of elections and the Six County organiser.[84]

Catney met with the leadership of the movement in Belfast at that time and expressed his criticisms:

> I made it clear to both the membership and the leadership of the organisation as I travelled around … that in my opinion the 1994 ceasefire was a mistake. It was handled from a position of weakness rather than a position of strength … I agreed with Gerry Adams' comment at the time that the Good Friday Agreement is not a republican document. Then as we got into the non-fulfilment of Patten I made it clear that the same rule of thumb that had been used to endorse the Good Friday Agreement, to bring about the IRA cessation in the first place, was being used in relation to policing – that policing was a fundamental cornerstone of the state and to cut corners – it wasn't going to be revolutionary change, it was going to be reform.[85]

Significantly, Catney went on to state:

> All those objections I was quite prepared to live with because I was dedicated and committed to the Republican Movement, the Provisional Republican Movement as it was, and was quite prepared to remain within and argue my corner from within. But I wouldn't allow myself to be silenced. Then in 2005 a number of changes were made in the sort of middle management of Sinn Féin within the Six Counties. It was clear that within that reshuffle the message was that I was to have no input into anything.[86]

Catney has argued that he subsequently 'made representation' to the chief of staff of the Provisional IRA, the adjutant-general of the IRA, the national chairperson of Sinn Féin, the president of Sinn Féin and the national director of elections of Sinn Féin. Catney claimed that everyone he met agreed it was a 'shocking situation' and that something would be done about it.[87] Catney waited six months and has stated that 'nothing happened'. Catney has argued:

> Look, I have no problem being in an organisation that is going in completely the wrong direction, as I see it, as long as I am allowed to argue my corner ... but I could not remain within an organisation that claimed that it was dedicated to putting an end to second-class citizenship and working on the very very minimum level on the basis of a parity of esteem when that couldn't even exist within the organisation.[88]

Catney subsequently resigned and has stated 'I was never in Sinn Féin and so I couldn't resign from Sinn Féin. So I resigned from the IRA and just bid people adieu.'[89] Until his death, Catney was one of the most prominent former Provisionals who considered themselves as having been 'an independent even within the Provisional IRA'.[90]

In reference to individuals who stayed with the Provisional Movement into the recent period, Brendan O'Brien's *The Long War: The IRA and Sinn Féin from Armed Struggle to Peace Talks* is particularly informative regarding the nature of the Provisional Movement. O'Brien makes reference to the Provisional Sinn Féin leadership's appeasement towards the membership regarding concerns about the overall direction in which the movement was going. He refers to an earlier failed attempt by the IRA leadership to change the position on abstentionism during an IRA convention which took place in Meath under the disguise of an Irish-language conference. In reference to the meeting O'Brien states, the 'South Armagh and Dundalk brigades split down the middle and mid-Ulster and Kerry were opposed'.[91] The IRA convention re-convened in Dublin and the required majority was attained, with, however, the following guarantees:

> (1) key positions on the Army Council were to be filled by hard-liners committed to a continued escalating armed struggle; (2) local units were to be given more freedom of action, 'local commander prerogative'; (3) Martin McGuinness was to hold a pivotal role on Northern Command, as well as on the Army Council. Two hard-line militarists, Anto Murray and Danny McCann, who had been among those expelled for challenging the leadership, were re-admitted and returned to active service in Belfast. Kevin Hannaway, a cousin of Gerry Adams, became Adjutant General, number two to Martin McGuinness.[92]

O'Brien's characterisation of the nature of the movement is consistent with the arguments put forward by interviewees who have stated that guarantees were repeatedly given by the Provisional leadership regarding the direction in which the movement was going. Therefore, it is interesting to note at which points these 'independent thinkers' within the Provisional Movement departed and entered the 'radical republican' or 'independent' sphere. At what point did guarantees from the leadership prove futile?

Voices from the grave

Ed Moloney's *Voices from the Grave* was the first, and to date the only, book to be published from the Boston College Project on which Dr Anthony McIntyre was the lead researcher. Through the Brendan Hughes chapters, the book was the first to openly detail criticism of the Adams leadership in such a manner. The book charts Hughes's close relationship with Gerry Adams in Long Kesh prison in the 1970s and early 1980s and the deterioration of the relationship to the point where Adams was allegedly given the 'cold shoulder' at Hughes's funeral in West Belfast in 2008. Hughes's last interview was given to McIntyre in 2002, and Moloney states 'he was particularly exercised by the neglect shown towards ageing IRA veterans by the Provo leadership'.[93] Moloney claims that Hughes was especially angry about the death of Kieran Nugent, alleging that Provisional Sinn Féin called him the 'river rat' as he spent his final days drinking by a river in Poleglass in West Belfast.[94]

The book states that prior to his death Hughes spoke to Paddy Joe Rice, the leader of the D Company veterans' group, and requested that if he died Adams, Provisional Sinn Féin members and the Provisional IRA were to have 'nothing to do with the ceremonials' and they were not permitted to speak. Rice has stated, 'he was very adamant that none of them should have anything to do with it. He was afraid they would use his funeral to try and say that he ended up agreeing with Adams.'[95] Central to Hughes's criticism of the Provisional leadership is 'the way in which things were done'. Moloney has stated, 'what is striking with Hughes is that he was affected as much, if not more, by how it was all done as what was done; the deliberate running down of the IRA that he saw, the tolerance of informers and corruption, the lies, stealth and deception that he detected and, most of all, Gerry Adams' own denial of IRA membership.'[96]

Consistent throughout the radical republican narrative is the argument regarding how things were done by the Provisional leadership; which is particularly relevant to individuals who stayed with the Provisional Movement through major ideological shifts. When asked why he stayed with the Provisional Movement until 2007, Ciaran Mulholland, who is a member of the James Connolly Society in West Belfast,[97] has stated that he accepted that strategic compromises had to be made but argued:

> What I disagree with is changing your political ideology and changing the goal posts. For me the ultimate goal was the reunification of Ireland and the establishment of a thirty-two-county socialist democratic country. That appeared to be changing and being diluted throughout the years.[98]

Rejection of the Provisional leadership

Within radical republicanism a narrative has emerged regarding suspicion of the Provisional leadership as motives are questioned.[99] Suspicion of the leadership has contributed to a narrative which seeks to explain why the Provisional Movement developed in the way in which it did and has contributed to explanations from radical republicans regarding why such ideological shifts took place within the movement. This is reflected in Dan Hoban's comments. Hoban has referred to a period when he was active in republicanism in Derry around the time that Frank Hegarty was shot by the IRA as an 'informer'.[100] Hoban has commented:

> I'd say that [name withheld] was talking to the Brits for a long long time before it happened because … there was a man that was shot in Derry and I think it was to save a bigger fish. Now he was supposed to be a tout. I don't believe for a minute that he was. Now if he was, myself and this other man, we would have been uploaded and upturned because we were in charge of a lot of things that they'd have got to and they didn't get to. That was a fella in Derry now that was called Frank Hegarty that was shot.[101]

A prominent theme throughout the radical republican discourse is mistrust of the Provisional leadership. Jim McCrystal, a prominent radical republican in Lurgan and former member of the Provisional Movement who served fourteen years in jail, has stated 'I think the British government bought a lot of people and put them into Sinn Féin.'[102] McCrystal has detailed where his belief originated:

> Letters went out. I got a letter and on it it said 'there will be jobs coming up and you have been selected for your area and you will be told more about this at a later date'. It was very vague. It said that there would be an interview in this hotel in Market Hill and that a company car would lift you and bring you to this interview and I remember showing it to the wife … 'Who got my name? Who said I was looking for a job?' … A while after that I was talking to another fella, a prisoner who I was inside with too and he said to me 'sure I got one of those letters too'. He said 'I went to see about it you know' and I said 'what happened?' He said 'Oh a car arrived up with two well-dressed people in it and they said right we're going for the interview up to Market Hill.' These people were sitting at a table and they congratulated him and they said 'nice to see you and sit down there, we'll have a talk with you. Now we have to say this may not be exactly what you were thinking it was.' So he asked them 'well what is it?' Well they said who they were, from the British government and that 'we know you're a very educated person, we know that you used to be in Sinn Féin.' But he had left Sinn Féin. 'What we want you to do now is, we would like you to go back into Sinn Féin. Now we're not going to ask you to tout on anybody or anything like that because we know you wouldn't do it and we wouldn't ask you to do that. But what we would like you to do is go back into Sinn Féin. There'll be policies and things that we want put through.' They told

him 'don't worry you'll not be on your own.' At that stage they took out the money. He said 'forget about it.'[103]

Mc Crystal went on to ask: 'So if they wanted me to do that and if they got him to that stage, how many did they get?'[104] Anecdotes such as these were prominent throughout the ninety interviews and serve to fuel suspicion regarding the direction which Provisional Sinn Féin has assumed.

Conclusion

You've Sinn Féin, and they've broke away from all ideals and constitutional points of the Republican Movement.
　　　　　　　-Billy McKee, interview with the author, Belfast, 8 August 2013

The belief that Sinn Féin has moved away from its traditional message and base forms a dominant thread throughout radical republican criticism of the party. Upon the appointment of Michelle O'Neill, who succeeded Martin McGuinness as the head of the party in Northern Ireland, prominent radical republican Dr Anthony McIntyre commented '[T]he appointment of Michelle O'Neill is entirely consistent with Sinn Féin's ongoing and sustained abandonment of its revolutionary party and the comprehensive embracing of constitutionalism.'[105] McIntyre continued his criticism of the appointment: 'Sinn Féin has no shortage of former high-profile IRA prisoners serving as MLAs from which to choose a new leader for its Stormont assembly team. That it opted not to is indicative of its persistent and irreversible journey away from its former self.'[106] Pádraic MacCoitir, a prominent member of éirígí in Belfast, was a member of the Provisional IRA and served a prison sentence of fifteen years ending in 1996; while in prison he was part of the prison republican staff and took part in the Blanket Protest. MacCoitir joined the Republican Movement in 1970 when he became a member of Na Fianna Éireann. He has argued:

I started to see a change come about in the IRA especially. And Sinn Féin then at their Ard Fheiseanna, different statements they were putting out. They were moving further away from what they stated on paper what they were all about … I never for one minute thought that Sinn Féin would have gone as far as what they have gone today. And it makes me angry.[107]

The question 'why be a "dissident" republican?' must be examined within the wider context of 'why be a republican?', taking account of those radical republicans who were active in the Republican Movement prior to the formation of the Provisional Movement in 1969. McIntyre has argued that the Provisional Movement was set up as a response to how the British *behaved* in Ireland, not as a response to the British *being* in Ireland.[108] McIntyre's logic, taken to its ultimate conclusion, means that the British would have to simply alter their behaviour in Ireland (not depart) for the Provisional IRA to cease its campaign. McIntyre rejects the idea that the campaign came about as a result of the denial of Irish unity.

However, McIntyre's analysis is not shared by all those in the radical republican world: the contested narrative regarding the raison d'être of the Provisional campaign provides an insight into continued radical republican activity. In an address in Duleek in Co. Meath in September 2016, Francie Mackey (National chairperson of the 32CSM), recognised the reality of the situation regarding radical republicanism: 'as Irish republicans we know we are right. But we must equally know and accept that we are not winning this struggle.'[109] Recognition of this fact has led to interviewees from every republican group making reference to the 'need to keep building' and to 'keep the structures going'.[110] In his address Mackey stated that republicanism is not a spectator sport and concluded with:

> We have nothing to be afraid of open and honest debate. We won't have all the answers nor do we need to. This process has begun. The door is open. You are invited to step through.[111]

Notes

1 P. Nolan, 'The long, long war of dissident republicans', *Shared Space*, 16 (November 2013), p. 41. Published by the Community Relations Council.

2 D. Della Porta, *Clandestine Political Violence* (New York, Cambridge University Press, 2013), p. 23. In this book Della Porta examines four types of 'clandestine political violence': left wing (in Italy and Germany), right wing (in Italy), ethno-nationalist (in Spain) and religious fundamentalist (in Islamist clandestine organisations).

3 *Ibid.*, p. 23.

4 See Della Porta, *Clandestine Political Violence*, for an analysis of family and childhood influences on the development of ideology and politics in 'clandestine' organisations.

5 J. Tonge, 'Dissidents, ultras, militarists or patriots? Analysing the strategies, tactics and support for 'dissident' republicanism'. PSA Conference, Dublin Institute of Technology (October 2010).

6 J. Morrison, *The Origins and Rise of Dissident Irish Republicanism: The Role and Impact of Organizational Splits* (London, Bloomsbury, 2013).

7 J. Horgan, *Divided We Stand: The Strategy and Psychology of Ireland's Dissident Terrorists* (Oxford, Oxford University Press, 2013).

8 Speech by Martin McGuinness at Stormont after the murder of PSNI constable Stephen Carroll in March 2009. http://news.bbc.co.uk/1/hi/northern_ireland/7934894.stm. Accessed 6 July 2018.

9 Whiting, *Spoiling the Peace?*, p. 139.

10 The first letter of éirígí is not capitalised due to a decision taken by its founders to reflect the decentralised and egalitarian structure of the organisation.

11 Horgan, *Divided We Stand*, p. 40.

12 Tonge, '"No one likes us; we don't care"', p. 225.

13 *Ibid.*, p. 225.

14 J. Bowyer Bell, *The IRA 1968–2000: Analysis of a Secret Army* (London, Frank Cass Publishers, 2000), p. 95.

15 For further information on the Civil War period see M. Hopkinson, *Green Against Green: The Irish Civil War* (Dublin, Gill & Macmillan, 1988). In this work Frank Aiken quotes an old priest: 'War with the foreigner brings to the fore all that is best and noblest in a nation – civil war all that is mean and base' (p. 273). Hopkinson has stated 'The heavily regionalised conflict within such a small country left a permanent scar on the national psyche. Many other contemporaries have related that the civil war ended any social contact with anyone on the other side of the Treaty split' (pp. 273–4)

16 Kevin Hannaway, interview with the author, Belfast, 24 July 2013.

17 Under Operation Demetrius the 'hooded men' were subjected to sensory deprivation techniques by the British army in the 1970s. The hooded men are currently undertaking a legal challenge against the British government. See publication titled 'The Hooded-Men: British Torture in Ireland August 1971' by Father Denis Faul of Dungannon and Father Raymond Murray of Armagh. First printed in July 1974.

18 Kevin Hannaway, interview with the author, Belfast, 24 July 2013.

19 Billy McKee, interview with the author, Belfast, 8 August 2013.

20 E. Keane, *Seán MacBride: A Life* (Dublin, Gill & Macmillan, 2007), p. 14.

21 Brendan Madden, interview with the author, Galway, 4 June 2016.

22 Fra Halligan, interview with the author, Belfast, 19 November 2013.

23 Dan Hoban, interview with the author, Dublin, 3 November 2013.

24 *Ibid.*

25 *Ibid.*

26 Des Dalton, interview with the author, Dublin, 15 February 2013.

27 Richard O'Rawe is a Belfast republican and former IRA prisoner who first told his story to Anthony McIntyre during the Boston College Project. The Boston College Project (also known as the Belfast Project) began in 2001 and was directed by journalist and writer Ed Moloney. Dr Anthony McIntyre was the primary researcher on the project, which gathered a unique oral history archive of interviews with Irish Republican Army and Ulster Volunteer Force veterans, among others. The recordings, which have become known as the 'Boston tapes', were stored at Boston College, and interviewees were given a guarantee that their testimonies would not be made public until after their death. The inaugural publication from this project is Ed Moloney, *Voices from the Grave: Two Men's War in Ireland* (London, Faber & Faber, 2010). In 2011 the PSNI initiated legal proceedings to gain access to the tapes; they successfully gained access to two of the interview transcripts. In 2016 the PSNI subpoenaed Boston College for all the tapes. The legal battle continues. See http://thepensivequill.am/2012/10/the-belfast-project-and-boston-college.html and www.bbc.com/news/uk-northern-ireland-27238797. Accessed 6 July 2018.

28 In *Afterlives: The Hunger Strike and the Secret Offer that Changed Irish History* (Dublin, Lilliput, 2010), Richard O'Rawe has cited an interview conducted with Ruairí Ó Brádaigh for New York's WBAI radio station. Ó Brádaigh was asked

'... the Mountain Climber offer. As President of Sinn Féin at the time, did Gerry Adams, Martin McGuinness, or anyone else on the hunger-strike committee, make you aware of the existence of this offer?' O'Rawe continues: 'Ó Brádaigh, whom many believed to have been on the IRA Army Council at that time, was unhesitant in his answer: "I had no knowledge of any such offer, nor had Sinn Féin in general, and not alone that, I believe that the Army Council of the IRA were not aware of this offer either and I have gone on the record as saying that"' (p. 188).

29 See R. O'Rawe, *Blanketmen: An Untold Story of the H-Block Hunger-Strike* (Dublin, New Island, 2005) and O'Rawe, *Afterlives*.

30 Richard O'Rawe, interview with the author, Belfast, 12 September 2012.

31 *Ibid.*

32 *Ibid.*

33 Lita Campbell, interview with the author, Dublin, 21 October 2013.

34 *Ibid.*

35 *Ibid.*

36 Dan Hoban, interview with the author, Dublin, 3 November 2013.

37 Angela Nelson, interview with the author, Belfast, 17 September 2012.

38 R.W. White, *Provisional Irish Republicans: An Oral and Interpretive History* (London, Greenwood Press, 1993), p. 133.

39 'North Kerry Sinn Féin condemns deceit and treachery', *An Phoblacht* (February 1970). This was the first edition of *An Phoblacht*, which was established to replace the paper the *United Irishman* after the split in 1970. The *United Irishman* continued under the control of the Official Republican Movement.

40 *Ibid.*

41 *Ibid.*

42 White, *Provisional Irish Republicans*.

43 *Ibid*, p. 145.

44 *Ibid.*, p. 145.

45 Dan Hoban, interview with the author, Dublin, 3 November 2013.

46 *Ibid.*

47 *Ibid.*

48 *Ibid.*

49 Peig King is originally from Co. Tyrone.

50 Peig King, interview with the author, Dublin, 26 July 2016.

51 *Ibid.*

52 *Ibid.*

53 Paddy King, interview with the author, Dublin, 26 July 2016.

54 Peig King, interview with the author, Dublin, 26 July 2016.

55 Richard Behal, interview with the author, Killarney, 31 October 2013. Richard Behal joined the Republican Movement in the late 1950s. He was a republican prisoner in Limerick prison from September 1965 to February 1966, when he escaped after rubbing himself with butter to squeeze through the bars on the window of his cell. He was a member of the Sinn Féin Ard Chomhairle, as director of international affairs, from the early 1970s until 1983. In 1984 he was a Sinn Féin candidate in the European elections. He departed Sinn Féin in 1986 after the vote on abstentionism

at the party's Ard Fheis. See J. Bowyer Bell, *The Secret Army: The IRA 1916–1979* (Dublin, The Academy Press, 1997), pp. 342–3. Also see L. Clarke, *Broadening the Battlefield: The H Blocks and the Rise of Sinn Féin* (Dublin, Gill & Macmillan, 1987), pp. 215, 218. For a documentary on Richard Behal (part one) see: www.youtube. com/watch?v=UR3X3Alnono. Accessed 28 July 2018.

56 The text of resolution 162 is provided on CAIN: http://cain.ulst.ac.uk/issues/ politics/docs/sf/resolution162.htm. Accessed 6 July 2018. Also see, Sinn Féin, Ard-Fheis: Clár (31 October–2 November 1986), pp. 83–5.

57 The text of Ruairí Ó Brádaigh's 1986 speech is available at CAIN: http://cain.ulst. ac.uk/issues/politics/docs/sf/rob021186.htm. Accessed 6 July 2018.

58 For the full text of Martin McGuinness's 1986 speech see CAIN: http://cain.ulst. ac.uk/issues/politics/docs/sf/mmcg021186.htm. Accessed 6 July 2018.

59 R.W. White, *Ruairí Ó Brádaigh: The Life and Politics of an Irish Revolutionary* (Bloomington, Indiana University Press, 2006), p. 306.

60 *Ibid.*, p. 309.

61 Described to the author by RSF President Des Dalton in an interview for this book, February 2017.

62 Clarke's work also covers the period preceding the 1986 split.

63 Ruairí Ó Brádaigh had agreed to give an interview to this study; however, prior to the interview taking place he died from illness on 5 June 2013.

64 White, *Ruairí Ó Brádaigh*, p. 309.

65 *Republican Bulletin: Iris Na Poblachta*, Samhain (November 1986).

66 For a detailed account of who was assembled with Ruairí Ó Brádaigh at the West County Hotel, see *Republican Bulletin: Iris Na Poblachta*, Samhain (November 1986). Members of the executive are listed as follows: The Officer Board elected at the meeting of 2 November: Cathaoirleach – Dáithí Ó Conaill; Leas-Chathaoirleach – Des Long; Rúnaí – Cathleen Knowles; Cisteoirí – Joe O'Neill, Frank Graham; Urlabhraí – Ruairí Ó Brádaigh. The organising committee members are also listed.

67 Geraldine Taylor, interview with the author, Belfast, 14 October 2012.

68 *Ibid.*

69 Des Dalton, interview with the author, September 2017.

70 Micky McGonigle, interview with the author, Derry, 18 August 2013.

71 *Ibid.*

72 *Ibid.*

73 Lita Campbell, interview with the author, Dublin, 21 October 2013.

74 *Ibid. Irish Freedom: Saoirse na hÉireann* was the name of an earlier paper published by the IRB, starting 15 November 1910. See Gerard MacAtasney, *Tom Clarke: Life, Liberty, Revolution* (Sallins, Co. Kildare, Merrion, 2013). When *Saoirse: Irish Freedom* was established in 1987 historical continuity was emphasised. *History Ireland* has described *Irish Freedom: Saoirse na hÉireann* as the 'official' publication of the IRB. See www.historyireland.com/volume-23/concessions-be-damned-england-we-want-our-country/. Accessed 6 July 2018.
Also see D.J. Hickey and J.E. Doherty, *A New Dictionary of Irish History From 1800* (Dublin, Gill & Macmillan, 2003), p. 225: 'A paper published monthly from

15 November 1910 – it was suppressed in December 1914 – a vehicle for radical republicanism.'

75 Tomas Ó'Curraoin, interview with the author, Galway, 4 June 2013.

76 *Ibid.*

77 *Ibid.*

78 Fergal Moore, interview with the author, Monaghan, 14 October 2012.

79 Pádraig Garvey, interview with the author, Killarney, 30 October 2013.

80 Member of the 32CSM leadership (South of Ireland), interview with the author, 2013.

81 Nathan Hastings, interview with the author, Maghaberry prison, 8 March 2017. Nathan Hastings is from Derry and has been in Maghaberry prison since 2013 charged with possession of guns and explosives.

82 Bowyer Bell, *The IRA 1968–2000.*

83 Gary Donnelly, interview with the author, Derry, 21 August 2013.

84 Tony Catney, interview with the author, Belfast, 14 September 2012.

85 *Ibid.*

86 *Ibid.*

87 Tony Catney, interview with the author, Belfast, 14 September 2012.

88 *Ibid.*

89 *Ibid.*

90 *Ibid.*

91 B. O'Brien, *The Long War: The IRA and Sinn Féin from Armed Struggle to Peace Talks* (Dublin, The O'Brien Press, 1995), pp. 130–1.

92 *Ibid.*, pp. 130–1.

93 Moloney, *Voices from the Grave*, p. 295.

94 *Ibid.*, p. 295. Kieran Nugent was a member of the Provisional IRA. He was a prisoner in Long Kesh prison and was the first to be denied 'special category status'. Subsequently Nugent was the first prisoner to refuse to wear prison uniform and was labelled the first 'blanket-man', wearing only a blanket in protest. The Blanket Protest culminated in the Hunger Strikes of the 1980s.

95 Moloney, *Voices from the Grave*, p. 297.

96 *Ibid.*, p. 290.

97 At the time of this interview the James Connolly Society was affiliated with the 1916 Societies. It is now an independent collective.

98 Ciaran Mulholland, interview with the author, Belfast, 5 May 2014.

99 Moloney, *Voices from the Grave*; T. McKearney, *The Provisional IRA: From Insurrection to Parliament* (London, Pluto Press, 2011); A. McIntyre, *Good Friday: The Death of Irish Republicanism* (New York, Ausubo Press, 2008); White, *Ruairí Ó Brádaigh.*

100 Ed Moloney, *A Secret History of the IRA* (London, Penguin, 2007), pp. 387–9.

101 Dan Hoban, interview with the author, Dublin, 3 November 2013.

102 Jim McCrystal, interview with the author, Lurgan, 22 August 2013.

103 *Ibid.*

104 *Ibid.*

105 A. McIntyre, 'A day after a PSNI member is injured in a North Belfast shooting

Sinn Féin appoints Michelle O'Neill as their replacement for Martin McGuinness', *Belfast Telegraph* (24 January 2017).

106 *Ibid.*

107 Pádraic MacCoitir, interview with the author, Belfast, 4 October 2012.

108 McIntyre, *Good Friday*. Also see McKearney, *The Provisional IRA*.

109 Francie Mackey, oration delivered at the Hunger Strike commemoration in Duleek, organised by the Duleek Hunger Strike monument committee, 17 September 2016.

110 Francie Mackey, interview with the author, Omagh, 8 February 2013.

111 Francie Mackey, oration delivered at the Hunger Strike commemoration in Duleek, organised by the Duleek Hunger Strike monument committee, 17 September 2016.

2

The varied strands of 'dissident' republicanism: ideology and disunity

All I'd like to say is that I would like to see all republican groups, because there is great men and women, come together with an overall strategy as to how we can achieve a united Ireland. To give up the conflict amongst ourselves because we are falling into the hands of the enemy.

Christy Burke, interview with the author, Dublin, 19 March 2013

We feel that unity that is not based on fundamental values and fundamental principles is a flawed unity, and there are a number of people out there who would say that somehow or another it's possible to agree to disagree on certain issues and set them aside but come together around wider issues, and you know again we would point to the lessons of history on that where that has been attempted in the past; again the inherent flaws are there and they will surface and unfortunately from a republican perspective they tend to surface at the most critical period.

Des Dalton, president of Republican Sinn Féin (Kildare), interview with the author, Dublin, 15 February 2013

Introduction

The mainstream narrative on so-called 'dissident' republicanism has emphasised the divided and heterogeneous nature of radical republicanism. References are frequently made to the number of republican groups which exist: RSF, 32CSM, RNU, RSM, IRSP, éirígí, Continuity IRA, REAL IRA and the New IRA, among others (as well as a significant body of independents). This chapter provides an analysis of the divided nature of radical republicanism and focuses on the irreconcilable ideological and tactical differences between groups, which hinders any formal unity. It explores why republican groups have emerged in the more recent period (post-1998) and examines arguments put forward by the founding members regarding why formation of another republican group was necessary. Further, this chapter explores tactical diversity *within* organisations, which has proven highly divisive in relation to parades and elections – the significance of which is often under-represented in the dominant narrative on radical republicanism. Throughout the research it has emerged that significant division exists between some of the groups within Maghaberry prison. Through interviews with current prisoners in Maghaberry, the chapter presents an examination of the 'identity struggle' which has taken place within the confines of the prison, which provides an indication of significant points of division in wider group relations. The chapter also seeks to provide an insight into the nature of the relationship between Sinn Féin and radical republican groups.

A plethora of groups: 'republican traffic'

Each Easter Sunday and Monday in Milltown Cemetery in Belfast, a plethora of revolutionary republican organisations, as well as Sinn Féin, undertake their annual Easter commemoration. The centenary year of 2016 saw commemorations held in Milltown by RSF, the IRSP, éirígí, the Workers' Party and Sinn Féin, as was the case around Ireland North and South. It is not unusual to witness an organisation's colour party forming outside Milltown Cemetery gates as they await their turn while another group is in the process of finishing their commemoration and getting ready to depart the cemetery.

This 'republican traffic' through Milltown Cemetery is reflective of the divided nature of contemporary revolutionary republicanism. On a local level in Belfast, D Company on the Falls Road hold their commemorations separately from Sinn Féin, whose commemorations are organised by the Lower Falls commemoration committee; reflective of the fact that the company formerly known as D Company (also known locally as Dog D Company) has split. Just off the Falls Road sits the Clonard area of Belfast and this area is one of the few to maintain a unified commemoration where revolutionary republicans and members of Provisional Sinn Féin co-exist. Revolutionary republican Albert Allen, who is not a member of any organisation, has been instrumental in organising the inclusive commemoration and has commented on other commemorations:

> Some of them, when they get up and you hear it – they're not used in many ways for commemoration. They're used for political point gaining over different parties, so it's sad.[1]

Allen is referring to speeches made at commemorations which advocate a particular line or organisation. The unique Clonard commemoration does not permit political speeches but simply consists of a reading of the roll of honour of IRA volunteers who have died. Given that commemorations are as much about the present as they are about remembering the past, it is unsurprising that groups are reluctant to have shared commemorations.

Existing literature on 'dissident republicanism' has largely categorised radical republicans as disaffected ex-Provisionals. However, radical republicans are a heterogeneous group which consist of former Provisional Sinn Féin or Provisional IRA, former Fianna Fáil, IRSP or INLA, and individuals who have never been a member of any organisation. They also comprise individuals who were active in republicanism prior to the formation of the Provisional Movement in 1969 (see 'Introduction' for a list of pre-1969 interviewees). Failure to contextualise radical republicanism within this pre-1969 mould will limit understanding of such groups and individuals. As demonstrated by Robert W. White, individuals who were active in the Republican Movement prior to 1969 predominantly come from families which are deep-rooted in republicanism, in contrast to individuals who became active in republicanism in the post-1969 period in the North of Ireland, whose accounts 'show them to be less a product of family tradition and revolutionary ideals than a product of state violence'.[2] Regarding post-1969 recruits who live in the South of Ireland, White has stated that their accounts show that 'their recruitment is built upon a nationalistic ideological foundation'.[3] Despite pre- and post-1969 entry points into republicanism, radical republican interviewees have collectively asserted their allegiance to traditional republican principles and their loyalty to the Irish Republic declared in 1916.

Breaking points

The ideological and strategic position of radical republican groups must be viewed in the wider context of different 'breaking points' at which some of the founder members of these radical groups broke away from the Provisional Movement. The major breaking points were 1986 (over the ending of abstentionism), 1994 and 1997 (PIRA ceasefires), 1998 (Good Friday Agreement), 2005 (IRA decommissioning), 2007 (Sinn Féin's acceptance of the PSNI) and Martin McGuinness shaking hands with the British Queen in 2012.[4] The origins of radical groups have been well documented in the literature.[5] The various points of departure from the Provisional Movement or from Sinn Féin (coupled with the prevalence of personalities) go some way to explaining the disunity of republican groups. Geographical location has also proven a significant determinant regarding the prevalence of a particular republican organisation. RSF has proven strongest in Dublin (Head Office) and Lurgan (the Thomas Harte cumann), Republican Network for Unity is most active in Belfast (Office and conflict resolution services) and Newry/Dundalk, and the IRPWA has proven active in Belfast and Lurgan. Éirígí is strongest in Belfast and Dublin and the 32CSM is most active in Belfast, Derry and Dublin. Finally, the Republican Socialist Movement appears strongest in Derry and Belfast (Head Office).

An alphabet soup or the logical progression of fault lines?

While the contemporary period bears witness to a number of republican organisations (sometimes referred to as an 'alphabet soup' of groups), it must be noted that republicanism has never been categorised simply as one movement and that a unified radical republican base would be more surprising than the present divisive form. An examination of the 1916 period reveals various republican organisations, including the Irish Citizen Army, which was radical socialist, and the Irish Republican Brotherhood, which was militarist and separatist; each organisation espousing a unique position while being united under the common republican banner. Commenting on republican division in contemporary Ireland, Ciaran Mulholland, a member of the James Connolly Society in West Belfast, has stated:

> I suppose you have to get real. You're never going to get one leader as such for republicanism. Albeit there should be some formal means where those organisations could be brought together. We agree on those principles. We have more that we can agree on than separate us and together we are stronger.[6]

The dominant narrative on so-called 'dissident' republicanism has highlighted the fractured nature of 'dissidents'; and calls for 'republican unity', or at least the establishment of 'formal links' between groups (particularly from independent republicans), have been frequent. Such calls for formal unity between radical groups disregard the clear ideological and tactical water which exists between the groups. Joe Dillon, a senior member of the 32CSM in Dublin, has argued that:

> Every country in the world where a national parliament has been suppressed – you have different factions and groups … Resistance factionalism is sometimes part of a democratic necessity. Other times it is devious.[7]

Calls for republican unity may prove futile due to the historical nature of republicanism (which has never been one unified movement) as well as fundamental tactical differences between groups, which would make formal unity difficult and possibly unsustainable in the long term. In fact the existing narrative has under-estimated tactical diversity between republican organisations, which has proven highly divisive and can partly explain the persistence of 'splits' within the republican world. Interestingly, significant tactical diversity exists *within* radical republican organisations, thus dispelling any misconceptions that such groups are homogeneous in nature – as was demonstrated at the RSF Ard Fheis in 2014 regarding a motion on parades.

RSF: tactics versus principles

On 8 November 2014 RSF held their annual Ard Fheis in the historical venue of Wynn's Hotel in Dublin.[8] Resolution 20 on the clár, which was read by the session's chairperson, Mary Ward,[9] stated:

> That this Ard Fheis re-affirms that Republican Sinn Féin does not seek permission from the British-appointed parades commission or RUC/PSNI in the occupied six counties to assemble/parade or protest either in name or by proxy/third party, that

the use of such a commission deviates from our core principles of non-cooperation with the British occupation.

Charles Agnew Cumann, Armagh.

This seemingly innocuous resolution hit a raw republican nerve and the ensuing debate 'for' and 'against' proved highly charged as multiple speakers for each side queued to present their arguments to the Ard Fheis. Interestingly, speakers for and against the resolution could not be pre-determined by geographical location or by age group. Rather, northerners and southerners both assumed positions on either side of the debate. Further, positions could not be categorised by official position within RSF as the Ard Chomhairle appeared split on the issue. Early in the debate tempers flared between the speakers. At the heart of the debate was the age-old 'tactics versus principles' argument which has been present in republicanism since the treaty period of the early 1920s.[10]

The main speakers against the resolution were the Thomas Harte cumann from Lurgan. Central to their argument was that current security legislation has the potential to force republicans off the streets in Lurgan;[11] however, if an attending band has given 'notification' (not to be confused with seeking permission) to the parades commission, then all those attending the commemoration are protected against prosecution. The use of tactics to defeat security legislation has been used by the Republican Movement historically and has been used in the more recent period during events such as the anti-internment marches in Belfast at which representatives of all republican organisations were present. Within the radical republican context, groups such as the IRPWA have given notification to the parades commission. For the Republican Movement this was not a new position; in fact it is a position which was used by the Republican Movement throughout the 1980s in Derry.

Significantly, speakers in support of the resolution evoked the 'slippery slope' argument, stating that such 'compromises of principle' would eventually lead to a 'sell-out' or to 'entering Leinster House'. Speakers heatedly cited Cathal Goulding and Gerry Adams as people who had previously taken the path of compromising principles, and argued that if this resolution was defeated RSF would be following in the same vein; in republican terms this was arguably the most serious accusation that could be levelled at comrades. Members of the Thomas Harte cumann continued to take the platform, arguing the necessity to refuse to allow the security forces and British legislation to force republican commemorations 'behind graveyard walls' with a subsequent minimum number of people in attendance.

After a prolonged and highly emotive debate the chair put the resolution to the floor for a vote. The vote was deemed very close and it was revealed that two people present had voted when they did not possess voting rights due to the fact that they were not official delegates; therefore the controversial vote was held

again. As delegates held up their cards, tellers walked around the room count-
ing, as the chair asked people to remain in the same position during the vote
to enable the tellers to get an exact count. When the count was announced the
resolution had fallen by four votes. Tension ensued and heated verbal exchanges
took place as individuals exited the hall. RSF vice-president Cáit Trainor from
the Armagh cumann which had proposed the resolution later resigned on 19
November 2014.[12]

The debate outlined above provides an insight into the divisive nature of what
constitutes a tactic and what constitutes a principle within republicanism: this
question strikes to the heart of republicanism. As highlighted in chapter four,
Terence MacSwiney argued in 1921 that engagement with the state is unavoidable. However, the central point of contention within republicanism regards
the point at which engagement with the state is viewed as 'sell-out'. Republican
discourse regarding the 'road to constitutionalism' has provided a dominant
point of contention within and between radical groups in contemporary Ireland.
Tactical diversity among groups presents an immediate problem regarding any
potential formal unity. It is unclear how groups such as RSF, the IRPWA, the
Republican Socialist Movement, Republican Network for Unity or the 32CSM
could unite under one banner while assuming opposing positions regarding
tactics. When tactics are elevated to the position of principle, as was the case
in the 2014 RSF Ard Fheis, little room for compromise is present either internally or between groups. Central to the RSF position is the assertion that RSF
constitutes the true Republican Movement (is the true Sinn Féin) and is the
only organisation which has stayed true to republican ideology and principles.[13]
Consequently, discussion around tactics continues to take place within a context
of fidelity to core republican principles.

Maintaining principles within security legislation

Radical republican groups are operating within the context of all-encompassing
anti-terrorist legislation. Republican groups will need to find new ways to operate within the current legislation if they are to remain relevant. They will find it
necessary to explore new ways of holding public events that will not result in all
persons present being prosecuted. On 28 May 2016 RSF held an event in Lurgan
to unveil a monument to members of the IRA who had been 'killed in action'
in the North Armagh brigade. The event witnessed a heavy police presence and
twelve members of RSF were arrested as they left Lurgan following the event.[14]
Subsequently ninety letters were sent out by the PSNI to individuals who were
present at the event. The charges put forward stated that these individuals par-
took in an illegal parade. The youngest person questioned for attendance at this
event was a ten-year-old boy who was questioned at the side of Banbridge Road[15]
when the bus he was travelling on was stopped and detained by the PSNI; to the

charges the ten-year-old replied 'no comment'. PSNI prosecution of individuals attending radical republican events and parades within the North of Ireland will arguably threaten the sustainability of such events. It is probable that non-members of republican groups will not repeatedly attend such events which will end in their prosecution.

'One Ireland One Vote': the 1916 Societies

Debates around tactics reflect the fact that republicans share a common belief in the right to sovereignty – republicans are united in their assertion of the 1916 Proclamation that 'we declare the right of the people of Ireland to the ownership of Ireland and to the unfettered control of Irish destinies, to be sovereign and indefeasible'.[16] However, division exists within republicanism regarding how that sovereignty should be exercised. In 2012 the 1916 Societies (which were formed in 2009) launched the OIOV campaign, which sought to collectively advance the strategy of an all-Ireland vote on unity (under one umbrella campaign). To an extent, the campaign was a response to Sinn Féin's call for a border poll which would constitute a referendum within the state of Northern Ireland on Irish unity. Dee Fennell, a founder member of the 1916 Societies in Ardoyne in North Belfast, has described the societies as a 'single-issue group' and has commented on the formation of the Societies:

> I think that people are fed up with any sort of brand, a political party as a brand. I think that locally here people and republicans in general in this area would see themselves as having been at times overlooked, basically because what suited a particular party's policy at any given time over the last twenty years was perhaps greater than the demands and needs of the people of this area.[17]

The Societies' membership comprises individuals who are affiliated to different republican groups as well as independents. During the formative stage of the OIOV campaign, the 1916 Societies in Belfast held a 'mock debate' during which members presented arguments for and against a border poll and an all-Ireland vote.[18] The late Tony Catney, a prominent founder member of the Societies, comically assumed a Provisional Sinn Féin position arguing against the OIOV campaign of which he was a founder. Catney stated that debates such as this one would ultimately strengthen the societies' position on relevant matters and would allow the issues to be exposed from all angles, and stated 'the best way to identify your opponent's arguments are taking on your opponent's arguments'.[19] After the formal debate Tony Catney addressed the room with his true opinions:

> It is our job as republicans to change our reality. A referendum isn't the preferred position of republicans.
> [Speaking on the proposed Sinn Féin border poll] Even if people in the six

counties vote yes the triple lock kicks in. Very few people read the Good Friday Agreement.

People need to lift their heads up. I live in Ireland. Why do I have to go to someone like Peter Robinson to ask permission to have a say? The border poll is a sectarian head count. Republicanism is non-sectarian.[20]

The central premise of the OIOV campaign is based upon the traditional republican position that the Irish people (as a whole) have not undertaken an act of self-determination since 1918.[21] Tony Catney proceeded to outline the case for an all-Ireland vote and argued that in schedule one of the Good Friday Agreement 'the Irish aren't mentioned. There is a mistaken belief that the British and unionists will allow the vote to take place.'[22] Catney's speech was followed by passionate comments from the floor which included one speaker stating 'we need to expose the lies of Sinn Féin. We need to expose the myth that a border poll will lead to a united Ireland.'[23]

Significantly, the call for an all-Ireland vote is not shared by all republican groups and republicans have not united in support of the campaign. RSF has rejected the OIOV campaign, as illustrated by the organisation's President Des Dalton at the 2013 RSF Ard Fheis:

Another campaign under the title 'One Ireland – One Vote' is in clear contradiction of the unequivocal statement contained within the 1916 Proclamation. The constitution of Sinn Féin is equally clear in declaring 'that the sovereignty and unity of the Republic are inalienable and non-judicable'. In other words, this is not a right that is negotiable or one that can be given away.[24]

At the 1986 Ard Fheis, Ruairí Ó Brádaigh had stated that the sovereignty and unity of the Republic 'can't be given away and are not a matter for reconsideration. They are absolutes.'[25] Echoing the position of his predecessor, Dalton continued:

The right to exercise national self-determination should not be confused with holding a referendum to determine if such a right exists in the first place. You cannot put to a ballot something that is fundamental to our very definition as a nation.[26]

The 32 County Sovereignty Movement

Francie Mackey,[27] national chairperson of the 32CSM, has not ruled out the coming together of republican groups and has cited the period leading to the 1916 Proclamation:

In the lead-up to 1916, republicans from various views came together with the Rising of Easter 1916 and they produced the 1916 Proclamation which all republican groups, including Sinn Féin, would have us believe that they revere and yet they violate the message in it of the sovereignty of their nation.[28]

The 32CSM (which began as a lobby group within Sinn Féin) have argued that sovereignty is the key issue, as stated by the organisation's honorary president Phil O'Donoghue in Kilkenny:

> We came to the conclusion [within the Provisional Movement] that this just wasn't acceptable. The Mitchell Principles for one. That was an infringement on sovereignty as far as we were concerned but it was also an infringement on the Green Book[29] as well, and that is more or less how we started.[30]

The 32CSM has accepted RSF's Éire Nua policy and the two organisations articulate a similar position on sovereignty, as demonstrated by O' Donoghue:

> The sovereignty of the nation is inalienable. It is therefore not in the competence of any generation of the people to surrender that sovereignty for each generation holds it in trust for the nation. The question of surrender of national independence may not be submitted to an electorate.[31]

The 32CSM and RSF have rejected the One Ireland One Vote campaign propagated by the Societies, and have re-emphasised their allegiance to the First Dáil Éireann and to the Republic.

Saoradh: 'Liberation'

The most recently formed radical republican group is Saoradh, which was launched at the organisation's first Ard Fheis in the Canal Court Hotel in Newry in September 2016.[32] The most prevalent questions facing Saoradh are why they felt the need to form another radical republican group and in what way is this group different from existing groups? Point 3.2 of the party's constitution under 'objectives' states 'to effect an end to the partitionist institutions of Stormont and Leinster House'.[33] Further, point 4.5, under 'means', states:

> Through the contesting of elections where the contesting of such elections is deemed to advance our national objectives. This shall be based upon a clear strategic analysis of the prevailing conditions and balance of forces. (Participation in elections to Westminster and the partitionist institutions of Stormont and Leinster House can only be permitted on an abstentionist ticket.)[34]

Adhering to traditional republican ideology, the organisation has declared that it will be abstentionist regarding Leinster House, Stormont and, unsurprisingly, Westminster. The first chairperson of the party is Davy Jordan, a former republican prisoner from Tyrone.[35] The top table (assumed national executive) at the first Ard Fheis included prominent republicans such as Mandy Duffy from Lurgan (IRPWA), Nuala Perry from Belfast (Independent) and Dee Fennell from Belfast (1916 Societies). In attendance were other well-known republicans such as Colin and Paul Duffy from Lurgan. The organisation claims to have branches in the North and South of Ireland.

Since the party's inception Saoradh has been vocal regarding the issue of prisoners in Maghaberry. Current republican prisoner (and Saoradh member) Nathan Hastings from Derry has stated that Saoradh are the official spokespersons for the prisoners in Roe Four (a wing within Maghaberry prison which houses republican prisoners).[36] Interestingly, at the party's launch a greeting message was read out from veteran republican Billy McKee in Belfast, who has not affiliated with any republican group since RSF. Until around 2009/10 Billy McKee was loosely associated with RSF and unveiled the plaque on the RSF Office on the Falls road in April 2005 to mark the centenary of Sinn Féin. Given that the organisation is in a formative period, little is known about the policies of the party; however, Nathan Hastings[37] has provided an insight into its thinking. Hastings, a former spokesperson for the 32CSM movement in Derry, was in Maghaberry during the formation of Saoradh but has affiliated with the new party. He has argued that there was a need for something new:

> I view the thirty-two county sovereignty movement as a lobby group. There is a need for an organisation which is scientifically socialist along Marxist and Leninist lines.[38]

Hastings has argued that there was a need for a 'revolutionary' republican organisation and has responded to criticism which has been levelled at the party regarding 'a lack of policies'. He has asserted that the party is in its infancy and has stated, 'but who was going to make the policies? They need a ruling executive or Ard Chomhairle as I call them, first and then those things will come.'[39] It remains to be seen how Saoradh will develop and what strategy they will adopt in pursuit of their objectives. The emergence of Saoradh has led to speculation on the current position of the 32CSM, particularly due to the fact that a number of prominent members of Saoradh are former members of the 32CSM. It is also interesting to note that Nathan Hastings has commented 'in my opinion the thirty-twos made a mistake in not coming in as a group within Saoradh'.[40] This suggests that this idea was at least floated and subsequently rejected by the 32CSM. When commenting on his move to Saoradh, Hastings has argued that a clear strategy is absent from some of the existing groups. The reputation of the 32CSM (widely believed to be the political wing of the REAL IRA) never fully recovered from the Omagh bomb of 15 August 1998 that killed twenty-nine people. It remains to be seen whether the emergence of this new organisation will significantly alter the landscape of contemporary radical republicanism.

Loyal to the Republic: attitudes to Leinster House

Radical republicans continue to profess their loyalty to 'the Republic', as proclaimed in the 1916 Proclamation read out by Patrick Pearse under the portico at the front of the GPO in Dublin on Easter Monday. Fundamental to republican ideology is loyalty to the 1916 Republic; and of equal importance is a rejection of the current twenty-six-county state. Consequently, attitudes to Leinster House are a further point of disunity between republican groups. RSF has remained consistent in its opposition to taking seats in Leinster House. RSF President Des Dalton has commented:

> There are groups out there that are ambiguous to say the least about their attitude to that and some of them would see it ... [that] at this particular moment in time yes it probably is of advantage to hold an abstentionist position but [they] would not rule out a change in that somewhere down the road, whereas we would hold the opposite view to that.[41]

Division within republicanism regarding recognition of Leinster House dates back to the Civil War period in 1922–3. In the late 1960s Ruairí Ó Brádaigh had a discussion with Seamus Costello[42] where Costello advocated entering Leinster House as a 'staging post' and a tactical issue. When Ó Brádaigh pointed to past analogies Costello replied that he didn't live through that, to which Ó Brádaigh responded:

> It's like a sausage machine. When you put meat in one end of a sausage machine it will still come out a sausage at the other end. You basically want to put the whole movement through the sausage machine just so that you can be convinced.[43]

Dalton has asserted, 'these are discussions that already took place within our movement'.[44]

The ideological and tactical differences between republican groups make the formation of a broad front unlikely. This view was also demonstrated by the chairperson of éirígí, Brian Leeson in Dublin, who has stated:

> There has been a couple of attempts in trying to create a unified republican front and so forth and our view is that there's not sufficient ideological and strategic ground there ... in essence you don't walk into a marriage that you believe is going to end in divorce.[45]

Éirígí and the Societies: decentralised structures

At the éirígí Ard Fheis in May 2009 the membership voted in favour of registering the party with Leinster House. The party's chairperson, Brian Leeson, has commented, '[F]ollowing a lengthy period of internal debate, the party membership took the decision last May to challenge these institutions both from within and without.'[46] Therefore it appears that the option to contest elections to Leinster House remains open to the party. Éirígí was created in Dublin in 2006 by a group of former Provisional Sinn Féin members who opposed the direction in which Sinn Féin was moving.[47] In 2007 the group took the decision to become a political party. The discourse of éirígí has been dominated by opposition to Sinn Féin's movement away from leftist politics, towards the political centre. Commenting on the emergence of éirígí, Brian Leeson stated:

> The question is – why did we feel the need to start something new and it's a long story that we didn't think any of the existing groups at that point in 2006 had got the mix of social and economic, national, cultural, ideology right in theological terms or strategic tactical terms.[48]

Notably, éirígí has rejected the highly centralised structure of Sinn Féin. From its inception, éirígí adopted a flat structure formed around 'ciorcal' (local branches), which is the Irish word for circle.[49] It is also notable that the party has chosen to use a lower case é at the beginning of éirígí, to reflect the egalitarian structure of the organisation. Each ciorcal has a chairperson who simultaneously occupies a position on the organisation's national executive. The group has also rejected the traditional delegate system which is used by Provisional Sinn Féin and RSF at Ard Fheiseanna; as stated by Leeson, 'we work on a one member one vote principle.'[50]

The adoption of a flat structure was not exclusively based on what the organisation rejected in Provisional Sinn Féin; significantly the éirígí discourse has also rejected what it views as 'authoritarian structures' in RSF. The 1916 Societies have shared éirígí's rejection of the authoritarian structures of Sinn Féin and RSF; subsequently the dominant organising principle of the societies was a decentralised structure. Ciaran Mulholland of the James Connolly Society in West Belfast has described the organisation as:

> Very much the opposite of the Sinn Féin movement where a lot of people came from. You don't have this hierarchical movement.[51]

Given that a significant number of radical republicans (and founder members of radical groups) are former members of Provisional Sinn Féin or the Provisional Movement, it is unsurprising that the form which radical groups have assumed is largely based on what is rejected in Provisional Sinn Féin.[52]

The mantle of true socialism?

Historically, republicanism has been characterised by a strained relationship between nationalist and socialist elements. Contemporary radical republican groups have collectively adopted socialist ideology and principles; however, the emphasis placed on socialist principles has served as a point of contention within the republican world, as groups such as éirígí and RNU have criticised others for being weak on socialist principles and have presented themselves as holding the mantle of 'true socialism'.[53] Republican groups collectively profess an allegiance to the 1916 Proclamation, but some groups emphasise nationalist elements whereas others emphasise Connolly's socialism. In 1897 James Connolly stated:

> If you remove the English army tomorrow and hoist the green flag over Dublin
> Castle, unless you set about the organisation of the Socialist Republic your efforts
> would be in vain. England would still rule you. She would rule you through her
> capitalists, through her landlords, through her financiers, through the whole array
> of commercial and individualist institutions she has planted in this country and
> watered with the tears of our mothers and the blood of our martyrs.[54]

Citing Connolly, groups such as the RSM have proven critical of RSF for holding what they view as an 'ultra-nationalist' outlook, and have stated 'a lot of
people give their lives up for a flag and I find that really really hard to understand.
You know it should be pure allegiance, as Gustavo said, to the working class.'[55]

The late Tony Catney, who was a member of the 1916 Societies in Belfast,
has commented on the wide spectrum that exists within radical republicanism
by stating:

> There are people that I know who are involved in republican struggle and their
> politics are as right wing as Maggie Thatcher ever was. They just want to be right-
> wing Irish rather than right-wing English.[56]

The discourse propagated by each group around socialist principles is reflected
throughout their strategy for moving forward. RSF's Éire Nua document has
been widely accepted by republican groups; however, Francie Mackey of the
32CSM has stated:

> The issue of sovereignty applies to everyone, not just those left-wing groups and
> whilst republicans tend to have their support base in the left of centre the issue of
> sovereignty applies to everyone equally as outlined in the proclamation.[57]

Francie Mackey has cautioned against advocating a particular type of Ireland that
they would want to see after a British withdrawal as:

> You could alienate other people from the issue which you wouldn't want to do
> because whether you're centre or right or left the issue of sovereignty is still the
> same.[58]

For Mackey and the 32CSM the issue of obtaining sovereignty is paramount –
once this has been achieved the *form* which a united Ireland will take is up for
discussion.

Sinn Féin: the 'desire for embourgeoisement'

A dominant theme throughout radical republican discourse has been the argument that Sinn Féin has moved away from its traditional working-class base.
Radical republicans have argued that Sinn Féin has implemented budget cuts
in the North of Ireland while standing on a socialist platform in the South –
arguably leading to the development of a different type of party on each side of
the border. Fra Halligan of the RSM in Belfast has stated:

[Sinn Féin say] 'stop the child benefit, stop the DLA [Disability Living Allowance], stop the working-class credit and let them suffer in Ballymurphy, we don't need them anymore'. They [Sinn Féin] would go wild with rage at you [for saying that], they'd say 'how dare you?' But that is what the people in Ballymurphy say. Not me.[59]

As the message of Sinn Féin has moderated, the target audience of the party has changed. Murray and Tonge have argued that the party's electoral base has expanded to include the Catholic middle class.[60] Independent republican Tommy McKearney, who is a member of the Independent Workers' Union, commented on Sinn Féin's election candidates in the 2002 election in the South of Ireland, making specific reference to the decision by Head Office to replace the local candidate in the Dublin Central constituency, Nicky Kehoe (an ex-IRA prisoner), with a more 'photogenic and middle-class Mary-Lou McDonald'.[61] McKearney has argued that 'while there was no immediate spate of resignations, there was a groundswell of unease with what many saw as a desire for embourgeoisement and an obsession with image. In time this, coupled with the series of u-turns made by Sinn Féin, led to a number of influential activists departing the organisation and in time establishing a new socialist republican party, éirígí.'[62]

In 2009 Sinn Féin president Gerry Adams commented on the party's movement from a more 'defensive stage of struggle into a more offensive stage' and stated, 'there's no reason absolutely why you can't keep the contact with the base in all the ways that are necessary'.[63] However, crucially Adams went on to say 'it might just be a different type of terrain that you are trying to occupy but it requires exactly the same tie-in'.[64] Radical republican groups have rejected Sinn Féin's targeting of a 'new terrain' and have perceived Sinn Féin as abandoning socialist principles. However, a more nuanced picture is presented by independent Tommy McCourt, a former member of the Provisional Movement in Derry, who has argued:

> The Provisional Movement from its inception had never a clear class or socialist policy. It adopted strategies and policies as and when it suited them. I remember way back when the Provos were first coming on the ground they were writing on the wall in the Brandywell – Better dead than red. Then they become suddenly – we are a revolutionary organisation.[65]

Reflective of McCourt's analysis, Tommy McKearney has referred to the absence of 'a coherent analysis and understanding of what it meant to be socialist or how it might be implemented, apart from a broad and sometimes uncertain view that the details could be worked out in the aftermath of an IRA victory'.[66] As well as the Provisional Movement's ambiguous position on socialism, McKearney has highlighted the fact that 'the Provisional IRA was largely a movement of the working class, the unemployed working-class and less well-off rural population. Its support base was made up of those who found themselves doubly disadvantaged as they were excluded and marginalised both by reason of their class and community origins.'[67] It is therefore unsurprising that the radical republican criticism of Sinn Féin is dominated by references to the party 'moving away from socialism and the working-class base'.

Breaking points

Radical republicans have largely failed to successfully articulate a clear strategy for advancing their goals,the absence of which has contributed to a lack of republican unity. Tony Catney of the 1916 Societies in Belfast has argued that:

> A clear analysis of an alternative republican way forward would throw up the points of linkage with other groupings or individuals and I think the republican struggle needs to get to that point as quickly as it can.[68]

However, a strategy for moving forward is inevitably intertwined with views on the struggle (from a radical republican perspective, why the Provisional campaign failed). Radical republicanism is heterogeneous in nature and is highly nuanced regarding perceptions of the past and the development of the Provisional Movement. Groups and independents have remained divided regarding their analysis of the trajectory which the Provisional Movement has taken to the present day.

Existing literature has cited the various 'breaking points' at which individuals departed from the Provisional Movement.[69] RSF, which was formed in 1986, has criticised republicans who left after that year as failing to see the 'writing on the wall'. Whiting in particular has commented on RSF's attitude towards radical republicans who have departed the Republican Movement in more recent years.[70] It would appear that individuals who stayed with the Provisional Movement or with Provisional Sinn Féin until recent times (2005) accepted ideological shifts in position, including the acceptance of Leinster House, entering Stormont or IRA decommissioning – the first time the latter had ever taken place in the history of Irish republicanism. The decommissioning of IRA weapons was a complete departure from previous 'dump arms orders' or declarations of ceasefire from the Republican Movement. IRA decommissioning, the final act of which took place in 2005, saw the IRA leadership engage in a process which put its weapons 'verifiably beyond use', a step unprecedented in Irish republican history.[71] Radical republican Nuala Perry in Belfast has argued:

> I would still have been there for a year or two after the Good Friday Agreement because, contrary to what everybody was telling me at the time, I still believed that 'we'll give it a chance and see how this pans out'. There was still this thinking that all these people that I was with all my life, people that I joined the movement with

and gone through some pretty hard and dangerous times with, were still there and you're saying well if you're still there, contrary to what other people are saying, you have to give it a go. You have to see what will happen in a year.[72]

RSF's isolationist stance is rooted in the belief that it maintains the continuity of the Republican Movement. This position is reflected through language, as the party continues to assert that it is the true Sinn Féin and has repeatedly called on Provisional Sinn Féin to stop using the name Sinn Féin. As recounted earlier, in 1986 Ruairí Ó Brádaigh led a walkout from the Sinn Féin Ard Fheis in the Mansion House in Dublin. Ó Brádaigh and those who went with him reassembled at the West County Hotel and regrouped as RSF. Approximately 130 individuals were present in the hotel, including Ó Brádaigh's brother Seán, Joe O'Neill, Dáithí Ó Conaill, Frank Glynn, Tommy O'Neill and Denis McInerney.[73] Some individuals who were present at the time have argued that a mistake was made in adopting the name Republican Sinn Féin rather than simply maintaining the name Sinn Féin. Among those assembled in the Mansion House was Co. Kerry RSF member Pat Quirke, who has stated:

At that time there was a decision made to call ourselves Republican Sinn Féin. Looking back at what happened I think it was [a mistake]. That they should've stayed Sinn Féin. But I don't condemn. Condemn is a strong word. I went along with it at the time. I went along with it. But I still think it was a mistake.[74]

As illustrated by Pat Quirke, the name Republican Sinn Féin was adopted for pragmatic purposes. RSF is opposed to formal unity with other republican groups (based on resolutions passed in 1999 and 2006) on the basis that RSF is the legitimate Republican Movement. Former vice-president of RSF, Geraldine Taylor in Belfast has stated:

We walked out with the Republican Movement intact. Those who remained in the Mansion House that day were the dissidents.[75]

While RSF members maintain links on an individual basis with members of other groups, no formal organisational links are permissible. At the 2006 RSF Ard Fheis, a resolution was passed which stated that the organisation is prohibited from having links with other republican groups.[76] Further, the RSF code of conduct for members states:

4 Other Political Groupings: As agreed by the 1999 Ard-Fheis, members of Republican Sinn Féin may not take part in political activities with political groupings such as the IRSP or the 32 County Sovereignty or any other political body that either: (A) recognises either the Six or 26-County States or: (B) lays claim to the name of the Republican Movement.

Therefore members of RSF are unequivocally prohibited from engaging in unity with other groups, as it is in violation of their organisation's constitution.

The Continuity IRA and Limerick

In the radical republican world, where various groups co-exist, further confusion has been caused through the emergence of 'CIRA' statements, blogs and graffiti in areas such as West Belfast. The Continuity IRA (which shares an ideology with RSF) has claimed that this is not the Continuity IRA but is a breakaway faction led by Joe Lynch and Des Long in Limerick, former members of RSF who were in favour of 'republican unity'. Existing literature has documented this as a 'split' in RSF and in the Continuity IRA.[77] However, it appears that the Continuity is still intact, with senior figures of the RSF movement such as Dan Hoban reiterating that the 'Limerick group' have broken away and are not the Continuity IRA.[78] In June 2010 the editorial of RSF's newspaper *Saoirse* stated:

> Today yet another group has emerged who by their actions and words are attempting to confuse and demoralise the Republican people of Ireland. This latest group refused to accept the democratic decisions of Republican Sinn Féin as expressed at four successive Ard-Fheiseanna to reject participation in a 'Broad Front'. Having failed in their attempts to subvert the Republican Movement from within they are now trying to do so from outside.

Following this statement, declarations of support for RSF and the Republican Movement were published from Cumann na mBan, Na Fianna Éireann, the prisoners' organisation CABHAIR, and from prisoners in Maghaberry and Portlaoise prisons. A media statement was released from the Continuity IRA which stated:

> The leadership of the Republican Movement wishes to make it known publicly that contrary to claims made privately by those attempting to set up a splinter group no General Army Convention of Óglaigh na hÉireann – popularly known as the Continuity IRA – has been held. An unauthorised meeting which included non-members of the Movement was held under the pretence that it was a conference of local OCs (officers commanding). Some persons attending did so on the understanding that it was a genuine Army meeting. The numbers attending were much smaller than is claimed. When it turned out to be an attack and an undermining of the leadership a number of people departed and reported to Headquarters Staff on what had taken place. As a result the principal people involved were dismissed from membership in accordance with the long-standing General Order No 13. Others were suspended pending an investigation of their position.[79]

Des Long (a leading figure of the Limerick group) was among those reassembled in the West County Hotel in 1986 along with Ó Brádaigh; therefore his departure from RSF in such a manner was unexpected. It also signified the intense level of feeling within RSF and the Continuity IRA regarding opposition to 'broad fronts'. However, it remains unclear why mainstream media continue to appear 'confused' regarding the Limerick group and what took place in 2009/10 within the movement. Events surrounding this breakaway group illustrate issues of central importance to the radical republican world – namely legitimacy, organisational identity, calls for a broad front and groups' 'parroting' of other groups.

A paranoid world

Aside from 'tactical' diversity, a major element of division derives from suspicion and lack of trust within the highly insular radical republican world, as demonstrated by Belfast republican Billy McKee:

> I don't trust the way it's working now. The Special Branch seem to be able to tell you who you were talking to yesterday and so forth. I don't mind talking to people I know, but people I don't know – I steer clear of them.[80]

It is unsurprising that in this atmosphere of mistrust, no formal unity between groups has taken place.[81] A researcher in this area will witness first-hand the level of personal mistrust as they are repeatedly warned to 'stay clear of him' or 'everyone knows that group is full of informers'. A former high-profile prisoner in Maghaberry has claimed that he was imprisoned because 'the groups are infiltrated. There are a number of operations where people were set up.'[82] The narrative around infiltration has intensified in the recent period (since 2005) due to media reports which have claimed that republicans have been approached by MI5. In January 2017 the *Derry Journal* reported one such incident in Dungiven in Derry. The piece stated that a republican male had been approached six times in the previous two years by MI5, in a bid to recruit him as an 'informant'. The individual claimed that one such incident took place while he was on holiday in Spain. In response to the claim a spokesperson for the UK Home Office stated that they would neither confirm nor deny the allegation.[83]

Fluidity in the 'dissident' world

Paranoia is further heightened within the radical republican world due to the high levels of movement between republican groups. In the course of this research many interviewees had moved groups between the time of their interview and completion of the manuscript, some individuals having moved group more than once during this period. As a result of this high level of fluidity, the radical republican discourse has emphasised fears around group infiltration by the security services, particularly in the armed groups. A spokesperson for the Continuity IRA in North Armagh has stated:

> We would try and not [link with other groups] because the simple fact is once you start branching out to other organisations you might compromise your own security. In certain circumstances there might be a bit of co-operation but generally not.[84]

Suspicion is particularly prevalent towards radical republicans who stayed with the Provisional Movement until recent years. The Continuity IRA spokesperson continued:

> There's genuine republicans in the REALs and ONH but there's also people there that in my opinion stayed too long with the Provisionals. For whatever reason they came along in the last number of years. That I would see as a threat. It's a possible security threat.[85]

Prisoners: legitimacy, identity and allegiance

Historically the issue of republican prisoners has assumed a central place in the republican position and message, particularly in relation to the struggle for recognition and legitimacy which culminated in the Hunger Strikes of the early 1980s. When Northern Ireland secretary Merlyn Rees ended special category status in March 1976 a bitter battle ensued between the H-Block prisoners and the British government. Margaret Thatcher's policies of criminalisation resulted in H-Block prisoners embarking on the Blanket Protest in 1976, which led on to Hunger Strikes in 1980 and 1981. On 17 September 2016 Francie Mackey, chairperson of the 32CSM, delivered an oration at a Hunger Strike commemoration in Duleek during which he stated 'just like the Anglo Irish treaty in 1921 the policy of criminalisation was a strategic British effort to fundamentally undermine the sovereign legitimate basis of the republican struggle.'[86]

The issue of current prisoners has assumed a central position in the discourse of radical republicans regarding legitimacy. On 23 October 2016 Ulster Unionist Doug Beattie called for the ending of segregation in Maghaberry prison between republican prisoners and criminal prisoners. When entering Maghaberry prison on a 'visit' instructions will be given to turn right in order to enter into the meeting room for republican prisoners; those visitors turning left enter the meeting room for prisoners who have been jailed for criminal offences. This distinction is made by the prison authorities and republican prisoners are housed in Roes Three and Four after being held for a period of approximately three months in Bann House for assessment to determine where the prisoner will be placed within the prison.

Current relations between republican groups can be examined through the lens of Maghaberry prison, where republican prisoners include members of (or are affiliated to) Republican Network for Unity (Cogús), Óglaigh na hÉireann, CABHAIR[87] (Continuity IRA), the IRPWA, the New IRA, the REAL IRA and non-aligned. Roe Three houses republican prisoners who are affiliated to Cogús, the prisoner's organisation for members of Republican Network for Unity or Óglaigh na hÉireann. Roe Four houses the IRPWA, the New IRA, the REAL IRA and CABHAIR prisoners. Historically, relations between republican groups within the prison have proven largely genial as each group maintained their separate organisational structure; however, periods of high tension between the groups have taken place, particularly during the early 1970s in the context of the split between the Provisional and Official IRA.[88]

In 2014 CABHAIR prisoner Willie Wong in Maghaberry prison stated 'Links between the groups are good. Morale is high … we need to keep the flame burning.'[89] Interaction between prisoners within Maghaberry and their respective leadership outside the prison appears regular, leading to the assumption that relations between the groups within the prison impact (or are indeed reflective of) wider group relations. Despite largely genial relations within the prison, in the intense setting of Maghaberry a struggle regarding identity has played out on Roe Three resulting in CABHAIR prisoner Gabriel Mackle moving to Roe Four. Mackle is the only current CABHAIR prisoner in Maghaberry in comparison to 2010 when there were six CABHAIR prisoners in Roe Three. He has stated:

> They're trying to take my identity … I came into this prison a CABHAIR prisoner and I will leave as a CABHAIR prisoner.[90]

The struggle for identity began when a Cogús rota was posted on the wall in Roe Three which included tasks for CABHAIR prisoners Willie Wong and Gabriel Mackle, who do not come under the Cogús organisational structure. This led the CABHAIR prisoners to reject the instructions on the rota. When Gabriel Mackle expressed his objection to a senior member of Republican Network for Unity from Belfast on Roe Three, the response was 'this is a Cogús landing'.[91] Subsequently relations between Cogús and CABHAIR deteriorated within the prison, resulting in Mackle requesting to be moved to Roe Four, a move which was accepted by Roe Four. While this incident may not reflect the overall positive nature of relations within the prison, it does illustrate the importance of organisational identity and allegiance within the radical republican world, which may be amplified within the confines of the prison. While in Maghaberry Martin Corey has argued 'larger groups are trying to dominate smaller groups'.[92]

Mackle has stressed his loyalty to RSF, stating that when a person enters his cell the first thing they will see is an RSF hankie on the wall. As the only CABHAIR prisoner he has stated 'it's a numbers game. It's because they now have the numbers in here. Republican Sinn Féin fought to get that landing.'[93] Mackle has stated that relations between CABHAIR and RNU prisoners further plummeted regarding relations with the prison staff. Mackle has argued 'Roe Three are not putting it up to the screws. We on Roe Four are the only ones putting it up to the screws.'[94] A confrontation ensued between Mackle and a senior member of RNU who allegedly told Mackle to 'scale it down'. Mackle responded, 'I'm a republican prisoner of course I'll be putting it up to the screws … Roe Three are definitely treated differently to us on Roe Four.'[95]

In 2010, after a dirty protest[96] which lasted approximately nine months, an agreement was reached[97] between the prison authorities and the prisoners through the use of outside facilitators.[98] Similar to the no-wash/dirty protest in Long Kesh prison (from the late 1970s until the 1981 Hunger Strike), the dirty protest in Maghaberry prison in 2010 involved republican prisoners smearing excrement on the walls and floors of their cells as well as emptying urine into the prison landing.[99] The 2010 protest demanded an end to strip searches and more freedom of movement. It appears that republican prisoners were not fully unified in the lead-up to the agreement. Problems have also arisen between the groups regarding the issue of individuals entering the prison on criminal offences and being admitted onto republican landings. In response to this problem RSF President Des Dalton has commented:

> This dishonours all those who went before. I find it offensive to the memory of all republican prisoners and to the memory of those in the past that somebody like that would be classed as a republican prisoner. It devalues the concept.[100]

Similarly, the honorary president of the 32CSM, Phil O'Donoghue, has stated 'yes that was an issue there for a while.'[101]

The August 2010 agreement has not yet been implemented and delegations from Sinn Féin, the Red Cross and the SDLP have entered the prison and met with the prisoners. Alex Attwood from the SDLP and Declan Kearney from Sinn Féin have been among those entering the prison, notably on a 'humanitarian basis'. Current prisoner Nathan Hastings, who is affiliated with Saoradh, has commented 'they [Provisional Sinn Féin] deal with us as political prisoners'.[102] Hastings has stated that Sinn Féin have requested to come into the prison again; however, the prisoners have rejected this and have refused a further meeting based on the fact that 'the 2010 agreement isn't implemented and they're [Sinn Féin] part of the people who could implement it. Why are they saying they agree with us and then don't implement it?'[103]

The lack of co-operation between groups regarding the highly emotive issue of prisoners suggests that any formal organisational co-operation or unity is merely aspirational. The issue of current prisoners has not emerged as a 'single issue' campaign in the traditional sense that was witnessed at the time of the anti-H-Block protests in the early 1980s.[104] Independent councillor for Lisburn, Angela Nelson has called for unity on this issue and has stated:

> Leave whatever hat you are wearing at home. Let's all come on board and be under the one umbrella for the single issue. And that's the human rights of prisoners that exist now … because it has always been the republican way that once you are a POW you are a POW. You have no other affiliation to anybody else.[105]

Nelson has argued, 'under the Hunger Strikes, they weren't all Provisionals … there was never any – that you fought more for Bobby Sands than you did for Mickey Devine. That was never an issue on the outside.'[106] In contrast to the 1981 anti-H-Block protests, current republican groups have not come together around the issue of prisoners. In a Hunger Strike commemoration oration Francie Mackey recognised this fact and stated:

> The same unity of purpose that existed in 1981 does not exist today. We need to address this. There can only be one national army and those taken prisoner for its activities are national prisoners. The practice of republican POWs being somehow relegated to the status of a given prison landing is a farce ... in an almost tragic irony, with the perceived differences we conjure between ourselves; it was the British establishment who always viewed us as one. And in doing so they treated us in kind. For the British, volunteers of the Republican movement and the Republican social-ist movement were united in criminal intent against British interests in Ireland.[107]

However, the less than perfect relations within Maghaberry prison reflect a wider identity struggle within the radical republican world as each group has positioned itself as best placed to move republicanism forward. While calls for unity around prisoners have formed a central point in the radical republican message, there have probably always been minor, if not major, divisions among prisoners. For example, as described in R.W. White's *Out of the Ashes*, Bobby Sands intervened and stopped the INLA from going forward on their own with a second Hunger Strike.[108] It may also be worth noting that White cites min-utes from a meeting on 29 May 1981, just prior to the Irish general election, in which a suggestion by Gerry Adams (if successful) would have eliminated INLA/IRSP candidates.[109]

Independents

The contemporary period in Ireland can be characterised by the emergence of a large body of republicans who assume the label 'independent', resulting in RSF Ard Chomhairle member Martin Duffy stating:

> Independent from what? They say 'we just don't like joining any groups'... I just don't know what they mean by being an independent republican. I think they should join a party and commit themselves to the party and help it gain supporters and go down that road. [110]

'Independent' is not commonly used to mean an elected representative who is not affiliated. Rather, it is used to describe republicans who are not a member of any group. Many radical republicans who identify as 'independent' are former members of the Provisional Movement or Provisional Sinn Féin, who departed in the recent period (post-2005). These individuals have cited the high level of central control which existed in the organisation they left and have argued that their experience within the Provisionals has made them wary of partaking in any other organisation which could restrict their activity and message. Many independents have stated that they questioned the direction of the Provisional Movement while they were still members.

Independents have cited a feeling of isolation and a failure to connect with the overall republican base. Formerly an independent republican in Belfast (since approximately 2000), Nuala Perry was a founding member of Saoradh, which emerged in 2016. Prior to the formation of this organisation she commented 'there are people like myself, and I know at least twenty or thirty other independent republicans who feel very isolated because they don't belong to a certain group'.[111] Regardless of a lack of formal unity between independents, most independent interviewees were united in rejection of an armed campaign at present. While there is no formal coming together of independent revolutionary republicans, some have informally connected in small groups around a particular issue. The most notable example of this concerns the hooded men. A number of the hooded men[112] have come together as a group, a move which was initiated by independent republican Jim Mc Ilmurray in Lurgan. The group are currently engaged in a lengthy legal battle regarding the treatment to which they were subjected in the 1970s.[113] Beyond the coming together of groups such as this, the cause for unity among the groups has not progressed, nor is it likely to in the foreseeable future.

The difficulty in labelling what constitutes 'dissident'

This chapter opened with a quote from Irish republican Christy Burke in Dublin, who is predominantly referred to as an 'independent' by the mainstream. The decision to include Burke in this study on 'dissident' republicanism is based on the fact that he formerly occupied a senior position in the Republican Movement and was an elected representative under the Sinn Féin label. Christy Burke was a Sinn Féin councillor in Dublin City Council and (as an 'independent') was lord mayor of Dublin (2014–15). He was at the final talks in 1998 which led to the Good Friday Agreement; when leaving the talks (after spending the night in Stormont) the car in which he was travelling was overturned by unionist protestors. Burke was never officially a member of Sinn Féin; however, he joined Na Fianna Éireann aged seven and progressed into the IRA, siding with the Provisionals during the split with the Officials in 1969/70. In 2009 Burke resigned from the Sinn Féin Movement and continued as an independent councillor. As an independent Burke was involved in the 'free Marian Price' campaign.

Burke has commented on Sinn Féin: 'they knew I didn't toe the line. If my conscience told me that's wrong I said "that's wrong. I'm not having that" and they detested me for it but they knew I was straight and honest.'[114] In reference to his resignation in 2009, Burke has stated 'I could see a group coming in that was careerist … I'd no problem moving politically and progressing and growing and blossoming. I have no problem with any of that but it was the element of the clientele.'[115] Burke has recalled:

I went to a meeting in Parnell Square one night which I believed was with three or four people and when I went into the room there was about thirty non-elected people all telling councillors what they are going to do and what they are going to not do and I said 'listen I had the balls to go out there and put my face on a poster and knock on doors in my area where I know what's wanted and what's needed and I've done it for twenty odd years. I really don't need any of you lot telling me what to do.' 'Well you'll have to toe the line.' So I said 'I am out of here' and the next morning at six o'clock I picked up the phone and told the media and I said 'I've resigned as the Sinn Féin councillor' and that was it.[116]

The status of independents such as Christy Burke illustrates the difficulty of labelling what constitutes a 'dissident' republican and who should be considered as part of this constituency. Similar to other independents, Burke has commented that he maintains good relations with some members of Sinn Féin and has stated:

I hung in with Adams, I hung in with the likes of Brian Keenan, Lord rest him, who would have been a great friend of mine. I hung in with the guys that were on the Hunger Strikes, friends of mine who gave their lives ... and it began to start to fester. It was as if, like well the war is over and we got what we could out of the working class ... now we are moving on.[117]

Christy Burke is a prominent activist against drugs and was a founder member of 'Concerned Parents Against Drugs' in 1982 in Dublin. Commenting on the more recent period (since 2005) Burke has stated:

There was people in areas who were activists who put their necks on the line on the understanding of the protection of the Republican Movement against drug dealers, they began to get ostracised and they'd be saying to me 'what's going on? Nobody seems to really want to know, only you' ... there was an element in Dublin who despised me, probably because of the broad Dublin accent. I didn't have the degree out of Trinity, but I had the streetwise degree and one out of Mountjoy and one out of Portlaoise.[118]

Wider relations: Provisional Sinn Féin and radical republican groups

The dominant narrative has failed to adequately address the relationship between the Provisional and radical republican worlds. Communication between Sinn Féin and so-called 'dissident' groups has been minimal. Sinn Féin has publicly called for talks with republican groups; however, such talks have not taken place. In 2008 the RSM severed all formal communications with Sinn Féin. Fra Halligan, a prominent member of the RSM in Belfast, has stated:

The IRSP has refused to meet Sinn Féin on numerous occasions. Has refused to meet Gerry Adams and there has been numerous correspondence. We decided four or five years ago, maybe longer, to sever all connections with Sinn Féin and that was a political decision that was relayed to them in written form. They totally disagreed with that obviously and wanted to meet to have further in-depth discussions. That would be a waste of our time and theirs.[119]

Public communications between Sinn Féin and the groups have also been minimal; seldom have they shared a platform at an event. A rare public debate between Sinn Féin and RNU took place in February 2012 in the Waterfront Hall in Belfast. The platform comprised Jim McVeigh for Sinn Féin, Ciaran Cunningham for RNU, author Sam Millar, and former member of the RUC Special Branch Peter Sheridan. The debate was among the first of its kind to take place and provides a unique insight into relations and narrative between the Provisional and radical republican worlds. It was characterised by bitter exchanges between Cunningham and McVeigh as McVeigh referred to radical republican groups as 'small micro-groups that have no support'.[120] McVeigh went on to comment 'we have a strategy that will take us to where we want to be. This is what's missing from these micro-groups.'[121]

A clear narrative developed throughout the debate where the Sinn Féin representative commented on things 'changing' and 'moving on' and RNU's Cunningham cited Sinn Féin persecution and demonisation of radical republicanism. Cunningham commented 'we have been at the tough edge of provisional persecution. This was the reality of trying to organise.'[122] Jim McVeigh stated 'people like Ciaran don't have a strategy. They talk about socialism etcetera',[123] to which Cunningham replied 'you guys used to say the same thing.'[124] Cunningham's quip elicited strong applause from the audience and as the debate proceeded to the question and answer session it became apparent that the audience contained prominent figures from the radical republican world such as Martin Óg Meehan from the Ardoyne area in North Belfast who stated 'I voted yes for the Good Friday Agreement but Sinn Féin aren't going anywhere and the socialist Republic has vanished from the vocabulary of Sinn Féin.'[125] McVeigh stated that Sinn Féin wanted to bring 'dissident groups in from the cold' to which Cunningham replied 'we don't need to be brought in from the cold thanks very much. We need debate about how to get back to social revolutionary.'[126]

This unprecedented public debate highlighted dominant points of contention between the radical republican and Sinn Féin narratives. Sinn Féin's McVeigh reiterated 'we are up for a discussion with other republican groups.'[127] Sinn Féin has made formal approaches to radical republican groups including RSF and the 32CSM (invitations from Sinn Féin were issued from the party's chairperson, Declan Kearney).

32CSM and wider relations

The common belief that the Provisional IRA killed the leader of the REAL IRA in Belfast in 2000[128] strained relations between the 32CSM and Sinn Féin. However, in 2005 the 32CSM distributed documents to political parties including the DUP, UUP and Sinn Féin. Documents sent to the unionist parties asked for an assessment of 'where they see themselves at present', 'where they see themselves going' and 'was a united Ireland free from British interference an inevitable outcome?'[129] The document sent to Sinn Féin asked the party whether the Good Friday Agreement is interim, medium or long term and addressed the issue of sovereignty. The 32CSM also sent documents to the British and Irish governments. Tony Blair's office acknowledged receipt of the document and stated that it had been passed to the secretary of state in Belfast. The Dublin government also acknowledged receipt of the document. Francie Mackey has commented:

> None of the political parties including Sinn Féin acknowledged that they received it, even though it was handed in person into the Sinn Féin office for the attention of Gerry Adams at their office on the Falls road in Belfast.[130]

Relations between Sinn Féin and the 32CSM hit a low point when Sinn Féin asked the latter to enter into discussions. As stated by Mackey:

> Particularly in the lead-up to an important election, they tried to use the issue of meeting and discussion and said they'd invited the Sovereignty Movement to talk to them and that's quite true. But before we even answered they were on the media announcing it. So we have to treat it that it was deliberate that they'd invited us for discussions because they see that as advantageous by muddying the waters in the republican base … it was divisive.[131]

Mackey has commented that the 32CSM are still awaiting a response to the questions outlined in the document they sent to Sinn Féin, as a foundation for any talks which would take place between the two organisations. The 32CSM have sent documents to RSF in the past and RSF has acknowledged receipt; however, no formal meetings have taken place. The most recent correspondence from the 32CSM to RSF came in July 2016 regarding the fallout from Brexit. Richard Behal has commented:

> The sovereignty committee have actually agreed to adopt the Éire Nua plan of RSF… and that's a very important development. I don't understand that every time a demand is made [from the 32CSM] for a meeting, RSF and the Continuity IRA turn it down. Is it, it's my football and you are not going to play with it?[132]

Shortly after the formation of the 32CSM, the organisation's honorary president Phil O' Donoghue initiated contact with Ruairí Ó Brádaigh and a former member of RSF from Limerick. O'Donoghue has stated that he outlined the 32CSM position and that:

they were interested but not so much on the political level as the military. I said, I can't speak for you on that end of it but can we arrange to meet? Whatever took place at that meeting is between them ... Just before he [Ó Brádaigh] died he was going to meet Francie and myself but we were just too late.[133]

RNU

The emergence of RNU in 2007 was an attempt to form an umbrella organisation which would house a wide spectrum of non-mainstream republicans. However, the organisation developed in such a way as to form its own distinct group identity, allegedly sharing an ideology with the armed group ONH. A decade later, in October 2017, the entire Ard Chomhairle of RNU, along with several members, resigned from the organisation. On 10 October *The Pensive Quill* published a statement by 'a collective of former RNU and Cogús activists' regarding the resignations. The statement, which was drafted by the former Ard Chomhairle of RNU, described the decision as unanimous. The statement revealed that in August 2017 RNU had held a national workshop at which the organisation explored the 'long term viability of the movement'. The workshop highlighted the 'lack of any political strategy, and more precisely one to differentiate it from the other republican groupings – poor morale, stunted growth and a growing issue with the unmanageable and ambiguous organisation of Cogús'.[134] The statement revealed that the resignations took place due to the conclusion that 'RNU was a party no longer capable and functioning in the current political climate'.[135] Interestingly, the statement argued 'Irish republicanism in its current state is fractured while what it requires is unity.'[136]

Conclusion

I've seen too many splits, many over personalities. Cliques. The thing is too big for that. You are dealing with life and death and we have to move on from being children.

-Richard Behal, interview with the author, Killarney, 31 October 2013

There is recognition from radical republican groups and independents (with the exception of RSF) that working together would be beneficial to the republican cause. However, as outlined throughout this chapter, the prospects for formal unity are dim, particularly given the recent formation of a new organisation, Saoradh. In 2013 Billy McKee commented 'I'm not in touch with any of these groups now. I'm not even associated with them. But I would never turn my back on them. I would never condemn anything they do.'[137] McKee's stance in 2013 makes his declaration of support in 2016 for the new party Saoradh notable and poses the question of why McKee has declared support for this particular organisation. Speculation includes McKee's support of (and friendship with) some of the key figures in Belfast. It appears that personalities have proven influential within the radical republican world and often dictate whether or not individuals are willing to associate with particular groups. Central to the discourse propagated by each group is the argument that *their* group will best advance the republican cause.

Notes

1 Albert Allen, interview with the author, Belfast, 17 October 2013.

2 White, *Provisional Irish Republicans*, p. 11.

3 *Ibid.*, p. 11.

4 The Queen's official title is 'Queen of the United Kingdom and the other Commonwealth realms'.

5 See Frampton, *Legion of the Rearguard*; Morrison, *Origins and Rise*; Horgan, *Divided We Stand*; Whiting, *Spoiling the Peace?*.

6 Ciaran Mulholland, interview with the author, Belfast, 8 May 2014.

7 Joe Dillon, interview with the author, Skerries, 19 March 2013.

8 For information on Wynn's Hotel please see J.A. Gaughan, *Austin Stack: Portrait of a Separatist* (Dublin, Kingdom Books, 1977). Also see Connell, 'Founding of the Irish Volunteers', *History Ireland*, 21: 6 (November–December 2013).

9 Mary Ward née Lawler is a member of RSF and Cumann na mBan living in Donegal. She is originally from County Cork and was an organiser for Sinn Féin in Munster in the 1970s. Mary is the widow of Pat Ward from Burtonport in County Donegal, who as a republican prisoner took part in Hunger and Thirst Strikes in the 1970s in the South of Ireland. Pat Ward died in 1988 due to the effects of the Hunger Strikes.

10 A. Maillot, *In the Shadow of History: Sinn Féin, 1926–70* (Manchester, Manchester University Press, 2015); B.P. Murphy, *Patrick Pearse and the Lost Republican Ideal* (Dublin, James Duffy & Co. Ltd, 1991). Also see C.H. Fallon, *Soul of Fire: A Biography of Mary MacSwiney* (Cork, Mercier Press, 1986).

11 Under section 41 of the Terrorism Act 2000 suspects can be held without a warrant for forty-eight hours.

12 See *Saoirse: Irish Freedom*, December 2014 and, 'No co-operation with British forces of occupation! Build RSF in North Armagh', *The Pensive Quill*, 21 November 2014. For Cáit Trainor's statement on the resignation please see www.politicalworld.org. Accessed 17 July 2018.

13 R. Ó'Brádaigh, *Dílseacht: The Story of Comdt. General Tom Maguire and the Second (All Ireland) Dáil* (Dublin, Irish Freedom Press, 1997). Also see Frampton, *Legion of the Rearguard*; Whiting, *Spoiling the Peace?*.

14 C. Young, 'One man charged after masked colour party takes part in Lurgan parade', *Irish News* (30 May 2016).

15 Banbridge road appears to be the preferred location for the PSNI to arrest and question those coming from republican events in the republican Kilwilkee estate in Lurgan.

16 1916 Proclamation, 24 April 1916.

17 Dee Fennell, interview with the author, Belfast, 28 November 2013.

18 1916 Societies debate on 'One Ireland One Vote' campaign, West Belfast, 2009.

19 *Ibid.*

20 *Ibid.*

21 In the 1918 election Sinn Féin candidates won seventy-three seats in twenty-four counties on an abstentionist basis. On 21 January 1919 the Dáil met in Dublin. For more information see J. Bowyer Bell, *The Secret Army: The IRA 1916–1979* (Dublin, Poolbeg Press Ltd, 1990).

22 Tony Catney, 1916 Societies' debate on 'One Ireland One Vote' campaign, Belfast, 2009.

23 *Ibid.* Anonymous speaker.

24 Des Dalton, presidential address, RSF Ard Fheis, Dublin, 2013. See *Saoirse: Irish Freedom*, No. 320 (December 2013).

25 Sinn Féin Ard Fheis, 1986, speech by Ruairí Ó Brádaigh. Text available at http://cain.ulst.ac.uk/issues/politics/docs/sf/rob021186.htm. Accessed 17 July 2018.

26 Des Dalton, presidential address, RSF Ard Fheis, Dublin, 2013.

27 As well as being a senior member of the 32CSM, Francie Mackey was a Sinn Féin councillor in Omagh and was chairman of the Mountfield area renewal scheme in Omagh.

28 Francie Mackey, interview with the author, Omagh, 8 February 2013.

29 The Green Book (which emerged within the prisons in the 1970s) is the IRA's training manual, setting out the leadership structure, election procedures for leadership, overall structure of the organisation, the IRA constitution and general army orders.

30 Phil O' Donoghue, interview with the author, Kilkenny, 4 November 2013.

31 *Ibid.*

32 C. Young, 'New revolutionary republican party Saoradh launched', *Irish News* (26 September 2016).

33 www.saoradh.ie. Accessed 17 July 2018.

34 *Ibid.*

35 Young, 'New revolutionary republican party Saoradh launched'. The position of chairperson will be rotated.

36 Nathan Hastings, interview with the author, Maghaberry prison, 8 March 2017.

37 For information on Hastings' imprisonment see www.bbc.co.uk/news/uk-northern-ireland-foyle-west-29080251. Accessed 17 July 2018.

38 Nathan Hastings, interview with the author, Maghaberry prison, 1 March 2017.

39 *Ibid.*

40 Nathan Hastings, interview with the author, Maghaberry prison, 8 March 2017.

41 Des Dalton, interview with the author, Dublin, 15 February 2013.

42 Seamus Costello was a leader of Official Sinn Féin and latterly the IRSP.

43 This was told to Des Dalton by Ruairí Ó Brádaigh. Des Dalton, interview with the author, Dublin, 15 February 2013.

44 *Ibid.*

45 Brian Leeson, interview with the author, Dublin, 1 February 2013.

46 'Éirígí registers as political party in 26 counties', *Irish Republican News* (29 March 2010).

47 For details on the emergence of éirígí see Frampton, *Legion of the Rearguard* and Whiting, *Spoiling the Peace?*.

48 Brian Leeson, interview with the author, Dublin, 1 February 2013.

49 The ciorcal was the organising unit for the Fenians. See F. McCluskey, *Fenians and Ribbonmen: The Development of Republican Politics in East Tyrone, 1898–1918* (Manchester, Manchester University Press, 2011).

50 Brian Leeson, interview with the author, Dublin, 1 February 2013.

51 Ciaran Mulholland, interview with the author, Belfast, 8 May 2014.

52 Saoradh, the most recently formed republican group, has emphasised the flat structure of the organisation and the bottom-up approach. The organisation was founded in 2016 around former republican prisoners. At the time of its formation, Saoradh was described by the founding members as a political vehicle rather than a political party. Saoradh rejects authoritarian structures such as those in Provisional Sinn Féin. Notably the majority of its founding members are individuals who remained within Sinn Féin or the Provisional Movement until the more recent period – post-1998. For an interview by Martin Galvin with Saoradh's Packy Carty in February 2017 see http://thepensivequill.am/2017/02/saoradh-rebuilding-republican-movement.html.

53 Éirígí has been most visible in Belfast and Dublin through its public meetings on austerity.

54 James Connolly, *Shan Van Vocht* (Socialist Newspaper), January 1897. Reprinted in P. Beresford Ellis (ed.), *James Connolly: Selected Writings* (London, Pluto, 1997), p. 124.

55 Fra Halligan, interview with the author, Belfast, 19 November 2013.

56 Tony Catney, interview with the author, Belfast, 14 September 2012.

57 Francie Mackey, interview with the author, Omagh, 8 February 2013.

58 *Ibid.*

59 Fra Halligan, interview with the author, Belfast, 19 November 2013.

60 Jocelyn Evans and Jonathan Tonge, 'Social class and party choice in Northern Ireland's ethnic blocs', *West European Politics*, 32:5 (2009), 1012–30. Also see Murray and Tonge, *Sinn Féin and the SDLP*; and McKearney, *The Provisional IRA*.

61 McKearney, *The Provisional IRA*, p. 197.

62 *Ibid.*, p. 197

63 Gerry Adams, interview with the author, Belfast, 5 March 2009. Gerry Adams retired as president of Sinn Féin in February 2018 and was succeeded by the party's vice-president, Mary-Lou McDonald.

64 *Ibid.*

65 Tommy McCourt, interview with the author, Derry, 20 August 2013. McCourt is a former member of the Official IRA and a founder member of the IRSP.

66 McKearney, *The Provisional IRA*, p. 106.

67 *Ibid.*, p. 99.

68 Tony Catney, interview with the author, Belfast, 14 September 2012.

69 Frampton, *Legion of the Rearguard*; Morrison, *Origins and Rise*; Horgan, *Divided We Stand*; Whiting, *Spoiling the Peace?*.

70 Whiting, *Spoiling the Peace?*, pp. 130–1.

71 For information on IRA decommissioning see Chapter three 'Ceasefires and Decommissioning'.

72 Nuala Perry, interview with the author, Belfast, 15 August 2013. Nuala Perry was an independent when this interview was given; however, she subsequently became a member of the executive of Saoradh.

73 White, *Ruairí Ó Brádaigh*.

74 Pat Quirke, interview with the author, Tralee, 30 October 2013.

75 Geraldine Taylor, interview with the author, Belfast, 14 October 2012. Taylor was vice-president of the organisation from 2009–13 and was a member of Cumann na mBan.

76 While RSF does not have formal links with republican groups, the organisation does work with groups such as the Peace and Neutrality Alliance on common issues such as neutrality and opposition to the EU. Links also exist with trade unions and anti-austerity groups, among others.

77 See Morrison, *Origins and Rise*, pp. 197–8. Morrison states 'These two groups are now in immediate competition for both membership and support. They are in the final stage of a split' (p. 198). Also see Horgan, *Divided We Stand*, pp. 26–7. Horgan states 'The most recent divide occurred in 2010 when the paramilitary CIRA moved out from under the control of the RSF leadership, who they believed were stifling them militarily' (p. 26).

78 For an account of the emergence and development of the Limerick group (the Limerick Independent Organisation/'Real' Sinn Féin) see R.W. White, *Out of the Ashes: An Oral History of the Provisional Irish Republican Movement* (Kildare, Merrion Press, 2017), pp. 180–1.

79 'IRA speaks; Army Council intact and in control', *Saoirse: Irish Freedom*, No. 278 (June 2010).

80 Billy McKee, interview with the author, Belfast, 8 August 2013.

81 The recently formed Saoradh does not represent a coming together of existing groups; rather, it is a new group comprising former members of other groups and independents.

82 Male, 50s, interview with the author, Maghaberry prison.

83 'It's like something out of a movie says Dungiven man asked to work as informant for MI5', *Derry Journal* (24 January 2017).

84 Male, CIRA, interview with the author, North Armagh, January 2014. This individual has been a member of the Continuity IRA in North Armagh for more than ten years.

85 *Ibid*.

86 Oration by Francie Mackey, Hunger Strike commemoration in Duleek organised by the Duleek Hunger Strike monument committee, 17 September 2016. Text available at https://republican-news.org/current/news/2016/10/we_are_the_authors_of_this_str.html. Accessed 4 July 2018.

87 Commentators frequently compare Cabhair to the IRPWA; however, the distinction must be made that Cabhair deals solely with prisoners' welfare and the welfare of prisoners' families as opposed to being a political organisation.

88 B. Hanley and S. Millar, *The Lost Revolution: The Story of the Official IRA and the Worker's Party* (Ireland, Penguin, 2009).

89 Willie Wong, interview with the author, Maghaberry prison, 9 January 2014. Willie Wong was released from Maghaberry prison in 2016.

90 Gabriel Mackle, interview with the author, Maghaberry prison, 27 September 2016.

91 Cogús has not granted interviews with their prisoners.

92 Martin Corey, interview with the author, Maghaberry prison, 30 August 2013.

93 Gabriel Mackle, interview with the author, Maghaberry prison, 27 September 2016.

94 *Ibid.*

95 *Ibid.*

96 Éamon Ó'Cuív visited the prison at this time, as covered by media such as the *Irish News*.

97 For information on the background to the 2010 agreement see 'August 2010 agreement: a brief historical and political context' on the IRPWA website: www.irpwa.com. For details on the agreement see www.irsp.ie/news/?p=184. Accessed 17 July 2018.

98 See www.irsp.ie/news/?p=184. Accessed 17 July 2018.

99 In 1976 special category status was removed from prisoners, resulting in a loss of political status and the associated 'privileges' and remission. In protest against this move, republican prisoners refused to wear prison-issue uniforms or to undertake prison work. Kieran Nugent, the first IRA member arrested after the ending of special category status, refused to wear the prison uniform and after being put in his cell without any clothes wrapped himself in a blanket and thus the 'Blanket Protest' had begun. In 1978 the protest escalated to the no-wash protest and then the 'dirty protest'. In 1980 the protest further escalated to Hunger Strike. See White, *Out of the Ashes* and English, *Armed Struggle* (2012).

100 Des Dalton, interview with the author, Dublin, 27 September 2016.

101 Phil O' Donoghue, interview with the author, Kilkenny, 4 November 2013.

102 Nathan Hastings, interview with the author, Maghaberry prison, 8 March 2017.

103 *Ibid.*

104 For details on the anti-H-Block campaign see D. Beresford, *Ten Men Dead: The Story of the 1981 Irish Hunger Strike* (London, Hunter Publishing, 1987): Clarke, *Broadening the Battlefield*.

105 Angela Nelson, interview with the author, Belfast, 17 September 2012.

106 *Ibid.*

107 Francie Mackey, oration at Hunger Strike commemoration in Duleek, 17 September 2016. Text available at https://republican-news.org/current/news/2016/10/we_are_the_authors_of_this_str.html. Accessed 4 July 2018.

108 For a detailed account of division in the lead-up to the Hunger Strike see White, *Out of the Ashes*, p. 177.

109 *Ibid.*, p. 184.

110 Martin Duffy, interview with the author, Lurgan, 24 August 2013. During this interview Martin Duffy (who was imprisoned in November 1998) revealed that he was the first republican prisoner in Maghaberry prison in the post-Good Friday Agreement period.

111 Nuala Perry, interview with the author, Belfast, 15 August 2013.

112 The fourteen men who comprise the group known as the 'hooded men' were subjected to sensory deprivation interrogation techniques by the British army and RUC, including the use of white noise, sleep deprivation, food and drink deprivation and hooding in the 1970s. They have mounted a legal challenge in Belfast under the representation of Kevin Winters Solicitors claiming that the police, secretary of state and justice minister have failed to investigate allegations that they were tortured.

113 In 1978 the Irish government took the British government to the European Court of Human Rights, which ruled that the hooded men had been subjected to inhuman and degrading treatment but not torture. In 2014 the Irish government received a number of documents which had not been disclosed by the British government in 1978, leading the Irish government to seek a revision of the 1978 ruling; this was refused by the European Court of Human Rights in 2018. The Irish government is seeking a referral to the Grand Chamber of the European Court of Human Rights. The case is on-going. See https://madden-finucane.com/2018/06/12/hooded-men-case-now-to-be-referred-to-grand-chamber-by-irish-government/. Accessed 17 July 2018.

114 Christy Burke, interview with the author, Dublin, 19 March 2013.

115 *Ibid.*

116 *Ibid.*

117 *Ibid.*

118 *Ibid.*

119 Fra Halligan, interview with the author, Belfast, 19 November 2013.

120 Debate in the Waterfront Hall, Belfast, 11 February 2012, which the author attended.

121 *Ibid.*

122 *Ibid.*

123 *Ibid.*

124 *Ibid.*

125 *Ibid.*

126 *Ibid.*

127 *Ibid.*

128 Tonge, '"No one likes us; we don't care"' .

129 Francie Mackey, interview with the author, Omagh, 8 February 2013.

130 *Ibid.*

131 *Ibid.*

132 Richard Behal, interview with the author, Killarney, 31 November 2013.

133 Phil O'Donoghue, interview with the author, Kilkenny, 4 November 2013.

134 RNU, 'RNU no longer capable', *The Pensive Quill* (10 October 2017). http://thepensivequill.am. Accessed 17 July 2018.

135 *Ibid.*

136 *Ibid.*

137 Billy McKee, interview with the author, Belfast, 8 August 2013.

3

Ceasefires and decommissioning

Militant republicanism throughout our history has always been about defending the sovereignty of the nation. That was their only legitimacy and that remains their only legitimacy.

> Francie Mackey, interview with the author, Omagh, 8 February 2013

As a member of the Provisional IRA, legitimacy was given to me by the state that oppressed me. We asked for change in a peaceful and democratic fashion and we were shot down.

> Tommy McKearney, interview with the author, 4 October 2012

I didn't join to fight for civil rights. I went out to achieve a thirty-two-county Republic. I wasn't going to be beholden to Britain to grant me the right to have a vote, to grant me the right to get a job.

> Francie McGuigan, interview with the author, Belfast, 24 July 2013

Provisional IRA ceasefires (1994 and 1997)

At midnight on 31 August 1994, from my West Belfast home I could hear the sound of continuous gun-fire in the distance. The Provisional IRA had declared a ceasefire. The ceasefire was called amid a wider context of back-channel negotiations between the British government and the IRA, the Hume–Adams dialogue, electoral advances of Sinn Féin in the North and South of Ireland, and significant shifts in strategy by Provisional Sinn Féin, which was transforming into a constitutional nationalist party. The early 1990s heralded a new era for Provisional republicanism where the traditional republican position was reiterated *alongside* the promotion of an equality agenda within the North. The revised message, as articulated by the Provisionals, was the culmination of a rethink within the movement which had taken place since the mid-1980s. Provisionals continued to argue that the state of Northern Ireland was un-reformable and that the movement would reject any internal solution; however significant shifts were taking place within the organisation's thinking. Sinn Féin has propagated the argument that the pursuit of equality within the Northern state exists 'within' the pursuit of sovereignty. During this period there was also a shift regarding the relationship between the political and the military; in the post-ceasefire context the military side was relegated beneath the political (a significant reversal of traditional positions).[1]

At 6pm on 9 February 1996 the PIRA ended its cessation of activities. The Provisional Movement viewed the Conservative government under the leadership of John Major as acting with hostility towards the peace process, rather than demonstrating genuine engagement in a bid to make progress. Despite this, the wider movement continued its communication with the British government as well as the on-going talks between Gerry Adams and John Hume. In 1997 the winds changed and the British Labour Party under Tony Blair won the UK election, thus transforming the context in which Sinn Féin was operating. That year Sinn Féin made a historic announcement that the organisation endorsed the Mitchell Principles which committed the party to 'democratic and exclusively peaceful means of resolving political issues'.[2] The all-party talks in 1996 during the lead-up to the Good Friday Agreement had been chaired by George J. Mitchell. Sinn Féin was excluded from these talks on the basis that the IRA had resumed its campaign. The talks ceased in 1997; however, Mitchell produced a report which set out principles for inclusion of Sinn Féin in subsequent talks. The Mitchell report's principles stated that parties must commit to 1) democratic and exclusively peaceful means; 2) total disarmament of all paramilitary organisations; 3) disarmament taking place in a manner verifiable by an independent commission; 4) renunciation of the use of force; 5) acceptance of the agreement reached without attempts to alter it by force or the threat of force; and 6) an end to punishment beatings and killing.[3]

Sinn Féin's acceptance of the Mitchell Principles was a crucial step preceding the party's entry into all-party talks which culminated in the Good Friday Agreement of 10 April 1998.[4] 1997 also saw Sinn Féin reverse a long-held republican position through its acceptance of the principle of consent which is present in strand one of the Good Friday Agreement. The consent principle was fundamentally opposed to the traditional republican position, which had described consent as tantamount to a unionist veto. Sinn Féin's rejection of the premise of consent was a major point of division in correspondence between Sinn Féin and the SDLP during the Hume–Adams dialogue of the late 1980s and early 1990s.[5] The party's acceptance of consent, coupled with the Mitchell Principles, fundamentally altered the political landscape and solidified the end of the PIRA campaign. Acceptance of the consent principle was tantamount to acceptance of 'another way forward', thus removing the ideological rock upon which republicanism had rested in the modern period – that the Irish people as a whole had not conducted an act of self-determination since 1918.

Tommy McKearney has stated that the first post-ceasefire step for the Provisional IRA was to issue a statement saying that their war was 'definitively over' and (reflecting the language of the Mitchell Principles) they would 'henceforth adhere to purely democratic and peaceful means'.[6] However, as noted by Tommy McKearney, 'this was in some ways a meaningless statement, since no army council or GHQ [General Headquarters] staff can hope to bind the hands of future generations. What it did do though was to publicly humiliate the organisation by forcing it effectively to say "please" and then "pretty please" … [and then] … undergo the indignity of decommissioning its arms.'[7] Sinn Féin's acceptance of the Mitchell Principles saw prominent republicans such as Francie Mackey, Joe Dillon and Mickey McKevitt depart the Provisional Movement and form the 32CSM. The REAL IRA was also formed at this time, which shares an ideology with the 32CSM.

Dissention in the ranks

Alongside rejection of the Mitchell Principles and consent, the Provisional IRA ceasefires of the 1990s proved a significant departure point for some members of the Provisional Movement who are now termed 'dissident republicans' by the mainstream.[8] For those who departed the Provisional Movement in opposition to the ceasefires, a central component of their narrative rests on the manner in which the ceasefires came about and the way in which they were 'sold to the base'. Echoing arguments presented by O'Brien in *The Long War*, Richard Behal (a former senior member of the Republican Movement) has argued that the IRA ceasefires of the 1990s were sold to the base on the following grounds:

1) there will be a united Ireland by 2016
2) The Brits are pulling out.[9]

Behal has stated that he was deeply concerned about the above 'reassurances' which were being provided to the base and that he approached a 'top IRA commander' at the time:

> Come on. Don't give me bullshit. I've been through too much, seen too much and I know too much, what the fuck is going on? [the commander responded] 'Oh. I was at a meeting with GHQ today. It can't be said openly but I've got categorical assurance, if the Brits haven't shown the beginning of disengagement in six months the ceasefire is over and we are going back to war in six months.' I said – are you sure of this? 'Sure as I can be', he said, 'I got it from the chief of staff himself.'[10]

Evidently there were those within the Republican Movement who at this time doubted whether or not the leadership were serious about a permanent cessation.

External to discussions which were taking place within the republican family, the ceasefire of 1994 was greeted on the streets of Belfast with jubilance and, as recollected by the author, black taxis drove up and down the Falls road in West Belfast with tricolours hanging out of their windows and beeping their horns, reflective of the celebratory atmosphere. Richard Behal (who was not reassured by the words of the senior commander) recalled witnessing the scene in Belfast:

> I said, are these Belfast people going out of their fucking minds? What liberation? What the hell? It's a ceasefire that was called by the IRA! I said, there must be something I don't know about. I regret to say I was right. And unfortunate Belfast people in the euphoria, even the people in the streets, they all fell for it. It was like a victory parade, like VE day. It wasn't. It was the day they had lost all that had been sacrificed – a lot of it was lost.[11]

Similarly, independent republican Tommy Gorman in Belfast has recalled the period 'me and Mackers [Anthony McIntyre] – I remember one time standing on the top of the Whiterock road[12] when they announced this, their ceasefire and the decommissioning. And this cavalcade of cars went past with tricolours out the window. And we said it was the turkeys celebrating Christmas. And we laughed at them.'[13]

Billy McKee, active in Na Fianna Éireann since 1936 and the Republican Movement since 1939, has recalled 'the day the thing was made there was people actually cried, republicans when they heard about it being accepted'.[14] One such republican was Maire Óg Drumm from Belfast, who went on to join éirígí and is now independent:

> I remember driving through Glendalough, this traffic jam, and it came on the news saying that the ceasefire had been called and I remember sitting in our car and I just cried and I said 'that's it' and I just knew in my own head that was it, that it was over and I thought but where are they going to bring us now?[15]

During that period on-the-ground whispers permeated throughout nationalist areas in Belfast that Gerry Adams had a grand strategy which would advance republicanism – a card which hadn't yet been revealed or played. Geraldine Taylor, who was a member of RSF from its formation in 1986, recalled 'I went into one guy's house and he said he's [Adams] something up his sleeve. I says there's nothing else up there but his arm. It's proved to be true.'[16]

The Waterfront debate: 2012

The first public debate during which mainstream and radical republicans shared a platform took place in the Waterfront Hall in Belfast on 11 February 2012. The debate was dominated by a central point of contestation – the raison d'être of the Provisional IRA's campaign. From the platform Provisional Sinn Féin's Jim McVeigh categorically stated, 'our conflict began because we were second-class citizens. To defend our communities. We always said if there was another way we would take it.'[17] In response, also on the platform, Ciaran Cunningham from RNU vehemently rejected McVeigh's argument, reiterating the traditional republican position that the campaign was in pursuit of Irish sovereignty. Thus ensued a debate which strikes to the heart of the Provisional–'dissident' divide, that is, motivations for the Provisional IRA campaign and therefore justification (or lack of) for an armed campaign in current circumstances. Radical republicans who have continued to pursue the armed campaign have rejected the manner in which the ceasefires of the 1990s were called and subsequently handled. The central point of division regarding the ceasefires (and therefore the rasion d'être of the campaign) necessitates an examination of the birth of the Provisionals in 1969.

A phoenix rising from the ashes

In the late 1960s the Civil Rights Movement in America (against racial segregation) gathered momentum and adopted the slogan 'we shall overcome'. At the same time, momentum was gathering around civil rights in the state of Northern Ireland: the influence of the American civil rights campaign was evidenced through the adoption of the same slogan by the Northern Ireland Civil Rights Association. NICRA, which demanded equal treatment for Catholics, was 'met by the violence of Protestant loyalists, who in the summer of 1969, attacked a Catholic community left defenceless by a moribund IRA'.[18] The Provisionals emphasised an 'overriding need for a defence force to protect vulnerable Catholic communities from sectarian attack'.[19] Subsequently the ranks of the Provisional IRA were swelled with recruits eager to defend their communities throughout the North. As documented by English, the Provisionals 'began primarily in response to defensive need, to urgent danger'.[20] The violence which erupted in response to the Civil Rights Movement provided unanticipated momentum to the old IRA, as demonstrated by a radical republican in Belfast who has recalled 'I remember going to training camps from the early '60s believing that there is never going to be the opportunity to use this.'[21]

The Provisional IRA emerged within the context of systemic structural inequality and discrimination within the state of Northern Ireland.[22] The newly formed Provisional IRA reiterated the traditional republican position that the state of Northern Ireland was un-reformable. The pre-1969 IRA (Old IRA) had a formative influence in the emergence of the Civil Rights Movement directly through the Wolfe Tone Societies.[23] It is therefore unsurprising that traditional republican ideology seeped into the development of the civil rights message which reinforced that the partitionist state of Northern Ireland needed to be dismantled. Opposition to structural inequalities within the Northern state was perfectly compatible with the traditional republican anti-partitionist stance. The contemporary Provisional narrative has retrospectively emphasised the 'defender' element of the movement at that time. In contrast, radical republicans, while accepting the defender element within the Provisional campaign, have rejected the manner in which the Provisional Movement has developed since. Radical republicans have argued that Provisional Sinn Féin has embarked upon a path to constitutionalism which has incorporated the party further into the state of Northern Ireland, rather than seriously attempting to dismantle the state and 'smash Stormont' (a republican slogan which appeared on posters in the 1980s). Radical republicans have cited how far Sinn Féin has travelled from 'smash Stormont' to taking seats as Stormont ministers, and in the words of radical republican critics, they have gone on to 'administer British rule in Ireland'. Belfast republican Francie McGuigan has argued:

> We spent our time trying to take Stormont down to make British rule in Ireland impossible and we had a fair amount of success at it but now Sinn Féin today are the people that is stabilising the British position in Ireland by working within Stormont.[24]

Brian Leeson in Dublin, the chairperson of éirígí, has argued:

> in terms of cause and effect it is clear that in terms of the Provisionals the real motive engine within the Provisionals was the denial of civil rights to the Catholic middle class. At the point at which they were granted through the Good Friday Agreement it appeared that the reasons for the Provisionals' existence disappeared.[25]

The radical republican constituency has argued that, while this was the 'context' into which the Provisional IRA was born, these 'structural conditions' were not the primary *motivation* of volunteers. Whilst the Provisionals at this time admitted masses of volunteers who were joining in a 'defender' capacity, interviewees (who were in the Republican Movement prior to the formation of the Provisionals in 1969) have stressed their primary motivation as Irish sovereignty. Freedom and sovereignty were paramount. Jim McCrystal, an ex-republican prisoner in Lurgan, has stated:

> I was always told in the Republican Movement your mandate was as long as the Brits were here in your country. That was your mandate to oppose them and I still believe that.[26]

The dominant Sinn Féin narrative has promoted the 'defender' role of the Provisional IRA, citing notable instances such as Bombay Street in 1969. On 15 August 1969 (the Catholic feast of the Assumption) Bombay Street, situated near Clonard Monastery in West Belfast, was burned to the ground by loyalists, and fifteen-year-old Gerald McAuley, who was a member of Na Fianna Éireann, was shot dead. Ed Moloney has stated 'When the IRA split acrimoniously later that year, the Belfast men who led the breakaway Provisional IRA swore they would never leave their streets defenceless again. For their icon they chose the phoenix, the mythical firebird rising in vengeance from the ashes of Bombay Street.[27]

While acknowledging that the Provisionals did *arise* in a 'defender' capacity, radical republicans have criticised the Sinn Féin narrative as 'revisionist', evidenced by a review of the Sinn Féin message that was articulated at the time. An examination of *An Phoblacht* during this period illustrates traditional republican ideology. On 28 December 1969 the Provisional IRA issued its first statement: 'we declare our allegiance to the thirty-two county Irish Republic, proclaimed at Easter 1916, established by the First Dáil Éireann in 1919.'[28] The first issue of *An Phoblacht*, published in February 1970, carried an article on the front page titled 'On this we stand: The Rock of the Republic', which stated 'In the very first issue of this paper we wish to say bluntly and openly that we are standing on "The Rock of the Republic", and from that position we refuse to budge. Let us explain.' The article proceeds with a discussion of the 'Articles of Agreement for a Treaty between Great Britain and Ireland' (of 1921) and demonstrates the legitimacy of the Provisional IRA through its lineage to the First Dáil Éireann.[29] Further, in July 1971 *Republican News* carried a section titled 'What is our aim?' which stated 'Our aim is to secure the political, cultural and economic independence of all the Irish Nation … The Six County Statelet is invalid in its conception and unlawful in its maintenance … It must be destroyed.' The following year, on 18 August 1972, *Republican News* published the text of an oration given by Sean McKenna from Newry at the graveside of Colm Murtagh: 'He was foremost in the fight against British forces of occupation during the last 12 months.'[30] Such traditional republican ideology was articulated throughout republican literature until the mid-1980s. Arguably, articles which appeared in *An Phoblacht* or *Republican News* in the 1970s and early 1980s would not be out of place in the RSF paper *Saoirse* today.

Sovereignty – not civil rights

Competing narratives regarding 'justification' for the IRA campaign strike to the heart of the Provisional–'dissident' divide. The mainstream has presented an analysis which argues that altered structural conditions within the state of Northern Ireland have removed the justification for an armed campaign in current circumstances. Pádraic MacCoitir in Belfast has commented:

> The myth that is put out there by spokespeople for Sinn Féin is that if there had been civil rights … if the unionist government had have brought in reforms at that time and there would have been some more equality for Catholics that there wouldn't have been an armed campaign. In my opinion that galls me for anybody to even say that. I mean as if people who joined the IRA just joined the IRA as a reaction to Stormont.[31]

The president of Republican Sinn Féin, Des Dalton (successor to Ruairí Ó Brádaigh) has argued that:

> There has almost been a revisionist rewriting of history to suit a particular narrative. If you're to follow the official narrative of what's happened in Ireland over the last

forty-five years you would be led to believe that we've had thirty something years of an armed civil rights campaign … Ruairí Ó Brádaigh or Dáithí Ó Conaill or other such republican leaders of that particular period of the 1970s were very clear that civil rights were something which were attainable within the UK.[32]

Dalton is making reference to discussions and debate which took place within the Republican Movement in the 1950s and early 1960s when momentum was gathering around civil rights demands. In the lead-up to the 1955 general election in the Northern state, civil rights formed a core issue of the Sinn Féin manifesto, which focused on discrimination within the Northern state. Tom Mitchell and Phil Clarke contested the election as prisoner candidates and, as noted by Des Dalton, 'Paddy Mc Logan [the Sinn Féin president] actually sounded another warning about that and he said we need to be careful because an active Westminster can address all of those issues overnight very very quickly.'[33]

Deep division regarding the origins and justification of the Provisional IRA campaign is not confined to the Provisional–radical republican divide. Rather, *within* the radical republican world there exists a range of heterogeneous views regarding the formation of the organisation. Consequently, the radical republican world contains a wide spectrum of views on the current use of armed actions. There are notable examples of individuals who stayed within the Provisional Movement throughout the ceasefires only to depart during the latter period (post-1998); therefore it is unsurprising that their views on armed struggle may be closer to the narrative presented by the Provisionals than to current armed groups such as the Continuity IRA, REAL IRA, New IRA or ONH. Anthony McIntyre, who departed from the Provisional Movement, has argued:

> I think what made republican ideology fashionable was the anti-Brit campaign that the Provos, the INLA, the Official IRA waged. I mean you've British soldiers on the streets murdering Irish citizens, arresting Irish citizens, firing CS gas. It's easy to develop an intellectual framework, a prism that explains all that. Even though your initial reaction to the British presence in 1969 was not negative. It was the behaviour, not the presence that changed all that.[34]

Similarly, Tommy McKearney, who left the Provisional Movement in 1986, has argued 'when the Provisional IRA insisted in the post-Bloody Sunday period that only an end to British rule would satisfy its members, it was at least as much a condemnation of London mismanagement as an expression of the desire for self-determination.'[35] While the ranks of the IRA may have been swelled by the 'behaviour' of the British in the North, radical republicans have asserted the achievement of a thirty-two-county Republic as their primary motivation and have stressed the ideological continuity of their republicanism stretching back to the pre-1969 period.

The radical republican constituency has rejected any conflation of a civil rights agenda with the Republican Movement's desire for self-determination.

Sinn Féin and the wider Provisional Movement have failed to recognise the two issues of 'equality' within the Northern state and Irish 'sovereignty' as separate, and have argued that the achievement of 'equality' within the North is a stepping stone to Irish unification. An analysis of Sinn Féin literature since the mid-1980s demonstrates a change in language, as references to achieving 'freedom' were overtaken by references to the desire for 'equality'.

What was it all for?

The mainstream narrative has argued that things are better now, violence has largely departed the stage and that no one wants to return to the dark days of the past. References are frequently made to equal opportunities for Catholics and Protestants in housing, electoral practice and employment within the state of Northern Ireland. The mainstream has presented these arguments to radical republican groups engaged in an armed campaign; however, such a narrative fails to recognise a commitment to ideological republicanism regarding self-determination. Radical republicans have drawn a distinct division between the two issues and have cautioned that a civil rights agenda can be achieved within the state of Northern Ireland as part of the UK – was the Provisional IRA campaign fought to achieve equality *within* the UK? In contemporary Ireland, both Provisional and radical republicans have invoked the names of 'fallen comrades' such as Hunger Striker Bobby Sands in the justification of their current position. The invoking of prominent republicans (in relation to the contemporary political climate) is not new. Rather it can be located comfortably within republican tradition, as demonstrated by Robert W. White who recalled the case of Lily Moffatt. Moffatt, who joined Sinn Féin in 1917 and Cumann na mBan in 1919, assumed an anti-treaty position in the Civil War of 1919–23. White recalls an interview which Moffatt gave to *Iris: The Republican Magazine* in 1982 in which she was asked 'what do you think of the Free State today?' She replied 'Not much. It's awfully short of the Republic. And when I think of Liam [Mellows], Rory [O'Connor], Richard [Barrett] and Joe [McKelvey] shot in cold blood by the Staters [in 1922] … The people that died in my young days would have no regard for the Free State.'[36]

The contemporary Provisional Sinn Féin message has centred around the party's electoral mandate in the North and South of Ireland, as well as adherence to the Good Friday Agreement as 'the only show in town'. Non-mainstream republicans have argued that the Good Friday Agreement falls far short of what the republican campaign sought to achieve; as demonstrated by Richard English, 'they clearly had a right to ask whether the suffering they had endured and inflicted could be justified in pursuit of what the Provisional Movement eventually seemed to have settled for.'[37] Danny Morrison has argued:

You must understand that we were second-class citizens, Stormont was symbolic of our oppression. Fifty years there, we had no rights. We'd no Irish-language rights, no sporting rights, were harassed, you weren't allowed to fly a tricolour, you could be stopped on the street for carrying a hurl, so the Civil Rights Movement was set up and it was suppressed and then along came the IRA which had basically retired … the IRA argument was that we are not going to get our civil rights until we get our national rights and the only way to get our national rights is to take on the Brits. So that's how the armed struggle started, with that simple basic tenet.[38]

Inherent in the Provisional–'dissident' divide is the notion that the Good Friday Agreement constitutes a settlement. Sinn Féin has rejected the labelling of the Agreement as a 'settlement'. Further, Danny Morrison has argued 'so the people who are critical of Sinn Féin, I only respect them if they propose alternatives.'[39] Morrison's comment reflects a dominant point throughout the mainstream critique of radical republicanism – that it offers no alternative. Danny Morrison has also argued:

Fortunately there were people there who were able to transform their talents from military to politics almost overnight and the bulk of prisoners supported the change. That is what's very important. What the dissidents are saying to me is that I don't have a right to decide my political future, the political future of my children, the political future of my community. I do not have that right even though I went to jail and risked assassination, and there were a couple of attempts on my life.[40]

Morrison continued: 'I know for a fact, because I was in jail with hundreds of people, that 80 plus per cent of the former prisoners support the change and what a minority are saying is, "You don't have a right to change, you are sell-out bastards."'[41]

Overall plan of Provisional leadership

A central theme which runs throughout the radical republican narrative is the argument that the Provisional leadership had in place an overall plan to 'wind down' the republican campaign and the Provisional IRA. Danny Morrison has rejected this:

If the idea had been secretly hatched by a cabal in 1981 why would the IRA con- tinue to have sought huge arms shipments in '85, '86 and '87? … So you can see that in terms of the leadership they were preparing for a war. And also – we know from reports – and this is where you can't just blame the leadership all the time – when the leadership handed out weapons like the heavy machine-gun, like the 12.7 machine-gun which could hit helicopters etc., many areas couldn't cope with the size of the weapons, you know, with transporting them.[42]

There exists an element within the radical republican base which argues that the IRA campaign was not sustainable. These individuals are not critical of the

IRA ceasefires of the 1990s. This constituency is predominantly manned by 'independent' republicans (who left the Provisional Movement in the post-Good Friday context) and who are prominent critics of current armed groups such as the Continuity and REAL IRAs. Their opposition to Sinn Féin is articulated through criticism of how the movement developed in the post-ceasefire period. One prominent critic, Tommy McKearney, has argued that it became clear to the IRA in the 1980s that the 'spike' in operations that took place in the late 1970s could not be easily maintained.[43] This is a crucial point of contention *within* the radical republican world – a division between those who maintain that the campaign came to a natural end and those who argue that it was deliberately wound down by the leadership. A prominent republican who falls into the latter category is former adjutant-general of the Provisional IRA, Kevin Hannaway in Belfast.[44] Hannaway has argued:

> We as an army, that is to say the IRA, on four accounts, brought the British army to the table so we had won the war effectively but had lost the peace … we had only one [aim], it was standard IRA army procedure that it was British withdrawal. There was nothing else up for discussion. And all those who died and fought the war and paid the supreme sacrifice, gave their lives.[45]

Kevin Hannaway has pointed to British army papers which came into the possession of the IRA[46] in 1978:

> The brigadier-general of the British army in the North of Ireland and the chief constable of the RUC … and it was a report to the inner circle of the British cabinet and I had the privilege of reading some of these … and what was very adamant in it was this report was stating clearly from both sides, that is to say the chief constable and the GOC [general officer commanding], that the IRA were undefeatable from a military perspective and that the only way they could be defeated was through infiltration.[47]

Jim McCrystal in Lurgan, who was imprisoned with Gerry Adams, has argued:

> I think in my own mind we could have achieved it … had we not succumbed to the British government. I think we were on the verge of something … so I thought we were nearly there, only that the British being so smart and getting these politically minded people to come round and do what they did. I think that's what spoiled and stopped it and I think now with the way things are at the minute it will take a long time to get back to that.[48]

Gary Donnelly, an independent councillor in Derry and member of the 32CSM, has argued:

> The leadership had changed their political objectives to what they are now but didn't tell the people who were engaged. They had control of the army and they didn't tell the people in the army that they had changed, that they were no longer fighting for a thirty-two-county socialist republic. To me that's completely morally

wrong. So the use of violence by the Provisional Movement at some stage had become morally wrong because they had changed their objectives and just didn't tell their base.[49]

Donnelly has also questioned the use of Provisional violence on the basis of what has been achieved.

Decommissioning: 'The choke'

Final IRA decommissioning in 2005 came in the wake of electoral advances by Sinn Féin, culminating in 2001 when the party electorally surpassed the SDLP to become the largest representative of the nationalist population in the North. Sinn Féin's electoral success prompted some commentators to argue that it had 'stolen the clothes' of the SDLP.[50] With both parties singing from the same hymn sheet, the electorate in the North of Ireland had questioned the need for two constitutional nationalist parties which were similar in message. The end of the Provisional IRA's campaign had paid electoral dividends for Sinn Féin in the North and South of Ireland, having removed a moral objection for a number of Catholics to vote for Sinn Féin.[51] Gerry Adams has commented:

> I think there are a range of reasons why people that might not have previously voted for Sinn Féin came to vote for us and the issue of Sinn Féin's position on armed struggle is clearly one of those issues. It's impossible to measure that.[52]

Danny Morrison has recalled his experience canvassing in the Mid-Ulster constituency in the 1982 election:

> I was out canvassing in Mid-Ulster and on at least two occasions and certainly in one of those cases in Strabane a woman told me to my face at the front door, 'Son, I like the way that you talk about the national question, I like your politics but I cannot support those bombs.' That was a clear indication of the limits to the vote. And, by the way, it was something that we probably knew anyway, and it was something that I was well aware of when I made the armalite and ballot box speech back at the Ard Fheis in 1981. That is, that there was a ceiling on the support for Sinn Féin as a result of moral quandaries that people had over the armed struggle per se or aspects of the armed struggle.[53]

The transformation of the Provisional Movement from the mid-1980s led the Provisional IRA to one conclusion: final decommissioning of weapons. Sinn Féin had become incorporated into the system within the North of Ireland to an extent that it became untenable for the Provisional IRA to retain its weapons. More significantly, it appeared that there was no desire within the leadership of the Provisional IRA to keep the door open for any future return to an armed campaign. Danny Morrison has provided the rationale:

In a way the peace process and the political process was the IRA cashing in the chips of the armed struggle in return for access to power, the institutions, the structures. But such engagements, as well as building and contributing to society here, are still about influencing the situation, about keeping up the momentum for independence – which is why the unionists say Sinn Féin is 'relentless'.[54]

Dump Arms: 2005

On 28 July 2005 the Provisional IRA made a historic announcement:

> The leadership of Oglaigh na hÉireann has formally ordered an end to the armed campaign … All IRA units have been ordered to dump arms … All volunteers have been instructed to assist the development of purely political and democratic programmes through exclusively peaceful means … Volunteers must not engage in any other activities whatsoever … The IRA leadership has also authorised our representative to engage with the IICD [Independent International Commission on Decommissioning] to complete the process to verifiably put its arms beyond use.[55]

The Provisional IRA had committed to the decommissioning of IRA weapons, marking a historic departure in Irish republicanism: the first time that the Republican Movement had decommissioned its weapons. Previous 'dump arms' orders or ceasefires called by the movement did not result in the decommissioning of weapons. Rather, weapons were stored for a future time in which conditions would be more favourable to armed struggle. Weapons which were used by the Provisional IRA in 1969 were taken from IRA dumps where they had been stored after the 'dump arms' order in 1962. Kevin Hannaway's father Liam Hannaway was a quartermaster of the IRA in North Belfast during this period. His command stretched over Short Strand, Ballymacarret, New Lodge Road, Ardoyne, Old Park and New Barnsley. On 15 August 1969 Kevin Hannaway went alongside his father to an arms dump to 'get some gear out'. He has recalled:

> He said 'there is no dumps in Ardoyne' and I said 'why not?' He said 'we can't get one; nobody wants to know in Ardoyne.' And so the nearest dump was actually in New Barnsley. It was alleged a British soldier by the way was handling it.[56]

Kevin Hannaway was making reference to the lack of arms which were available and to the low level the campaign had reached; as well as the low level of interest in the campaign. As Hannaway stated:

> there had been good republicans in Ardoyne over the years but they had died off and their families didn't follow on – or it was dying out. And you had the like of my dad, his dad – big Frank McGlade, Billy Mulholland – people like that who were sort of basically considered jokes.[57]

Hannaway has highlighted two points of significance: first, the low ebb which republicanism had reached after the failed border campaign and secondly the manner in which republicans returned to 'arms dumps' to retrieve weapons which had been stored for conditions which would be more conducive to an armed campaign.

In reference to the 2005 decommissioning (as opposed to earlier periods) Des Dalton has commented:

> You would notice – to read back on the statements that were issued in 1923 and 1962 – there was no acceptance of the status quo. There was no acceptance or negation of a future generation's ability to take up arms and I think that is the difference between the position the Provisionals take. The Provisionals attempt to draw a line under Irish history and say that because this particular generation have made a decision we were also denying the right of future generations to do likewise and maybe take a different position and take a different viewpoint.[58]

The 'drawing of a definitive line' under the armed campaign by the Provisional leadership proved a step too far for some within the movement: significantly these individuals had stayed within the Provisional Movement or Sinn Féin through the ceasefires of the 1990s and throughout major ideological shifts within the movement. Evidently, the act of decommissioning had a profound effect on individuals who would depart the movement upon the realisation that there was no possibility of the resumption of an armed campaign. As with the IRA ceasefires, there were individuals within the movement who believed that decommissioning would never actually happen. In the years preceding decommissioning, slogans appeared on walls in West Belfast stating 'Not a bullet, not an ounce', 'Not an ounce, not a round' and 'Decommission? No mission.'[59] Albert Allen, who was with the Provisional Movement in Belfast until IRA decommissioning, has stated:

> The reason why I think a lot of them stayed right up until the army was stood down was out of loyalty and also there were a lot of issues which were fobbed by the movement from the leadership. The likes of decommissioning. People were actually told don't believe we're gonna be decommissioning because we're not.[60]

In an article in *The Blanket* in October 2003 Anthony McIntyre argued 'the only people lacking the ability to work out that the IRA has decommissioned its weaponry are to be found within the Republican Movement. Nobody outside the ranks is running around whispering, "It never happened."'[61]

A butterfly that flew away

In September 2015, a decade after IRA decommissioning, Bobby Storey, a prominent member of Sinn Féin in Belfast, addressed a press conference at the Roddy McCorley Social Club in West Belfast:

> The IRA has gone, the IRA have stood down, they have put their arms beyond use, they have left the stage, they are away and they are not coming back … I think the

chief constable and other perspectives out there see this in terms of the IRA being a caterpillar that's still there, where I think it's moved on, it's become a butterfly, it's flew away, it's gone, it's disappeared and they need to evolve to that as well.[62]

The radical republican narrative has argued that decommissioning was tantamount to 'surrender'. Barry McKerr, an independent republican in Lurgan, has described decommissioning as 'the choke for an awful lot of people who actually agreed with them at the start. People just saw that as surrender.'[63] Kevin Hannaway has argued:

> Sinn Féin, the last leaders of the IRA. They done what the British army couldn't do. The British army couldn't get the weapons off them. The British army couldn't defeat them. But they have done away with the IRA and they have handed in the weapons.[64]

Hannaway, a former adjutant-general of the Provisional IRA, continued, 'they have disarmed the Irish nation and they never owned the weapons to give them away in the first place. Those weapons belong to the nation.'[65] Compounding the point, Francie McGuigan in Belfast has stated:

> The weapons were being held in trust for the Irish nation to be duly handed over to an elected government of the thirty-two-county Republic. That was in the IRA constitution. So they had no right.[66]

IRA decommissioning has formed a central plank in radical republican criticism of the Provisional leadership. The arguments outlined above highlight how IRA decommissioning was viewed by some members of the organisation as in direct contravention of their ideology and constitution. A spokesperson for the Continuity IRA in North Armagh, who maintains fidelity to the Sinn Féin constitution of 1917 and the Green Book of the IRA, has argued:

> Right through history it's been stated that if there comes a period where you're getting nowhere – ground arms for a future generation … what the Provisionals done, they just handed over thousands of weapons – we saw it as a turning point.[67]

Billy McKee, a founder member of the Provisional Movement, has argued:

> These fellas [names withheld] and company, they took over and they, well we had a couple of peace conferences, they didn't materialise but they got going and they had secret talks which eventually led to what you call the handing over of the weapons. They weren't, they were sold. There was a bank raid, twenty-six million a few weeks afterwards and it was the handing over. If it had've been what you call an IRA job they would have pulled the country apart. There was hardly any raiding or anything.[68]

McKee's analysis is typical of the radical republican narrative which views the Provisional leadership with suspicion and asserts that there was an overall plan to 'wind down' the organisation. Billy McKee joined Na Fianna Éireann in 1936 when he was fifteen years old and was imprisoned in every decade between the 1930s and 1970s. McKee was first arrested at the age of seventeen for drilling with Na Fianna. In the *Irish News* in March 2016 he drew upon the traditional republican position:

> Them weapons belonged to the republican movement and if they wanted to drop out and go political that was up to themselves … I or none of the other republicans would have had any objections, go and do what they wanted to do, but they had no right to hand those weapons over and that was treachery … I condemn it and I condemn them.[69]

McKee has commented: 'I would never have handed over the weapons in the first place … because when they lost the weapons they lost everything. They just became tame dogs.'[70]

The publication of Jonathan Powell's memoir *Great Hatred, Little Room: Making Peace in Northern Ireland* in 2008 fuelled the radical republican narrative regarding an 'overall plan' orchestrated by the Provisional leadership by making reference to contacts between the British government and the leadership of the Provisional Movement. In the same year Deaglán de Bréadún published *The Far Side of Revenge: Making Peace in Northern Ireland*, which stated that in the lead-up to IRA decommissioning, some IRA statements were drafted by members of the British government. The Provisional IRA traditionally signed statements using the pseudonym P. O'Neill. De Bréadún has stated: 'P. O'Neill began to widen his cloak and, via Sinn Féin negotiators, accept contributions, suggestions and even drafts from impeccably respectable civil servants on both sides … these officials even became adept at making the usual gestures towards republican core values while at the same time trying to get in a couple of things we wanted.'[71] Such revelations inflamed the radical republican constituency and confirmed the belief that the campaign was wound down, with input from the British government.

The Féile: 2017

In August 2017 in St Mary's College in West Belfast, Reverend Harold Good addressed an audience as part of the West Belfast Féile. Reverend Good (along with Father Alec Reid of Clonard Monastery in West Belfast) 'oversaw' the decommissioning process of Provisional IRA weapons in 2005. Canadian general John de Chastelain was the chair of an international independent commission which oversaw the destruction of IRA weapons. The church leaders were independent eyewitnesses to the process and said in a joint statement, 'this role was to be clear and focused. It would involve watching the whole process of decommissioning, minute by minute, from beginning to end.'[72] During the Féile talk in 2017 Reverend Good commented on that period and provided an insight into the thinking of those undertaking the physical task of decommissioning the weapons. Good recalled being there when Provisional IRA members were actually handing over their weapons and stated:

> What I heard was as important as what I saw. Conversations in the evenings where men said we're doing this so that we don't hand on to our children what we've been through.[73]

This was a poignant insight from an independent witness who was in the presence of those carrying out decommissioning of their weapons.

Conclusion: the 'right' to armed struggle

The aforementioned Waterfront debate which took place in 2012 provided an insight into the competing narratives on the contemporary use of armed actions and provided an insight into the justification of contemporary armed actions by the radical republican base. During the debate Sinn Féin's Jim McVeigh characterised so-called 'dissidents' as people who were finding it difficult to come to terms with the legacy of serving significant time in prison, to which RNU's Ciaran Cunningham responded 'it is convenient for people to portray "dissidents" as a mental condition.'[74] Radical republicans have emphasised their *right* to engage in armed struggle as a 'principle'. This strikes to the heart of the Sinn Féin argument regarding structural conditions. Radical republicans have made a distinction between the right to wage an armed campaign as a principle and tactically choosing when to use armed struggle. This point is central to understanding why decommissioning was 'the choke' for individuals who left the Provisional Movement at this point. Decommissioning negated the historic *right* to engage in armed struggle at a future time.

At republican commemorations throughout Ireland, radical republicans cite the 1916 Proclamation in justification for continuing armed struggle:

> In every generation the Irish people have asserted their right to national freedom and sovereignty; six times during the past three hundred years they have asserted it in arms. Standing on that fundamental right and again asserting it in arms in the face of the world, we hereby proclaim the Irish Republic as a sovereign Independent State. And we pledge our lives and the lives of our comrades-in-arms to the cause of its freedom, of its welfare, and of its exaltation among the nations.[75]

Chapter five provides an analysis of the motivations of radical groups that are currently engaged in armed struggle. Armed groups have traced their lineage to the Proclamation and have stressed the continuity of the Irish republican struggle. Crucially, they have rejected the dominant narrative surrounding 'different campaigns' but rather have stressed highs and lows in republican military activity (which constitutes a continuous republican armed campaign against occupation). The depth of feeling among radical republicans regarding decommissioning was reflected in comments by Anthony McIntyre in *The Blanket* in 2003: 'no informer throughout the course of the conflict has been able to deal such a blow to the military capacity of the IRA as its own leadership has. Yet the very people who gave up the IRA's weapons have sat in judgement of others and sent them to their graves for "informing" on IRA munitions.'[76]

Notes

1 See McKearney, *The Provisional IRA*, p. 181.
2 See G. Mitchell, J. de Chastelain and H. Holkeri, 'Report of the International Body on Arms Decommissioning' (22 January 1996). http://cain.ulst.ac.uk/events/peace/docs/gm24196.htm. Accessed 18 July 2018. For a discussion of the respective positons of the political parties in the lead-up to Sinn Féin's acceptance of the Mitchell Principles see Hennessey, *Northern Ireland Peace Process*, pp. 107–14.
3 J. Powell, *Great Hatred, Little Room: Making Peace in Northern Ireland* (London, The Bodley Head, 2008), p. 87.
4 McKearney, *The Provisional IRA*, p. 181.
5 Northern Ireland Political Collection, Linenhall Library, Belfast, P3394, 'Papers and Correspondence from Gerry Adams and Sinn Féin to SDLP', 18 March 1988.
6 McKearney, *The Provisional IRA*, p. 181.
7 *Ibid.*, p. 181.
8 See Frampton, *Legion of the Rearguard*; Whiting, *Spoiling the Peace?*.
9 Richard Behal, interview with the author, Killarney, 31 October 2013.
10 *Ibid.*
11 *Ibid.*
12 The Whiterock road is in West Belfast, next to City Cemetery.
13 Tommy Gorman, interview with the author, Belfast, 3 October 2012.
14 Billy McKee, interview with the author, Belfast, 8 August 2013.
15 Maire Óg Drumm, interview with the author, Belfast, 6 March 2014.
16 Geraldine Taylor, interview with the author, Belfast, 14 October 2012.
17 Public debate in Waterfront Hall, Belfast, 11 February 2012, attended by the author.
18 R. English, *Armed Struggle: The History of the IRA* (Oxford, Macmillan, 2003), p. 81.
19 *Ibid.*, p. 338.
20 *Ibid.*, p. 338.
21 Male, interview with the author, Belfast, July 2013.
22 For references to the emergence of the Provisionals see White, *Out of the Ashes*; K. Bean, *The New Politics of Sinn Féin* (Liverpool, Liverpool University Press, 2007); McIntyre, *Good Friday*.
23 See English, *Armed Struggle* (2003), pp. 90–1.
24 Francie McGuigan, interview with the author, Belfast, 24 July 2013.
25 Brian Leeson, interview with the author, Dublin, 1 February 2013.
26 Jim McCrystal, interview with the author, Lurgan, 22 August 2013.
27 Moloney, *Secret History of the IRA*, p. 7. See also J. Bowyer Bell, *The Irish Troubles: A Generation of Violence 1967–1992* (Dublin: Gill & Macmillan, 1993), p.111: 'Billy

McKee had set up the Clonard defense [sic] with a handful of IRA men armed with shotguns and .22 rifles. Catholic Bombay Street off the Falls Road was burned out while the troops were still moving in a few streets away. While helping families move out of the burned street, a republican Fianna youth, fifteen-year-old Gerald McAuley, was shot dead at 4.00pm in an exchange of fire with the loyalists. The boy was the first IRA casualty.' Further, see S. MacStiofáin, *Revolutionary in Ireland* (Edinburgh: Gordon Cremonesi, 1975), p. 121: 'Heavily armed police, together with B-Specials and the Orange mobs, attacked Nationalist streets in Belfast. Five people were killed and two hundred injured. Almost two hundred homes were burned out, dozens of them having been clearly selected as premeditated targets. Bombay Street, off the Falls Road, was gutted, and many Catholic families were forced out of mixed areas.'

28 English, *Armed Struggle* (2012), p. 106.
29 *Ibid.*
30 *Republican News*, Vol. 1, No. 48 (18 August 1972).
31 Pádraic MacCoitir, interview with the author, Belfast, 4 October 2012.
32 Des Dalton, interview with the author, Dublin, 15 February 2013.
33 *Ibid.*
34 Anthony McIntyre, interview with the author, Dublin, 3 April 2013.
35 McKearney, *The Provisional IRA*, p. 201.
36 White, *Provisional Irish Republicans*, p. 161.
37 English, *Armed Struggle* (2012), p. 321.
38 Danny Morrison, interview with the author, Belfast, 7 May 2014.
39 *Ibid.*
40 *Ibid.*
41 *Ibid.*
42 *Ibid.*
43 McKearney, *The Provisional IRA*, pp. 145–7.
44 Kevin Hannaway is a first cousin of Gerry Adams. For information on the Hannaway family see P.M. O'Sullivan, *Patriot Graves: Resistance in Ireland* (Chicago, Follett Publishing Company, 1972), pp. 60–1: 'Kevin Hannaway is a fourth generation Republican; his Father and Grandfather were active members of the IRA spanning a period from 1916 to the 1970s. His Great-Grandfather was member of the Irish Republican Brotherhood (IRB) or Fenian Movement in the 1860s. Kevin Hannaway was interned on 9 August 1971 along with his brothers Dermot and Terry, their father Liam was arrested and interned later the same year.'
45 Kevin Hannaway, interview with the author, 24 July 2013.
46 The papers were in a briefcase which was taken from a car during a robbery in England. The papers, which were stamped 'Top Secret', were alongside machine-guns and a 9mm Browning pistol.
47 Kevin Hannaway, interview with the author, Belfast, 24 July 2013.
48 Jim McCrystal, interview with the author, Lurgan, 22 August 2013.
49 Gary Donnelly, interview with the author, Derry, 21 August 2013.
50 Murray and Tonge, *Sinn Féin and the SDLP*.
51 *Ibid.*
52 Gerry Adams, interview with the author, Belfast, 5 March 2009.

53 Danny Morrison, interview with the author, Belfast, 2 December 2008.

54 Danny Morrison, interview with the author, Belfast, 7 May 2014.

55 CAIN. 'IRA statement on the ending of the Armed Campaign', 28 July 2005. See http://cain.ulst.ac.uk/othelem/organ/ira/ira280705.htm. Accessed 19 July 2018.

56 Kevin Hannaway, interview with the author, Belfast, 24 July 2013.

57 *Ibid.*

58 Des Dalton, interview with the author, Dublin, 15 February 2013.

59 McIntyre, *Good Friday*, p. 63. (Article titled 'Sinn Feign', *Parliamentary Brief*, December 2001.)

60 Albert Allen, interview with the author, Belfast, 17 October 2013. Albert Allen was a member of the Republican Movement from the age of fifteen, joining Na Fianna Éireann in 1969.

61 McIntyre, *Good Friday*, p. 76. (Article titled 'Pulling the guns over their eyes', *The Blanket*, 27 October 2003.) *The Blanket* was an online magazine based in Belfast (2001–8). See www.ulib.iupui.edu/collections/blanket. Accessed 19 July 2018.

62 'IRA has vanished "like a butterfly": Bobby Storey', *News Letter* (13 September 2015).

63 Barry McKerr, interview with the author, Lurgan, 23 August 2013.

64 Kevin Hannaway, interview with the author, Belfast, 24 July 2013.

65 *Ibid.*

66 Francie McGuigan, interview with the author, Belfast, 24 July 2013.

67 Continuity IRA, interview with the author, North Armagh, January 2014.

68 Billy McKee, interview with the author, Belfast, 8 August 2013.

69 C. Young, 'Political process will not deliver a united Ireland – Billy McKee', *Irish News* (30 March 2016).

70 Billy McKee, interview with the author, Belfast, 8 August 2013.

71 D. de Bréadún, *The Far Side of Revenge: Making Peace in Northern Ireland* (Cork, The Collins Press, 2008), p. 372.

72 The text of this statement is available at http://cain.ulst.ac.uk/events/peace/decommission/hgar260905.htm. Accessed 19 July 2018.

73 Reverend Harold Good, speaking at Féile an Phobail, St Mary's College, West Belfast, 8 August 2017. Please note that this quote is not verbatim but is taken from handwritten notes by the author, who was present at the event. The author endeavoured to write Reverend Good's words as accurately as possible.

74 Public debate in Waterfront Hall, Belfast, 11 February 2012, attended by the author.

75 The 1916 Proclamation, 24 April 1916. Text available at http://cain.ulst.ac.uk/issues/politics/docs/pir24416.htm. Accessed 19 July 2018.

76 McIntyre, *Good Friday*, p. 74. (Article from *The Blanket*, 'Pulling the guns over their eyes', 27 October 2003.)

1 Press conference launching 'Irish Democracy: A Framework for Unity'. Dublin. Left to
right: 32CSM honorary president Phil O'Donoghue, 32CSM national chairperson
Francie Mackey and Joe Dillon

2 Left to right: Kevin Hannaway and Francie McGuigan at the first reunion of the hooded
men, Lurgan, 30 July 2011

3 Anti-internment march, Falls road, West Belfast, 8 August 2013

4 Republican Sinn Féin 1916 Centenary commemoration, GPO Dublin, 23 April 2016.
Speaker: RSF president Des Dalton. Bottom right corner: veteran republican John Hunt

5 Cumann na mBan colour party (followed by Na Fianna Éireann colour party), Republican Sinn Féin 1916 Centenary commemoration, O'Connell Street, Dublin, 23 April 2016

6 Cumann na mBan colour party standing to attention facing the GPO, Republican Sinn Féin 1916 Centenary commemoration, Dublin, 23 April 2016

7 Centenary 1916 Easter commemoration, Arbour Hill, Dublin, 26 March 2016.
Fifth from the right: Richard Behal

8 Funeral of Republican Sinn Féin member Matt Conway, Kilcullen, Co. Kildare,
23 May 2016. Carrying the coffin, front to back: Dan Hoban, Des Dalton, Adrian Haire

9 Republican Sinn Féin colour party, Republican Plot, Milltown Cemetery, Belfast, 28 May 2016

10 Republican Sinn Féin colour party comes face to face with An Garda Síochána, Monaghan, 10 January 2016

11 Éirígí election candidate Pádraic MacCoitir, Sleacht Néill GAA grounds, Co. Derry,
March 2017

12 Billy McKee's ninety-sixth birthday party, Belfast, 12 November 2017.
Top left: Nuala Perry. Top right: Kevin Hannaway. Seated: Billy McKee

13 PSNI move in and arrest members of the colour party at an RSF Easter commemoration
in Lurgan on 31 March 2018. All eight members of the colour party were arrested,
plus one other individual in attendance

4

The Good Friday Agreement and the disruption of 'normalisation'

However much I dislike it, I do believe that the Good Friday Agreement gives a democratic basis to partition. And that people have the right to disagree with me on it. And much as I dislike the decision they have made, I don't feel I have any grounds whatsoever for violently overthrowing their Agreement.

Anthony McIntyre, interview with the author, Dublin, 3 April 2013

If republican leaders are to do anything in their own time it is about making republicanism relevant in their own time. So it isn't 1916, it isn't 1798, it's 2009 and what we have to do is to try and make those broad principles of democracy and fairness and equality relevant to the Ireland of today and that's a process of engagement just with whoever wants to be a part of it and all of those are influences.

Gerry Adams, interview with the author, Belfast, 5 March 2009

I believe I'm on the right side. I believe that. If I didn't believe that I was on the right side I wouldn't be in it.

Tomas Ó Curraoin, Republican Sinn Féin Councillor, interview with the author, Galway, 4 June 2013

Introduction

The most significant ideological shift undertaken by the Provisional Movement since 1986 was acceptance of the consent principle. Set against a backdrop of Peter Brooke's speech (which asserted Britain's neutrality in relation to Ireland) the Sinn Féin president Gerry Adams engaged in a dialogue with the SDLP leader John Hume. The dialogue provides an important insight into the thinking of Sinn Féin during this period regarding consent; the party position stated that it constituted a unionist veto. Within five years of the ending of the Hume–Adams dialogue (1993) Sinn Féin had fundamentally altered its position on consent, thus abandoning a fundamental ideological cornerstone on which republicanism had rested. Through interviews with key players, this chapter provides an insight into what was happening within the Provisional Movement in the lead-up to this significant shift. Interviewees who departed the Provisional Movement at this time have cited the acceptance of consent as more fundamental than final IRA decommissioning in 2005.

The principle of consent is a central component of the Good Friday Agreement which was reached in 1998. The Sinn Féin narrative in the post-Agreement period has been dominated by references to the centrality of the Agreement to the political process coupled with calls for a border poll on unity. The radical republican constituency has rejected calls for a border poll on the basis that it would constitute a six-county vote (Northern Ireland) and has asserted the traditional republican position which states that the only valid unit of determination is the whole of Ireland (thirty-two counties). Republicans have rejected the mainstream argument that the Agreement received ratification throughout the thirty-two counties of Ireland, highlighting the fact that two different referenda took place on two different issues, that is, GFA and the removal of articles 2 and 3 from the 1937 constitution of the Irish state. Radical republicans have therefore rejected the referenda as an all-Ireland democratic exercise and continue to assert that the last act of self-determination by the Irish nation was in 1918.

This chapter examines the issue of 'mandate' and explores how radical republicans conceptualise the issue of 'democratic mandate' within a discourse that asserts traditional republican principles, that is, the right to sovereignty which is 'non-judicable'. In the post-Good Friday Agreement period, the radical republican message has been dominated by the assertion that views 'beyond' the status quo are not tolerated. As evidenced, the radical republican base views its actions (and position) as compatible with human rights and democratic principles, based upon the perceived illegitimacy of the partitionist institutions in the North and South of Ireland.

Consent principle

On 9 November 1990 Peter Brooke, secretary of state for Northern Ireland (1989–92) delivered his notable statement to an audience in London in which he asserted that Britain had no selfish, strategic or economic interest in Northern Ireland and would accept the unification of Ireland by consent. Brooke's speech did not go un-noticed by the Provisional Movement, nor by the SDLP. In fact it added weight to the argument propagated by John Hume since the 1970s regarding self-determination.[1] A private dialogue between John Hume and Gerry Adams (1988–93) became public in April 1993 when Adams was seen entering John Hume's house in Derry.[2] The dialogue comprised an exchange of documents, a review of which provides an invaluable insight into the formative thinking of Sinn Féin during this period, regarding what would ultimately become the party's position on self-determination. John Hume's letter to 'Gerry' dated 17 March 1988 quoted the diary of Theobold Wolfe Tone which contained a statement of his objectives and methods:

> To unite the whole people of Ireland, to abolish the memory of our past dissensions and to substitute the common name of Irishman in place of the denomination of Protestant Catholic and dissenter – these were my means.[3]

Notably, Hume had selected a section of text which made reference to the 'people' of Ireland, reflective of the central premise of Hume's argument regarding consent – that unification of Ireland in reality means unity of the people as a whole. Sinn Féin's response came on 18 March 1988 in a document to the SDLP titled 'Towards a strategy for peace'. The cover letter from Gerry Adams started with 'John a chara … I trust that you will find our document interesting and stimulating and sincerely hope that you find in it sufficient points of mutual agreement.'[4] In this document Sinn Féin rejected the neutrality of Britain's role in Ireland, stating 'Britain's massive military and financial commitment is in fact a reflection of her continuing strategic, economic and political interests in Ireland.'[5] Correspondence from Sinn Féin to the SDLP entitled 'Sinn Féin on national self-determination and a proposal on joint action on fair employment' (2 May 1988) stated 'nationalists and democrats cannot concede a veto to unionists over Irish re-unification. To do so would be to concede a veto on the exercise of national rights to a national minority and would flout the basic principles of democracy.'[6] Sinn Féin remained steadfast in its opposition to the principle of unity by consent.

On 13 June 1988 SDLP correspondence to Sinn Féin (commenting on a Sinn Féin document dated 2 May 1988) stated:

> From our discussions it has emerged that while we are both agreed that the Irish people have the right to self-determination, there is a major difference between us on how necessary it is to obtain the agreement of unionists if there is to be unity in Ireland.[7]

Subsequently an SDLP document titled 'SDLP response to questions raised in discussion and in previous papers' (dated 11 July 1988) stated:

> It is people who have rights, not pieces of territory, and it is the Irish people who have the right to self-determination …
> … whether or not the unionists may or may not have a right to a veto on Irish unity, they in reality possess such a veto and have done so for a very long time.[8]

On 5 September 1988 the SDLP released a statement revealing that the talks between the two parties had 'ended without at this time reaching agreement on the objective of the talks'.[9] The two parties had failed to reach agreement on the meaning of self-determination or how it should be exercised. However, the established dialogue was maintained between the two parties into the early 1990s, which was largely facilitated by Father Alec Reid, a Brother in Clonard Monastery in West Belfast. Despite the assertion of traditional rhetoric, the tide was changing within the Sinn Féin movement. Amid the party's electoral advances in the North and South, a PIRA ceasefire was announced in 1994 and a definitive cessation followed in 1997. The mid-1990s saw the Sinn Féin message moving closer to that of the constitutional nationalist SDLP, and the direction in which the organisation was developing created a level of dissention within the ranks.

A seismic shift: the consent principle

In 1997 the Sinn Féin party undertook a historic shift in policy through its acceptance of the Mitchell Principles and the principle of consent.[10] This acceptance led to the first significant point of departure from the Provisionals since the 1986 split over the ending of abstentionism. The departure in 1997 of individuals such as Micky McKevitt and Joe Dillon saw the formation of the 32CSM (which until then had existed as a pressure group within Sinn Féin).[11] The acceptance of the principle of consent overturned a fundamental ideological rock upon which Irish republicanism had historically rested. The significance of the issue to republican ideology was demonstrated during the aforementioned Hume–Adams dialogue (1988–93) when Sinn Féin refused to accept Hume's 'unity by consent' position and referred to the consent principle as tantamount to a 'unionist veto'.[12] Joe Dillon in Skerries, who is a founder member of the 32CSM, has recalled the period leading up to the Agreement:

> When I drove into Dublin that night to confront [name withheld] to know had they settled or negotiated the consent principle – [[name withheld] said] 'Ah I don't know.' I said you are fucking liars. You are illegally doing that and the constitution of Sinn Féin doesn't allow for it.[13]

Joe Dillon continued: 'I'm in the movement longer than Gerry Adams. Phil O'Donoghue the president of our organisation was on the raid with Seán South. We know what we are talking about.'[14] Francie Mackey, who similarly departed the Provisional Movement in 1997, and who is a leading figure in the 32CSM, has argued that 'undemocratic behaviour allowed the Provisional leadership to do what they wanted and led us to a position. They got to the negotiating table and failed to negotiate the republican position.'[15]

Around that time, in 1997, public meetings were taking place in Belfast, Dundalk, Dublin, Waterford and Cork. Francie Mackey has stated:

> Those were packed audiences of 400 or 500 people and it was clear that there was people within the republican base that wasn't happy with the direction that things were going. And it was also becoming increasingly obvious that the only thing that the leadership of Sinn Féin was going to get out of it was some form of internal settlement and that the issue of sovereignty wasn't on the table and we would be very critical of that leadership – either number one they didn't understand their

reasoning for their own existence or they deliberately didn't insist that the issue of sovereignty be on the table.[16]

According to the mainstream narrative, the centrality of the consent principle to the Good Friday Agreement, and the subsequent political arrangements (power-sharing), have removed the validity of the radical republican cause. Sinn Féin has emphasised the consent principle as a mechanism through which Irish sovereignty can be pursued. The contemporary narrative of Sinn Féin is dominated by calls for a border poll, particularly within a post-Brexit scenario. During the first televised Westminster election debate in June 2017 the Northern leader of Sinn Féin, Michelle O'Neill, demonstrated the centrality of a border poll to the party's current political strategy. O'Neill argued that Brexit had fundamentally altered the context, a point which was reiterated by the SDLP leader Colum Eastwood, who argued that the debate was no longer just about unity but was also now about re-entering the European Union. The radical republican narrative has rejected calls for a border poll, which would take place on a six-county basis. The unit of determination continues to form a central plank throughout radical republican discourse. Radical republicans adhere to the traditional ideological position of republicanism which asserts that the Irish nation as a whole (thirty-two counties) is the legitimate unit of determination regarding constitutional matters.

The consent principle, largely derived from the thinking of John Hume, makes recognition of the fact that the British presence in Ireland is in fact the unionist people. It is therefore underpinned by an acceptance of British neutrality on the position of Northern Ireland. Central to the radical republican ideology is a rejection of the British government as a neutral actor in the affairs of Northern Ireland. Radical republicans have reiterated the traditional republican position that Britain's role in Ireland is colonial and have therefore called on the British government to act as a persuader for Irish unity. Kevin Hannaway in Belfast has argued 'I believe that their [unionists'] strength is the British government and I believe that whilst Britain puts claim to here they'll always feel that they have the upper hand.'[17]

Acceptance of the consent principle strikes to the heart of republicanism and in fact has proven for some radical republicans more fundamental than the issue of IRA decommissioning. As Tommy McKearney has recalled, 'the US offered help and assistance to the SDLP for its "unity by consent" analysis, a position that republicans saw as tantamount to "first surrender and thereafter appeal to unionism to behave better".'[18] Independent republican Anthony McIntyre has referred to his departure from the Provisional Movement:

> The way the whole republican project has collapsed and the Sinn Féin leadership were effectively ordering the deaths of people who defended the consent principle, and they have become the greatest defenders of the consent principle themselves …

I thought all the effort that went in, the terrible taking of life that we inflicted, the misery that we visited on people, has to be authenticated in some way or explained. And I think the only way to continue or to try and authenticate it is by trying to argue for greater freedom for people.[19]

Good Friday

The legitimacy of the Good Friday Agreement (alongside the removal of articles 2 and 3 from Bunreacht na hÉireann) is not accepted by the majority of the radical republican base. The mainstream narrative has propagated the argument that the Agreement was 'ratified throughout Ireland', without recognition of the fact that two separate votes took place on two issues. In the North of Ireland the referendum was directly on the Agreement; simultaneously voters in the South of Ireland went to the polls to vote on the removal of articles 2 and 3, which laid territorial claim to the North of Ireland. The fact that voters in the South did not directly vote on the Agreement has formed a central plank in the discourse of radical republicans who reject that the referenda provide a legitimate mandate. In the North of Ireland 71.1 per cent of the electorate voted 'yes' for the Agreement. In the South of Ireland 94.39 per cent of the electorate voted for the removal of articles 2 and 3.

Radical republicans have rejected the legitimacy of the result of the referendum on the Agreement, on the basis that it took place exclusively in the six counties of Northern Ireland, as demonstrated by Ciaran Mulholland, a member of the James Connolly Society in West Belfast:

It's a democratic deficit that has never been addressed and the last all-Ireland election was back at the start of the [twentieth] century. It's something that has been denied and it's something that should be demanded. It's the right of every citizen in Ireland to decide how they intend to progress as a people and as a country.[20]

The radical republican narrative demonstrates continuity with the traditional republican position as articulated by Sinn Féin throughout the 1970s and 1980s. In June 1973 *An Phoblacht* detailed an oration by Martin McGuinness at Bodenstown, the burial site of Theobald Wolfe Tone, during which McGuinness stated:

There can be no solution within the context of a six county solution. The future of this country and its people is in a Democratic Socialist Republic … in the last few months we've had more elections and referenda, with still one in the offing, and all for what? To fool the people, that they have a say in decision making.[21]

Similarly, radical republicans have rejected the legitimacy of the referendum on articles 2 and 3 on the same basis. As stated by Tonge, Republican Sinn Féin was not dissuaded by the outcomes of these referenda: 'RSF argued that the small rejectionist vote offered potential, declaring that the 5.6 per cent "No" vote in the Irish Republic "compares to the core Republican vote in the 1981 H-Block (5 per cent plus) and 1957 (5.3 per cent) general election votes [periods of limited Republican support during an IRA border campaign and hunger strikes respectively]".'[22] When asked by the author 'what does the removal of articles 2 and 3 mean for the Republican Movement?' Dan Hoban, a senior member of RSF in Mayo, replied:

> They were never in earnest about it anyway. Sure they can change things and they can change the whole situation but they cannot change facts that the last time the Irish people voted in 1918 in elections, the people gave their allegiance to the thirty-two-county Parliament. That is the Parliament that we stand by and from that Parliament Mary MacSwiney and Commandant-General Tom Maguire handed that down to us republicans and we hold that the British have no right here, never had any right here and never will have any right and they can have all the border plebiscites they want but republicans will have no hand or part in it.[23]

Radical republicans have also rejected the referendum in the North on the basis of the questions which were asked and have argued that the wording was 'illegitimate' and 'narrow'. Republicans have highlighted the fact that no other options were presented on the ballot paper (a preference for Irish unity was not offered). A further central argument in the radical republican narrative is that the electorate viewed a 'yes' vote as a vote for peace. Tony Catney of the 1916 Societies has stated:

> You should speak to as many of the 74 per cent of the population that voted in favour of the Good Friday Agreement and ask how many of them ever read it. You will find very very few. And so people didn't vote for the text of the Good Friday Agreement. People voted for peace and I think that is the most laudable thing that people could have voted for. So yes I think mandates are important but you can't carve up the electorate to suit what you want as your mandate and then claim it as a mandate. So if in 1918 there had have been a democratic thought within the heads of the English parliamentarians then Ireland would never have been partitioned because the result of that showed very very clearly that 75 per cent, which is even greater than the percentage you had in the Good Friday Agreement, said yes we want an all-Ireland state and we want it run by Sinn Féin. That's what they said. That was the mandate.[24]

In reference to the referendum éirígí's Pádraic MacCoitir in Belfast has argued:

> If the referendum had been held in March 1916 the majority of people would have voted for peace. The same thing. If it had been two months after the Easter Rising in June 1916 the majority of people – it might have been less of a majority – but the majority of people of course, would have voted for peace … but it is how that referendum is worded and that's why people bought into the Good Friday Agreement so easily and so quickly. I'd say the majority of people who voted for the Good Friday Agreement weren't even aware of or cared about the print of the Good Friday Agreement.[25]

In this respect the radical republican narrative surrounding the Agreement has proven reflective of a 'false consciousness' Marxist narrative.

Historically, non-mainstream republicans have conceptualised the acceptance of negotiated 'settlements' and 'agreements' as demonstrative of the politics of fear. In the 1920s anti-treatyite Liam Mellows argued that 'support for the treaty represented not the will of the people but the fear of the people'.[26] John M. Regan has referred to the pre-treaty period: 'threatened British violence subverted the possibility of any free election or decision of any kind in Ireland in 1922, and this was to provide an important justification for the more doctrinaire nationalist republican perspective enunciated by the anti-treatyites.'[27] In fact, as recalled by Regan, in April of 1922 Austin Stack, while addressing the Mansion House conference, stated that 'no fair election' could be held while the threat of war remained.[28] The non-negotiable right to self-determination was emphasised by anti-treatyites in the same manner in which it is emphasised by radical republicans in contemporary Ireland.

Sovereign and indefeasible

In *1916: The Long Revolution*, Seamus Murphy has argued that nationalism and liberal democracy are compatible on many points but that they diverge regarding the 'appropriate order of priority' and has put forward this hypothetical question: 'if ninety per cent of the people of Ireland, north and south, voted in the morning to re-join the United Kingdom and be ruled from Westminster, should that be accepted?'[29] This question of mandate is relevant to radical republicanism and specifically to the 'One Ireland One Vote' campaign which has been propagated by the 1916 Societies in response to calls for a six-county border poll from Sinn Féin. Tony Catney, who was a founder and prominent advocate of the OIOV campaign, has stated: 'the people in this room are more pro-peace as the Good Friday Agreement consigns you to another round of violence.'[30] Belfast republican Dee Fennell has also been at the forefront in promoting the campaign and this study posed the following question to Fennell: what if an all-Ireland vote is held and the result is against Irish unity? In response Fennell has argued:

> Well for me I would just keep campaigning until you get a yes. If there was a vote tomorrow that would only be one generation of voters opposing reunification. Republicans have faced bigger obstacles than that.[31]

The radical republican world is not united around calls for an all-Ireland vote. RSF has rejected the campaign on the basis that Irish sovereignty cannot be determined by a vote that constitutes one generation. Therefore, in contrast to the 1916 Societies, RSF has deemed a vote (which will always be in one generation) on the issue of Irish sovereignty illegitimate. In a broader sense, the radical republican constituency has emphasised the 'inalienable right' of the Irish nation to sovereignty and does not believe that right to be (democratically) subject to referenda, as demonstrated by Jim McCrystal, an independent republican in Lurgan:

> I don't care if there was 99 per cent of the people in Ireland said I don't want a united Ireland. I can't agree with that and I won't accept that because I mean if they don't want to be in a united Ireland don't go into a united Ireland. Go wherever you want to go. I mean this is Ireland … I can't go over to England and turn them into Irish people and I won't try and I'm not going to let them people try to turn me into something.[32]

While the Good Friday Agreement was very clear in terms of the consent principle, 'constructive ambiguity' around language allowed unionist and nationalist leaders to sell the Agreement to their respective bases as a 'victory': Sinn Féin sold it as a 'stepping stone to a united Ireland'; simultaneously, unionist leaders presented it as 'securing the union'.[33] Beyond the framework of 'constructive ambiguity' present in the Agreement, radical republicans have asserted their position in relation to unionism – that unionists will occupy the same role as everyone else in a united Ireland. The Éire Nua policy of RSF outlines a federalist united Ireland in which unionists would have a level of autonomy within the North of Ireland.[34] Geraldine Taylor in Belfast has stated:

> We classify all those people as Irish people. They are our people and hopefully someday they'll understand that and realise that we are not out against them. We are out against the occupation of our country.[35]

Collectively, radical republicans have recognised unionism as an *identity* which would be accommodated in a New Ireland, as demonstrated by Anthony McIntyre:

> I do think that they [unionists] are Irish, that they are not British. But they see themselves as British. But people have a multiplicity of identities. The unionists just do not see themselves in this binary world, no more than we do as unionists or nationalists … They have a whole range of identities … Their role in the New Ireland will be the same as everybody else's.[36]

While republican groups have articulated policies that could be implemented in the case of Irish unity, they are faced with the fundamental issue of approximately one million unionists who maintain that they will never be persuaded into a united Ireland, an issue which is also relevant to Sinn Féin's outreach policy of persuasion.

Principles of freedom

The work of Murphy has also noted the importance of 'contextual analysis' regarding events such as the 1916 Rising, and has argued that 'evaluation of actions and the policies that give the actions their intentionality of meaning is central to the task. The synchronic aspect of context (crudely, what other groups were up to at the time) is directly relevant to that.'[37] The campaign waged by radical republicans must also be located within the wider context in which it operates. The Good Friday Agreement and subsequently the St Andrew's Agreement have significantly altered the context in which radical republicans are operating. Tommy McKearney has argued that:

> Some [republicans] are unwilling or unable to recognise the profound changes brought about by a post-Good Friday Agreement Ireland and believe they can return to the ways of the early 1970s. Blindly disregarding the almost total absence of popular support for armed insurrection, they continue to make a fetish of the use of arms.[38]

However, radical republicans reject the significance of the aforementioned Agreements and emphasise the location of radical republicanism within a historical continuum which expresses ideological continuity as a defining feature.

Murphy has argued that for the 1916 leaders 'democracy as currently experienced was flawed by their standards, or corrupted beyond redemption through being associated with any kind of submission to or involvement with Britain'.[39] Therefore the 'democracy' was deemed as lacking in moral or political authority. As stated by Murphy, the leaders of the Rising were 'nationalists first, and their understanding of democracy was subordinate to their understanding of nationalism'.[40] Similarly, contemporary radical republicans do not view the Northern or Southern states in Ireland as possessing any moral or political authority. In this respect, the associated structures and practices within each state are viewed as lacking in moral authority. The 32CSM has deemed the partitionist institutions illegal, as demonstrated through the legal challenge which it brought to the United Nations in 1998 (resubmitted in 2001).[41] Packy Carty, a member of the most recently formed group, Saoradh, has outlined the thinking behind his party's stance regarding opposition to contesting elections:

> While we don't recognise it [Northern Ireland] technically we realise the advantage of trying to push voter turnout below fifty per cent to divest this popular myth that somehow British rule, or its beachhead in Ireland which is Stormont, has some sort of popular mandate.[42]

The Saoradh position argues that the strategy of 'staying at home and not voting' in elections in the North of Ireland will 'divest this perceived support for British rule in Ireland'.[43]

The mainstream narrative has argued that the GFA fundamentally altered the landscape and drew a line in history. The Provisional Movement, which has been incorporated into the structures of Northern Ireland and has become part of the mainstream, has de-legitimised any actions by republicans (violent or non-violent) which are pursued outside the system and the status quo. Sinn

Féin has argued that the altered conditions in which republicans are operating (as well as the Sinn Féin electoral mandate) removes any justification for radical republican groups, including non-violent groups. The radical republican narrative on 'mandate' is conceptually framed by historical determinism. Radical republicans have rejected elections as a provider of legitimacy. They have argued that elections are inadequate measures of democratic standards and have stated that no election within an illegally formed partitionist state can assume any authority.[44] Fundamentally, the radical republican discourse is also infused with a rejection of the Sinn Féin narrative that conditions have significantly changed, as demonstrated on 16 October 2013 at the 1916 Joe McKelvey Society's event in Tyrone titled 'The burning of Long Kesh'. At the event Kevin Hannaway, one of the hooded men and an internee in cage twenty in Long Kesh prison in the 1970s, stated: 'We cannot talk about internment being confined to our past. It is here and now.'[45] Radical republicans contest the mainstream narrative that internment has ended and argue that they remain subjected to 'internment' under all-encompassing anti-terrorist legislation.

As highlighted by Cynthia Irvin, 'as many contemporary social movement theorists have demonstrated, the pluralist model extends only to competition by organised interests that are not challenging the status quo'.[46] Radical republicans do not seek to reform the system, rather they seek revolutionary change. The desire to fundamentally change the system has resulted in their steadfast opposition to participation in the institutions of the system; believing that participation in such institutions legitimises and reinforces the system and the status quo. Consequently, any analysis of the strategies employed by radical republican groups must extend *beyond* the framework of the mainstream institutions and elections. In this respect, radical republicans who operate externally to the status quo are constantly navigating the system regarding expressing their views outside the parameters of Stormont or Leinster House, on the basis that participation in such institutions would serve to legitimise these partitionist bodies.

The thin edge of the wedge

Throughout the history of Irish republicanism, prominent figures such as Terence MacSwiney have recognised that engagement with the system (on some level) is inevitable. The withdrawal of the state pension has been cited as a notable example.[47] References to the 'thin edge of the wedge' and 'the slippery slope to constitutionalism' have been paramount throughout the radical republican discourse since the 1980s, which culminates in the following questions: At what point does engagement with the system become 'sell-out'? What does opposition to the state extend to? A determination to avoid the conferring of legitimacy on institutions (through participation) may help to explain why republicans feel isolated and external to the system while simultaneously making no serious attempts to engage within the mainstream political system in either state, beyond occasionally contesting elections, mainly at a local level.

This navigation of the political arena by republicans is not merely a contemporary phenomenon but has been a constant throughout republican history, as demonstrated by Denis Carroll in *They Have Fooled You Again: Michael O'Flanagan (1876–1942)*. Carroll recounts an incident which took place in January 1936 regarding a broadcast by Radio Éireann to mark the anniversary of the opening of Dáil Éireann in 1919. He states that when the list of participants became known in the days preceding the broadcast, Father O'Flanagan was 'pressed by Cathal O'Murcadha [president of Sinn Féin] to withdraw from the programme'.[48] Subsequently he was approached by Sinn Féin's two vice-presidents and was again urged to withdraw. The reason for opposition to Father O'Flanagan's participation was the fact that Radio Éireann was the state broadcaster and some viewed participation in the broadcast as providing recognition of the Free State. However, the broadcast went ahead on 21 January with Father O'Flanagan'sinvolvement, after which the news sheet *An De* announced that 'Father O'Flanagan's participation automatically ends his connection with the Sinn Féin organisation'.[49] The headquarters of Sinn Féin subsequently confirmed that an order regarding Father O'Flanagan had been made by the standing committee. The issue drew media attention, resulting in the *Irish Independent* contacting Father O'Flanagan to comment on the matter. Carroll states: 'something more than the standing committee of Sinn Féin would be required to prevent him from repeating publicly before the Irish people the part he had taken on January 21 1919.'[50] This incident is reflective of tensions which have always existed in the Republican Movement regarding the extent to which engaging with institutions of the state moves beyond strategy into compromise.

The contemporary mainstream has highlighted 'parity of esteem', which is enshrined in the Agreement, as fundamentally altering the landscape. The Sinn Féin discourse is dominated by arguments that the Agreement is not a final 'settlement' but is a stepping stone to Irish unity and is an interim Agreement. In contrast radical republicans have cautioned about a normalisation agenda in the post-Agreement period. A central theme throughout the radical republican discourse is the rejection of normalisation within the state of Northern Ireland. Independent republican Cáit Trainor in Co. Armagh (formerly a vice-president of RSF) has stated 'it is unimaginative and a slave mentality to believe that only by going into the occupier's parliaments in our country can we make any progress.'[51] Radical republicans have cautioned about 'going into the system' and the dominant discourse throughout reflects the Machiavellian tactic pointed to by Terence MacSwiney: 'a town that has been anciently free cannot more easily be kept in subjection than by employing its own citizens.'[52]

The removal of the 'hard border' (approximately 1997–8) between the North and South of Ireland as well as the ending of British army patrols in 2007 have resulted in the appearance of a more 'normal' Northern Ireland. Crossing the border between the North and South of Ireland is not notably marked by any other occurrence than phone service and currency changing. In reference to general opinion in Ireland Richard Behal in Kerry has stated that 'people feel that everyone is equal now. It's up to you what you do now. You have no oppression unless you bring it on yourselves. And there is peace and happiness and we don't have prosperity due to the stupidity of our own politicians but that's nothing to do with England. And that has been sold fairly successfully to the mass of the population.'[53] Jim McDonald, a member of RSF in Nottingham, has stated 'if I tell people over here that there's British troops in the North of Ireland they laugh at you. "No they're all in Afghanistan." They're in Ireland and they don't believe you. And I think a lot of people in Ireland would be the same.'[54] In this respect, in the recent period (post-1998), radical republican groups have prioritised highlighting the 'nature' of the state of Northern Ireland and the on-going effects of partition.

Anti-normalisation

President of RSF Des Dalton has cautioned against normalisation and has highlighted the impact which a 'normalising agenda' has had. Dalton has stated:

> It's one of the things I'd counter to those who'd support normalising in the six counties as a stepping stone to Irish freedom. Where have you heard those words before? But you know there's no guarantee with the sectarian headcount at the end of it … that because you'll have 51 per cent Catholics that they'll all be 51 per cent nationalists or republicans. That's the road you go down because when you normalise something that's what you do, you make it normal. For people in the twenty-six counties the reality of British rule for them was removed in 1921. It didn't have British soldiers on the ground and it didn't have immediacy for them.[55]

Dalton compounded his point when he recalled a GAA match which he attended in Crossmaglen GAA grounds in Co. Armagh where the home team were playing Kildare. He attended the event with a group of friends from Kildare who are not politically active and has recalled:

> We were standing in Crossmaglen grounds … the national anthem was playing … and the two teams Armagh and Kildare stood facing the Tricolour and the Tricolour was right at the barrier of the British army base and one of the fellas said to me afterwards 'Des I now know what you'd be talking about … it brought it home to me – there are British soldiers in Ireland and I didn't realise it.'[56]

Pádraic MacCoitir in Belfast has stated:

> They [Provisional Sinn Féin] have the confidence there because they know that people want to have a normal society – whatever that normal society may be … the

normalisation policy coming in which has been pushed far more than it ever did in the 1970s and it's been far more successful from the British point of view and from Sinn Féin and the unionists, Stormont's point of view … and that's very very difficult and it's a big factor.[57]

The process of normalisation is reflected in language which dominates the mainstream. References to being Northern Irish have become commonplace. Radical republicans have rejected the term 'Northern Irish'; as Jim McCrystal from Lurgan has illustrated, 'I don't think you can say anything about Northern Irish. That's only a made-up name. You're either Irish or you're not and if you are born in Ireland how can you be anything else?'[58] Further, the phrase 'the island' has become dominant in the mainstream. Dalton has commented:

> The term 'the island' is another one that grates greatly with me and I hear the Provisionals at it constantly and it's becoming that sometimes you can't even refer to Ireland any more now as Ireland, as a nation. It's the island of Ireland or the island.[59]

In challenging the normalisation agenda radical republicans rejected Derry being chosen as the UK City of Culture in 2013 and campaigned on the issue. In this respect, the radical republican narrative is dominated by references to 'cultural imperialism', as illustrated by Lita Campbell in Dublin: 'culture has nearly been stolen from us. It was misused in Derry this year … UK City of Culture was absolutely obscene as far as I'm concerned. If you have no pride in your own history then you have no pride in anything.'[60] Further, radical republicans have viewed the removal of 'History' from the Leaving Certificate curriculum in the South of Ireland as further evidence of an 'air-brushing' of Irish history and the promotion of a revisionist agenda. Lita Campbell has argued 'I mean like what's their problem with history? Are they afraid when people learn their history and realise they are not little Britons or a subculture of the USA they might have a bit of pride in themselves and not put up with what they are putting up with at the moment?'[61]

Radical republicans have also expressed opposition to classes in the Irish language being funded by the British government. In the sporting arena, radical republicans have rejected the 'hierarchy of the GAA attending funerals of state agents such as Ronan Kerr' and 'welcoming the Queen of England to Croke Park'.[62] At the 2017 annual Ruairí Ó Brádaigh autumn school on 23 September in the Abbey Hotel in Roscommon town, Mary Ward, a member of RSF in Donegal, noted the fact that the GAA is discussing the possibility of not playing the Irish national anthem at games and no longer naming clubs after republicans such as Thomas Ashe as it may prove offensive to unionism.[63] In 2016 a GAA club in Co. Antrim removed the club's gates which contained the names of two IRA men after whom the club is named, due to a grant which the local unionist-dominated council were giving the club. In true Irish republican form the club split over the issue.[64]

Dee Fennell in Belfast has referred to republicanism as facing a 'cultural war against assimilation'.[65] Fennell has argued:

> It is up to republicans and the grassroots members of the GAA and other move-ments to combat that, because at the end of the day, if we are British in everything except for the island in which we are born, we might as well just throw in the towel and admit that we are British … The colonial message has been used for hundreds of years and they are still being used now. It's just that they are being used in a more subtle way by the use of media.[66]

However, not all radical republicans are united on the concept of 'cultural imperialism', as demonstrated by Anthony McIntyre:

> Cultural imperialism? What is it? People like to watch Liverpool? Like to watch Manchester United? So what? It's not the end of the world. Bobby Sands used to like Aston Villa. He loved Aston Villa. Does that make him less of an Irishman? People could say he's a stooge of cultural imperialism. Rubbish.[67]

McIntyre's analysis returns to the pressing question for republicans: what consti-tutes 'cultural imperialism' and at what point does engagement with the system become objectionable?

Donatella Della Porta has made reference to 'anti-colonial frames', a theory which was advanced in the Basque case by Frederico Krutwig in his book *Vasconia*. Della Porta has stated that 'from the awareness of anticolonial lib-eration struggles and of the European New Left came an inclusive conception based on the will to be Basque.'[68] Anti-colonial framing is evident in the radical republican narrative through an emphasis on 'the will to be Irish'. The contem-porary context in which radical republicans are operating has impacted upon the trajectory which this will to be Irish (and to be seen as Irish) has taken. Bert Klanderman has detailed motivations for involvement in social movements – the third ideological motivation is 'wanting to express one's own views'.[69] There is a strong perception among radical republicans that they are unable to express their views in the post-Agreement period in which everything is defined as mainstream and peaceful or 'dissident' and violent. Simply declaring opposi-tion to the mainstream narrative, even through peaceful means, has resulted in the label 'dissident' and the negative connotations which are attached. Richard Behal in Killarney has commented on the post-Good Friday Agreement period by stating:

> The direction of the public now – because they've been sold the line that the Good Friday Agreement was a settlement – and sure it stopped the killings in the North. There's no murders and no bombings. Look, you can go up there now [North of Ireland], they can come down here [South of Ireland] and Ireland is at peace. So what in the hells bells are you doing starting it all off again? … In other words, for a lot of people it's over.[70]

Radical republicans are operating in an atmosphere of arguably unprecedented hostility and interviewees frequently referred to the media not carrying statements from their organisation. Pádraic MacCoitir of éirígí has stated that the organisation frequently sends articles and letters to newspapers which are not carried.[71] At the Ruairí Ó Brádaigh autumn school in Roscommon town on 23 September 2017 RSF president Des Dalton argued, 'the media will speak to us on certain things, for example Willie Frazer wanting to march in Dublin. But the media doesn't want to hear what we are for or our strategy for going forward.'[72]

Democratic values and human rights

In the same spirit as the men and women of 1916, radical republicans do not view their actions as incompatible with liberal democratic values nor with human rights. They do not accept their actions or stance as 'undemocratic' due to their perception of the illegitimacy of the partition of Ireland and the 'illegal' creation of two partitionist states. Understanding this conceptualisation by radical republicans is crucial to understanding the basis on which they believe their legitimacy to rest. Radical republicans such as Ciaran Mulholland locate their views within a human rights framework which includes the right to hold a political opinion. While divided around cultural imperialism and how far is too far, radical republicans have united in their condemnation of the repression of any views outside the status quo in the post-GFA period. Radical republicans do not identify with the mainstream narrative and are operating within legislation which does not make provision for their views, and Robert W. White has noted that consequently 'attempts to intimidate anti-GFA activists are frequent'.[73] Nuala Perry in Belfast has stated 'they have gone with legislation that is designed to completely stop anything republican … they [Provisional Sinn Féin] have openly aided and abetted the criminalisation of republicanism.'[74] Perry has made reference to the post-1998 context stating:

> It's actually in legislation that you can be refused employment if you have sympathies against the Northern Ireland state … the unthinkable has happened in republicanism.[75]

Ciaran Mulholland has argued 'at the end of the day we are all human beings. I want to reach the stage where people can respect me for who I am and can sit down and engage in dialogue.'[76] Further, Mulholland has stated:

> I think as a human being, as an Irish citizen on the island of Ireland, I have a legitimate right to have a political persuasion … now I think that's perfectly reasonable. It's perfectly rational and it's something that should be respected and that's why I use the word legitimate because what you have, you have the status quo whether it's through conformists, red rag media, faceless securocrats and fifth columnists

suppressing anyone who doesn't think in the form of the status quo, and essentially you're being ridiculed, you're being put down.[77]

The sentiments expressed by Mulholland form a central plank throughout radical republican thinking; republicans continue to assert their frustration regarding the inability to express opinions which are beyond the mainstream Provisional analysis. The label 'dissident' is quickly applied and connotations of violence manifest. Mulholland has argued:

> [When] they are expressing themselves through protests on the streets they are subject to draconian legislation through the PSNI, stop and searches. Their voices are put down by people like Provisional Sinn Féin. When you can't express yourself and you see on the other hand how unionism can hold the state to ransom, they do as they want. The perfect example of that was through the flag protests; the louder they scream and hold the state to ransom … the more they seem to get … that sends the wrong message out where people can go 'well why don't I just lift a rifle up. That seems to be the only way I can express myself.'[78]

At the launch of the most recently formed republican party, Saoradh, Davy Jordan, the organisation's first chairperson, alluded to Sinn Féin by stating 'those who sit in the pay of our oppressor while claiming to champion our liberation are false prophets who have been defeated and consumed by the very system they claim to oppose. That is not republicanism.'[79] The Saoradh organisation contains individuals who may have voted for the Good Friday Agreement (or stayed with the Provisionals until the recent period, post-2000) but are opposed to the way in which Sinn Féin's politics have developed since. Radical republicans have criticised Sinn Féin's implementation of the welfare cuts and the party's movement away from socialism as it has moved into the centre. Gerard Hodgins, an independent republican in Belfast, has argued 'Despite their sort of socialist window dressing that they put on down south – Sinn Féin in power would just be like Fianna Fáil in power or Fine Gael in power. So I have my disappointments in them that way. I think they failed the communities which gave rise to them.'[80]

Shaking hands with the Queen of England: a step too far

The highly publicised handshake between the Queen of England and Martin McGuinness was a further step in the normalisation of Anglo-Irish relations and of the state of Northern Ireland. In the more recent period (post-2005) individuals who stayed with the Provisional Movement through ideological shifts and through acceptance of the PSNI departed over Martin McGuinness's handshake with the Queen in the Lyric theatre in Belfast in 2012. For some it was a step too far. As recognised in existing literature, the disruption of the process of 'normalisation' in the state of Northern Ireland has been a prominent aim of radical republicanism.[81] Commenting on the handshake, Tony Catney has stated:

I have no doubt that Martin McGuinness walked away from shaking hands with his sovereign monarch still feeling he was a republican. But even a definition outside an Irish context would sort of say Martin you are skating on a wee bit of thin ice there. This isn't just a visiting sovereign. This is your sovereign and one of the fundamental tenets of being a republican is that you are anti-monarchist and for God's sake catch yourself on.[82]

One of the most prominent departures from Sinn Féin at this time was that of Councillor Angela Nelson, who is now an independent councillor for Lisburn. Angela Nelson joined Sinn Féin in 1970 and was a member until 3 July 2012. Nelson announced her resignation through a letter in the *Irish News* and has commented:

I see the Queen and what she represents as commander-in-chief of the armed forces which still occupy the six counties of Ireland, who in the past murdered Irish men and women and examples are the Ballymurphy massacre, Bloody Sunday and all those things I witnessed as a young girl living in West Belfast … She pinned medals on the Paratrooper regiments' chests and said 'well done lads.'[83]

Nelson commented on her departure from the Provisionals by stating 'If I walk down that road and meet somebody from the Ballymurphy Massacre victims campaign group I have to be able to look them in the eye … So I made a decision to resign.'[84]

Further, Nelson has objected to the way in which the decision was taken regarding the handshake and has stated 'you don't meet the Queen of England and make a decision to do that on a Friday for it to happen within a week or two. So you knew it was already a done deal.'[85] Nelson's departure from Sinn Féin resulted in the party arguing that Nelson should give the seat to Sinn Féin as she had won it as a party candidate. However, Nelson refused to relinquish the seat and continues to be an independent councillor for Lisburn (retaining the seat won at the 2014 local elections).[86]

For some the handshake was entirely consistent with the change of direction of the Provisional Movement. Pádraig Garvey of RSF in Co. Kerry argued 'I feel there was a lot of noise made about Martin McGuinness meeting the Queen of England yet all I would see that as – she is the woman who employs him. She's the woman that pays his bills and it was no different to any other employer meeting their employee.'[87] Danny Morrison has argued:

The point about it is, for making peace and when you make peace with people you have to do strange things. You have to revise former positions. Now in this case here it's just being courteous. It would have been the height of ignorance, and it would have been remarkable had McGuinness gone there and sat down. Why would he have done that? So the Queen came to Ireland. She went to the garden of remembrance, she bowed her head.[88]

Repertoire of repression

Donatella Della Porta has emphasised the findings of social movement studies which point to an escalation of demands when groups feel 'excluded from the political system'.[89] Radical republicans not only feel excluded from the political system, but they also emphasise a repertoire of repression and harassment from the system in both the North and South of Ireland. A dominant theme throughout this narrative is the argument advanced by radical republicans that they are not permitted to express an alternative view to that of the mainstream, mainly Provisional Sinn Féin. As Della Porta has stated, this is not unique to the Irish republican case but is evident in the wider context of social movements, including the Basque Movement where 'ethno nationalists resorted to the long-standing narrative of oppression of the ethnic minority'.[90]

In April 2015 independent republican Dee Fennell in Belfast was arrested following a speech which he gave on Easter Sunday in Lurgan, the content of which included:

> Armed struggle must be a contributory factor to a wider struggle. The use of arms prior to 1916 was legitimate. The use of arms in Easter 1916 was legitimate. The use of arms after 1916 was totally legitimate. In the existing political context of partition, illegal occupation and the denial of national self-determination, armed struggle, in 2015, remains a legitimate act of resistance.[91]

Fennell's arrest has been described by academic Mark Hayes as 'essentially a thought crime. The real tragedy is that because Dee Fennell is a "dissident" republican, few people will hear of his case and even fewer people will care.'[92] Contemporary policy definitions of radicalisation processes have emphasised the adoption or expression of radical opinions and views.[93] Donatella Della Porta has pointed to the EU's definition of violent radicalisation as 'the phenomenon of people embracing opinions, views and ideas which could lead to acts of terrorism (European Commission 2005)'.[94] She goes on to state 'ideological radicalisation (such as the adoption of certain ideas) has thus been defined as "the mental prerequisite to recruitment" (Jenkins 2007:2).'[95]

In the post-Good Friday context, radical republicans have drawn public attention around the activity of parades, as was evident in the RSF case in Lurgan in May 2015.[96] In August 2017 five members of GARC were on trial in Belfast magistrates courts due to a republican parade which took place in September 2016 and which strayed from the route given to the parades commission.[97] The parade was a protest over the deal which had been reached to allow a contentious Orange Order parade through North Belfast. The organisers of GARC told the judge that they changed the route to 'ensure the safety of up to 600 demonstrators amid reports that menacing crowds of youths were gathering'.[98] During the trial Fennell argued that the event was 'a legal opportunity for residents to show their opposition to a deal "imposed on the community by Sinn Féin and the Orange Order"'.[99] Such incidents regarding republican parades tell a story – about radical republicans – the day-to-day activity which they are undertaking, and significantly their conceptualisation of their place in the wider society of the state of Northern Ireland.

Republican parades are largely the interface between the radical republican world and the wider society. Fennell highlighted the peaceful nature of the protest and many interviewees have stated that political violence continues in proximate dimension to 'suppression of peaceful protest'.[100] Robert W. White has conducted extensive oral history with activists in Irish republicanism throughout the past few decades and has drawn significantly on personal testimony of such activists. White has made reference to one such activist who joined the Provisionals in 1970 in Portadown. This activist 'changed his mind' regarding peaceful protest. White has revealed that the activist was influenced by Bloody Sunday and 'the state's response to events which included suspending civil liberties'.[101] White also concluded that 'for this respondent political violence became an option because of the perceived failure of peaceful protest'.[102] However, White went on to state that the respondent's involvement in the Republican Movement was a political decision and 'not a simple reaction that he wanted to hit back in response to Bloody Sunday'.[103]

Donatella Della Porta has observed that 'political violence throughout the world is intertwined with state responses to social movements in a sort of macabre dance'.[104] As stated by White, 'the nature of state repression has changed'.[105] Using the methodological approach of visual sociology, White has documented the changed nature of state repression through an examination of RSF events over the Easter weekend of 2016 when the organisation commemorated the centenary of the 1916 Easter Rising. White documented incidents which took place throughout the event; the parade began at the Garden of Remembrance in Parnell Square and proceeded to the General Post Office on O'Connell Street. White has noted the customary heavy police presence along with members of the counter-terrorism Special Detective Unit (commonly referred to as Special Branch). The author, who also witnessed the commemoration, saw members of Special Branch take onlookers' names and addresses, including members of the public who are not members of RSF but stopped to watch the parade which was led by a piper. An altercation developed regarding the fact that the colour party were covering their faces with green scarves. White has described the incident which took place outside the GPO: 'after the group took their positions in front of the podium from which speakers would address a sizeable crowd, Special Branch officers walked into the formation and pulled the scarves down … It was a petty and provocative display of the ability of state agents to interfere with an event. If someone had resisted s/he would have been arrested.'[106]

White's description of the events which took place that day echoes testimonies by the majority of interviewees. Discourse around 'suppression' and 'repression' occupies a central position throughout the radical republican narrative. Interviewees have emphasised their right to hold a political opinion and have argued that legislation such as section 30 of the Offences against the State Act (1939) is being used to stamp out alternative viewpoints to that of the state in the wake of the Good Friday Agreement. Donatella Della Porta has observed that 'in the cases analysed in this text [*Clandestine Policitical Violence*, 2013], a reciprocal adaptation brought about an escalation of protest forms and approaches to policing. Policing was in fact perceived as tough and, especially, indiscriminate and unjust; transformative repressive events contributed to justifying violence and pushing militant groups towards clandestinity.'[107] During an interview with the author, the following question was put to independent republican Francie McGuigan in Belfast: 'what do you think is the biggest challenge to being a republican at present?', to which McGuigan replied 'Admitting it.'[108] Also present was Kevin Hannaway, who subsequently added 'the second part is to be dubbed something that you're not. You see I am not against peace. No way. My struggle was about peace. But not a temporary peace. It was about a permanent peace.'[109] A central argument in the radical republican narrative is the belief that the British state along with Stormont are deliberately attempting to blacken the name of non-mainstream republicans. Fergal Moore in Monaghan, who joined RSF in 2009, has argued:

> It's things like Ricky O'Rawe's book and things like that that will give people heart to speak up and say well I'm not putting up with this anymore. And Anthony McIntyre, they were standing at the side of his house trying to put him out of it, you know. So things like that will get the ordinary man on the street to say well I'm fed up with the Provos too. And all we can do is offer the best alternative we can and we think we're doing that and hopefully they'll come towards us.[110]

Conclusion

Radical republicans have highlighted Sinn Féin's acceptance of the consent principle as a fundamental step in the group's transformation from revolutionary organisation to constitutional party. The radical republican discourse has rejected the mainstream argument that the Good Friday Agreement (and latterly the St Andrew's Agreement) have fundamentally altered the political landscape in which republicanism is operating. In contrast, radical republicans have asserted their fidelity to the traditional republican position and to the Republic declared in 1916. Independent republican Cáit Trainor has argued:

> As a republican the Good Friday Agreement was never a question for me, it is an internal settlement, a concession. I have never described myself as an anti-GFA republican as others do. I am not anti-GFA, the GFA was never something to even

consider. As a republican I do not believe in acceptance of British rule, even in the short term. The GFA legitimises British rule in Ireland until such times as a majority of the population say otherwise, such a vote would also be ran under the constructs of British institutions. I reject the GFA much the same as republicans rejected the 1921 treaty, the Sunningdale Agreement or any other such Agreement that does not give independence to Ireland.[111]

Crucially, any examination of radical republicanism must extend *beyond* the status quo due to the fact that radical republicans seek revolutionary change, not reform. Interviewees have provided insight into the 'navigation' of the system which is undertaken by radical republicans who have continued to argue that engagement with the partitionist institutions in Ireland serves to 'legitimise' them.

The arguments advanced by interviewees have offered insight into the radical republican perspective on the point at which engagement with the system becomes 'sell-out'. Collectively, radical republicans have rejected 'cultural imperialism', particularly in opposition to the mainstream 'normalisation' agenda in the state of Northern Ireland. Further, examination of the interface at which radical republicans encounter the state (mainly protests and marches) increases our understanding of the way in which they conceptualise their position within the state of Northern Ireland. In this respect the 'repertoire of repression' has formed a central component of republican discourse within the post-Good Friday Agreement period where the mainstream has suppressed dissent.

Notes

1 See P. McLoughlin, *John Hume and the Revision of Irish Nationalism* (Manchester, Manchester University Press, 2010).

2 S. Farren, *The SDLP: The Struggle for Agreement in Northern Ireland, 1970–2000* (Dublin, Four Courts Press, 2010), p. 283.

3 Northern Irish Political Collection, Linenhall Library Belfast, 'The Sinn Féin/ SDLP talks' (January–September 1988). P3396.

4 Northern Irish Political Collection, Linenhall Library Belfast, 'Gerry Adams and Sinn Féin, correspondence to John Hume and the SDLP' (18 March 1988). P3394.

5 *Ibid.*

6 Northern Irish Political Collection, Linenhall Library, Belfast. P3394.

7 Northern Irish Political Collection, Linenhall Library Belfast, 'Sinn Féin/ SDLP'. P3395.

8 Northern Irish Political Collection, Linenhall Library, Belfast, 'Papers and correspondence from John Hume and the SDLP to Sinn Féin, 1988'. P3395.

9 Northern Irish Political Collection, Linenhall Library Belfast, SDLP statement, written 30 August 1988. Released 5 September 1988. P3395.

10 Article 1 (ii) of the Good Friday Agreement says that the participants 'recognise that it is for the people of the island of Ireland alone, by agreement between the

two parts respectively and without external impediment, to exercise their right of self-determination on the basis of consent, freely and concurrently given, North and South, to bring about a united Ireland, if that is their wish, accepting that this right must be achieved and exercised with and subject to the agreement and consent of a majority of the people of Northern Ireland.'

11 An IRA convention was held in October 1997 regarding the Mitchell Principles, after which the REAL IRA was formed. See Frampton, *Legion of the Rearguard*.

12 Commenting on the outcome of the talks, a statement released by Provisional Sinn Féin in September 1988 (which was embargoed until 12 noon on 5 September) stated: 'the Sinn Féin delegation, in attempting to explore the SDLP policy of "unity by consent" was dismayed to discover that contained within this policy was a recognition and acceptance by the SDLP of the loyalist veto.' Northern Irish Political Collection, Linenhall Library Belfast, 'Papers and correspondence from Gerry Adams and Sinn Féin to SDLP, 1988'. P3394.

13 Joe Dillon, interview with the author, Skerries, 19 March 2013.

14 *Ibid.* Dillon is making reference to the IRA attack on Brookeborough RUC barracks on 1 January 1957.

15 Francie Mackey, interview with the author, Omagh, 8 February 2013.

16 *Ibid.*

17 Kevin Hannaway, interview with the author, Belfast, 24 July 2013.

18 McKearney, *The Provisional IRA*, p. 149.

19 Anthony McIntyre, interview with the author, Dublin, 3 April 2013.

20 Ciaran Mulholland, interview with the author, Belfast, 8 May 2014.

21 'Bodenstown oration by Martin McGuinness', *An Phoblacht* (10 June 1973).

22 J. Tonge, 'An enduring tradition or the last gasp of physical force republicanism? "Dissident" republican violence in Northern Ireland', in P.M. Currie and M. Taylor (eds), *Dissident Irish Republicanism* (London, The Continuum International Publishing Group, 2011), p. 112.

23 Dan Hoban, interview with the author, Mayo, 3 November 2013.

24 Tony Catney, interview with the author, Belfast, 14 September 2012.

25 Pádraic MacCoitir, interview with the author, Belfast, 4 October 2012.

26 Quoted in J.M. Regan, *The Irish Counter-revolution 1921–1936* (Dublin, Gill & Macmillan Ltd, 1999), p. 69.

27 *Ibid.*, p. 69.

28 *Ibid.*, p. 69.

29 S. Murphy, 'Easter ethics', in G. Doherty and D. Keogh (eds), *1916: The Long Revolution* (Cork, Mercier Press, 2007), p. 333.

30 Tony Catney, 1916 Societies debate on the One Ireland One Vote campaign versus a border poll, West Belfast, 2012. Attended by the author.

31 Dee Fennell, interview with the author, Belfast, 28 November 2013.

32 Jim McCrystal, interview with the author, Lurgan, 22 August 2013.

33 See English, *Armed Struggle* (2003) and Hennessey, *Northern Ireland Peace Process*.

34 Republican Sinn Féin, Éire Nua policy. See https://republicansinnfein.org/rsf-policies-2/. Accessed 20 July 2018.

35 Geraldine Taylor, interview with the author, Belfast, 14 October 2012.

36 Anthony McIntyre, interview with the author, Dublin, 3 April 2013.

37 Murphy, 'Easter ethics', p. 332.

38 McKearney, *The Provisional IRA*, p. 213.

39 Murphy, 'Easter ethics', p. 334.

40 *Ibid.*, p. 334.

41 See Whiting, *Spoiling the Peace?*, p. 127.

42 *The Pensive Quill*, 'Saoradh – rebuilding the republican movement; Martin Galvin speaks to former Irish republican prisoner Packy Carty' (7 February 2017). http://thepensivequill.am/. Accessed 20 July 2018.

43 *Ibid.*

44 For an assessment of the 1916 Rising within a 'liberal democratic ethical-political framework' see Murphy, 'Easter ethics'.

45 1916 Joe McKelvey Society event in Tyrone, 'The burning of Long Kesh' (16 October 2013). Attended by the author.

46 C. Irvin, *Militant Nationalism: Between Movement and Party in Ireland and the Basque Country* (Minneapolis, University of Minnesota Press, 1999), p. 9.

47 There is an unwritten understanding within republicanism that certain engagement with the state is unavoidable, for example state pension or payment of taxes. Drawing a pension is seen as a practical necessity.

48 D. Carroll, *They Have Fooled You Again: Michael O'Flanagan (1876–1942): Priest, Republican, Social Critic* (Dublin, The Columba Press, 1993), p. 211.

49 *Ibid.*, p. 211.

50 *Ibid.*, pp. 211–12.

51 Cáit Trainor, interview with the author by email, 15 January 2018.

52 T. MacSwiney, *Principles of Freedom* (Dodo Press, 2008), p. 103.

53 Richard Behal, interview with the author, Killarney, 31 October 2013.

54 Jim McDonald, interview with the author, Nottingham, 14 November 2013.

55 Des Dalton, interview with the author, Dublin, 15 February 2013.

56 *Ibid.*

57 Pádraic MacCoitir, interview with the author, Belfast, 4 October 2012.

58 Jim McCrystal, interview with the author, Lurgan, 2 August 2013.

59 Des Dalton, interview with the author, Dublin, 15 February 2013.

60 Lita Campbell, interview with the author, Dublin, 21 October 2013.

61 *Ibid.*

62 Dee Fennell, interview with the author, Belfast, 28 November 2013.

63 For further information see S. Moran, 'The GAA has no need for flags and anthems', *Irish Times* (30 September 2017).

64 C. Young, 'GAA club chairman quits over plans to remove IRA men gates', *Irish News* (23 August 2016).

65 Dee Fennell, interview with the author, Belfast, 28 November 2013.

66 *Ibid.*

67 Anthony McIntyre, interview with the author, Dublin, 3 April 2013.

68 Della Porta, *Clandestine Political Violence*, p. 219.

69 *Ibid.*, p. 116.

70 Richard Behal, interview with the author, Killarney, 31 October 2013.

71 Pádraic MacCoitir, interview with the author, Belfast, 4 October 2012.

72 Ruairí Ó Brádaigh autumn school, Abbey Hotel, Roscommon town, 23 September 2017. Attended by the author.

73 R. W. White, 'From state terrorism to petty harassment: a multi-method approach to understanding repression of Irish republicans', *Studi Irlandesi: A Journal of Irish Studies*, no. 7 (2017), pp. 45–64.

74 Nuala Perry, interview with the author, Belfast, 15 August 2013.

75 *Ibid.*

76 Ciaran Mulholland, interview with the author, Belfast, 8 May 2014.

77 *Ibid.*

78 *Ibid.*

79 Davy Jordan, chairperson of Saoradh, First Ard Fheis, Canal Court Hotel, Newry, 24 September 2016. See www.facebook.com/Saoradh/videos/334441560235968/. Accessed 20 July 2018.

80 Gerard Hodgins, interview with the author, Belfast, 13 September 2012.

81 Tonge, '"No-one likes us; we don't care"', pp. 219–26.

82 Tony Catney, interview with the author, Belfast, 14 September 2012.

83 Angela Nelson, interview with the author, Belfast, 17 September 2012.

84 *Ibid.*

85 *Ibid.*

86 Similarly, Louise Minihan in Dublin won a Dublin council seat as a Sinn Féin candidate; however, she departed the party in 2010 and went on to join éirígí. Minihan lost her council seat in 2014 when contesting it as an éirígí candidate.

87 Pádraig Garvey, interview with the author, Killarney, 30 October 2013.

88 Danny Morrison, interview with the author, Belfast, 7 May 2014.

89 Della Porta, *Clandestine Political Violence*, p. 207.

90 *Ibid.*, p. 207.

91 H. McDonald, 'Irish republican detained for calling armed attacks legitimate', *The Guardian* (20 April 2015).

92 M. Hayes, 'The ESRC university project on "dissident" Irish republicanism: some reflections on the relationship between research, academia, and the security state', *Contemporary Social Science* (published online 5 February 2018), p. 16. www.tandfonline.com/doi/abs/10.1080/21582041.2018.1427884. Accessed 25 July 2018.

93 The Terrorism Act (2000) puts emphasis on individuals who are 'inviting support' for proscribed organisations. Section 12(2) of the legislation states that a person commits an offence if 'he arranges, manages or assists in arranging or managing a meeting which he knows is–
    (a) to support a proscribed organisation
    (b) to further the activities of a proscribed organisation, or
    (c) to be addressed by a person who belongs or professes to belong to a proscribed organisation'.
    The Act can be viewed at legislation.gov.uk. Accessed 20 July 2018.

94 Della Porta, *Clandestine Political Violence*, p. 205.

95 *Ibid.*, p. 205.

96 See chapter two.

97 'Fennell: protest took new route to avoid a riot', *Irish News* (16 August 2017).
98 *Ibid.*
99 *Ibid.*
100 White, 'From state terrorism to petty harassment'.
101 *Ibid.*, p. 51.
102 *Ibid.*, p. 51.
103 *Ibid.*, p. 51.
104 Della Porta, *Clandestine Political Violence*, p. 33.
105 White, 'From state terrorism to petty harassment', p. 54.
106 *Ibid.*, p. 59.
107 Della Porta, *Clandestine Political Violence*, p. 33.
108 Francie McGuigan, interview with the author, Belfast, 24 July 2013.
109 Kevin Hannaway, interview with the author, Belfast, 24 July 2013.
110 Fergal Moore, interview with the author, Belfast, 14 October 2012.
111 Cáit Trainor, interview with the author by email, 15 January 2018.

5

Current armed republicanism

I think there's an onus on you especially, as an academic and author, and it's such
a serious piece of research, to ask them what the strategy is.

Danny Morrison, interview with the author, Belfast, 7 May 2014

The sympathy that there was for the H-Blocks, for the Armagh girls, for the
Portlaoise men, all that is gone because the peace process and all the millions poured
into revisionism and papers write pure poison. That has quite a bearing.

Martin Corey, interview with the author, Maghaberry prison,
30 August 2013

Republicans involved in current military activity should be questioned on their
actions and what they are seeking to achieve because if you're born and reared in
this place you've every entitlement to ask that question.

Martin Óg Meehan, interview with the author, Belfast, 12 December 2012

Introduction

Why should we fight for freedom? Is it not strange, that it has become necessary to
ask and answer this question?

Terence MacSwiney, *Principles of Freedom*, writing in 1921[1]

This chapter examines the heterogeneous nature of radical republicanism, which
encompasses a wide spectrum of views on the armed campaign within the current context. The radical republican base includes individuals who were supportive of the IRA ceasefires in the 1990s, or who voted 'yes' for the Good Friday
Agreement, but who are opposed to the current armed campaign, such as Gerard
Hodgins in Belfast who has stated:

I was actually in support of a ceasefire being called, when it wasn't very popular to
be saying so in the IRA. From my own experience I agreed with the Adams line
that we had fought it to a standstill ... I don't understand the mind-set which says
you have to constantly be at war.[2]

Fundamentally, radical republicans have united in their recognition of the
'right' to exercise armed struggle; however, they remain divided on when that

right should be exercised and whether or not it should be exercised in present conditions and amid the absence of popular support. It is for this reason that a significant portion of the radical republican constituency falls within the 'non-condemnation' category regarding the current use of armed actions.Prevalence of the 'non-condemnation' stance towards armed struggle is not a new phenomenon; rather, it has occupied a prominent position throughout the history and development of Irish republicanism.[3]

At various junctures, strategic decisions have been taken by the leadership of the Republican Movement to cease military activity, such as the 'dump arms' order in 1923 or the 1962 cessation of armed activity,[4] reflecting strategic decisions by the leadership based on wider conditions.[5] As evidenced by opposition to decommissioning, radical republicans have rejected any attempts to negate (what they regard as) a future generation's right to take up armed struggle. Significantly, until PIRA decommissioning in 2005, at each juncture throughout the history of the Republican Movement the cessation of activities was accompanied by the reassertion of the right of the Irish people to rise up in arms at a future time. Interviews conducted with members of armed organisations reveal an insight into the motivations and aims of those continuing armed activity, as well as their views on the morality of armed actions and where they take legitimacy from. Interviews were also conducted with prominent radical republicans outside armed groups who have provided their views on the armed campaign; including individuals who were formerly active in the Provisional Movement (some of whom were at a senior operational level). It is relevant to examine the position of individuals who have asserted the legitimacy of the Provisional campaign while simultaneously rejecting the legitimacy of the armed campaign conducted by groups such as the Continuity and REAL IRAs.

Location of the current campaign by radical groups (Continuity IRA, REAL IRA, ONH, New IRA) within the long trajectory of republican armed struggle demonstrates the cyclical nature of armed republicanism and highlights the reoccurrence of significant questions around utility and morality. It is useful to provide an examination of the current use of republican violence in the context of Just War Theory.[6] A significant question which has arisen for the republican leadership at each juncture is: at what point is violence no longer justified? In the more recent period the Omagh bomb in August 1998 led to an assessment within the radical republican base of the utility of the armed campaign in current circumstances.

Just war

In his chapter 'Easter ethics' published in *1916: The Long Revolution*, Seamus Murphy has analysed the morality of the 1916 Rising and applied Just War Theory, stating that '"Just war" theory focuses on the morality of the respective actions of the protagonists.'[7] Murphy has argued that 'it would be better to think of it as a theory laying down the criteria for permissible resort to force or justifiable use of military power'.[8] Murphy's application of Just War Theory emphasises criteria which must be met prior to resorting to war and subsequently regarding the conduct of war, which provides a useful theoretical frame through which to analyse arguments presented by radical republicans who are involved in or are supportive of a current armed campaign. Murphy has noted a crucial criterion as 'reasonable prospect of success' and that an armed campaign is a last resort.[9]

Quoting Just War Theory, Shanahan states 'some just war theorists require that before a group initiates war, all other options must have been exhausted'.[10] Shanahan has argued that 'in the standard republican narrative, the resumption of the [Provisional] IRA's armed struggle is presented as a last resort to achieve for Catholics their basic civil rights after all peaceful means to achieve reforms had been tried and had been brutally suppressed.'[11] Shanahan has rejected this narrative. However, the majority of radical republicans have also rejected this narrative. As detailed in chapter three, the contested narrative surrounding the origins and aims of the Provisional IRA highlights a fundamental point of departure in the Provisional–'dissident' discourse on the legitimacy of armed struggle. Anthony McIntyre, who served a life sentence in Long Kesh prison as a Provisional IRA volunteer (1976–93), is a prominent critic of the Provisional Movement and the Provisional Sinn Féin leadership. However, he has notably drawn a distinction between the Provisional IRA campaign and the campaign waged by current republican groups:

> Armed struggle in any society should be the last resort rather than the first resort. These people seemed to have made it a first resort. I don't regard them as criminals. I regard them as people caught up in a legacy, or the product or victims of a legacy.[12]

Reflective of the nuanced nature of the radical republican narrative, Tommy McCourt, an independent republican in Derry who joined the Republican Movement in 1968, has rejected the Provisional discourse on current radical groups and has argued:

> The difference is now between this broad dissident base and Provisional Sinn Féin … [it] is much broader than just those who wish to use a gun or don't. I think Sinn Féin, behind the scenes – Sinn Féin have no moral objection to using weapons and would use them tomorrow if they felt like it.[13]

McCourt's analysis reflects a discourse, evident throughout the radical republican base, which rejects the Provisional argument which emphasises changed structural conditions within the North.

Principles of democracy

The dominant discourse surrounding the contemporary use of armed struggle by republican groups has centred around questions of altered conditions within the state of Northern Ireland, human rights violations, utility and incompatibility with democratic values. Interestingly, Shanahan has highlighted the fact that according to some philosophers, acts of political violence 'are necessarily morally wrong because they always violate fundamental human rights'.[14] This argument is reflective of Haig Khatchadourian, who has asserted that any form of political violence is morally wrong based on the fact that the act in itself violates human rights.[15] This is an argument with which radical republicans have engaged, as demonstrated by Anthony McIntyre:

> I think that the groups today who are carrying on with armed struggle are in a strange way the antithesis of republican …: 'we, physical force republicans insist on our right to wage war and we will argue the case that the Irish people have the right, we feel'. Yet at the same time insist that [they] have no right to be free from their violence. And I think it's an absolute nonsense and for that reason I don't identify with the physical force tradition. I think it's anti-democratic.[16]

McIntyre's argument can be located within Seamus Murphy's critique, which states 'I consider the liberal democratic value system ethically superior to the nationalist one … it places the individual person at the centre of its value system.'[17] In contrast, Francie Mackey of the 32CSM has argued that republican values are reconciled with wider democratic values:

> Republicans are not about anti-peace. Far from it. The opposite would be the truth but conditions and the violation of our sovereignty has led republicans into armed conflict throughout our history and today; so from a sovereignty point of view we have to keep looking at ways to address the issue that leads to conflict and bring it to an end. Where in real terms – it's those who refuse the issue of sovereignty on the table are the real aggressors, the British government.[18]

Similarly, independent republican Jim McCrystal has located the radical republican campaign within the broader context:

> You take any of them countries – what do they do? Fly over and drop their bombs. Shoot people. Kill people … So I mean if it's right for one person it's right for the next person … The difference to me is when you're in your own country and you're fighting the people who came here to take all off you. I mean you're right. There's not too many other ways you can do it.[19]

McCrystal's comments are reflective of the broad tendency within radical republican discourse which locates the republican struggle within the wider context, arguing that the republican campaign is no less just than the British going to war. Radical republicans have largely refused to make a distinction between republican armed struggle and wars which have been propagated by the British, thus rejecting their war as 'terrorism' as distinct from wars undertaken by the British.

In a documentary titled *To Die for Ireland* (broadcast in the early 1980s) Dáithí Ó Conaill, who is a founder member of RSF, was asked by the presenter 'do you feel there is a moral question involved in the IRA's guerrilla acts?' Ó Conaill responded:

> One must be honest and admit that some of the actions carried out by the IRA were hard to justify. One can explain them. One can explain that warnings were not received in time with the result that civilians lost their lives when bombs exploded. One can explain that in some cases civilians were mistaken for military personnel. But one does not attempt to justify such things. As far as the IRA is concerned there is no moral question. We are quite clear as to the morality of the struggle we wage and we as a people have never renounced our claim to full freedom and sovereignty.[20]

However, in the contemporary period a discourse has developed within radical republicanism (particularly among independent republicans) which argues that an armed campaign in current circumstances is not compatible with human rights. Anthony McIntyre has stated:

> I do not engage in armed actions, not because I am a pacifist, because I am not a pacifist, but I do not engage in them because it would bring me into violation or conflict with far too many rights than I could ever hope to solve. In the sense that I would bring about fewer rights by armed campaign than the rights that I would violate and break by doing it.[21]

Legitimate targets

During the aforementioned debate in the Waterfront Hall in Belfast in 2012 (a unique insight into the Provisional–radical republican divide), the chair of the session asked with whom the armed 'dissident' groups were at war, given that a 'military stalemate' had been reached between the Provisional IRA and the British. However, this question fails to recognise that the radical republican world does not accept that a military stalemate has been reached. As early as the 1980s, radical republican discourse was dominated by a belief that the Provisional IRA campaign was on the verge of success but was defeated by individuals in the leadership. In *To Die for Ireland* Dáithí Ó Conaill made reference to the same document to which Kevin Hannaway referred in chapter three:

> There was a document captured by the Irish Republican Army. The document, thirty-seven, which was written by the General Glover. A confidential document for submission to the cabinet in London and in it he outlined a situation whereby the forces of the Crown could not militarily defeat the urban guerrillas. Glover asserted that the name-calling of the IRA as thugs and mindless people and so forth was

completely wrong … when we look at say over the last twelve months the British army have suffered a far higher casualty rate than they had have suffered in the preceding two years. It's a question of strike and disappear quickly and strike again.[22]

Clearly, this leaked document had an effect on individuals who viewed it as evidence that the IRA was on the verge of military success. Commenting on the Provisional campaign, a spokesperson for the Continuity IRA in North Armagh has argued 'in my opinion if they'd kept it going they'd have got somewhere. You know, it will achieve the end goal where politics won't.'[23]

The radical republican base is divided on the utility of an armed campaign in contemporary conditions, as demonstrated by Tony Catney, who has been critical of the armed groups:

> The fact that they have, to the best of my knowledge, in their entire existence never engaged the forces of the military occupation – I just think that says a lot about anybody who claims that they are involved in a republican struggle … my preference would be that nobody had to engage in armed struggle, that there genuinely was an alternative route. But anybody that feels that as the only way they have to go, then the onus on them is to inflict as little hardship and suffering on the nationalist and republican community and as much on the forces of occupation as possible.[24]

Timothy Shanahan has offered an interpretation of the 'jus in bello' discrimination conditions in Just War Theory which require a distinction between legitimate and illegitimate targets of military action, and has quoted 'in order for military action to be morally legitimate, it must only target individuals who pose a threat to the community's common good'.[25] As previously noted, the radical republican narrative rejects this concept and in fact this issue forms a central point of contention between the mainstream and radical discourse regarding basic motivations for the campaign. The Civil Rights Movement of the late 1960s altered the conditions in which republicanism was operating and had a significant impact on public opinion and the gathering momentum around a civil rights agenda. However, radical republicans continue to assert that the pursuit of equality was not the raison d'être of the IRA campaign. This is an important distinction to make. Radical republican armed groups have reasserted their war against colonialism in the pursuit of sovereignty.

Continuity IRA: the first 'dissidents'

The Continuity IRA was the first armed organisation to be commonly referred to as 'dissident' in the modern period. When the split took place in 1986, the newly formed Republican Sinn Féin made only one alteration to the Sinn Féin constitution, that is, that a change to the organisation's constitution on the issue of abstentionism from the Irish Dáil, Stormont or Westminster would require 100 per cent of the Ard Fheis to effect any change. Republican Sinn Féin continues to adhere to the same Sinn Féin constitution which has been in place since 1917. Therefore it is natural that the Continuity IRA formed in 1986 (which shares an ideology with Republican Sinn Féin and is widely believed to be the armed wing of the movement) continued to adhere to the Green Book which has been in place since 1978. Bowyer Bell has commented 'the IRA green book is not an ideological primer like Mao's Red Book but rather operating instructions for the involved'.[26] As recalled by Richard English, the Green Book emerged within the prisons in the early 1970s and was completed in 1978.[27]

According to Martin Dillon in *The Dirty War*, the Green Book was revised (by the Provisional Movement) in 1987 after the split between Provisional Sinn Féin and RSF.[28] Members of the Continuity IRA in North Armagh (in the North of Ireland) and in Co. Kerry (in the South of Ireland) have confirmed to the author that they presently adhere to the Green Book which was conceived in the early 1970s and that no alteration was made to the Green Book at the formation of the Continuity IRA, nor has any alteration been made since.[29] The Green Book states:

> The Irish Republican Army as the legal representatives of the Irish people are morally justified in carrying out a campaign of resistance against foreign occupation forces and domestic collaborators. All volunteers are and must feel morally justified in carrying out the dictates of the legal government, they as the army are the legal and lawful army of the Irish Republic which has been forced underground by overwhelming forces.[30]

This section of the Green Book reflects arguments by radical republicans which state that any recognition of partitionist states or parliaments removes legitimacy for the continuing struggle. Given the fact that the Green Book states that volunteers are members of the army of the Second Dáil Éireann, recognition of Leinster House (taken to its logical conclusion) would undermine the Second Dáil, thus undermining the associated army. Therefore members of RSF and the Continuity IRA have asserted their belief that the Provisional IRA abrogated its position as the legitimate Republican Movement in 1986.

The Green Book emphasises that the IRA is 'the direct representative of the 1919 Dáil Éireann parliament, and that as such they are the legal and lawful government of the Irish Republic'.[31] The continued use of the Green Book by the Continuity IRA is unsurprising given the organisation's assertion that, as the true legitimate Republican Movement, it draws a direct lineage back to 1916. The issue of legitimacy (and where it is derived from) is central to the republican narrative and has proved a dominant point in the contested discourse between the Provisionals and radical republicans, as well as within the republican constituency. Danny Morrison has argued:

> Even on his death bed Ruairí still believed that the Continuity IRA was the Government of Ireland, which is ridiculous … I mean, I don't believe that my

authority to fight the Brits came from some seventy-nine-year-old man who was the last surviving member of the Second Dáil, and who said to republicans in 1969/70 I invest my powers from 1920 to you, you are now the government of Ireland. I mean it's just nonsense.[32]

Crucially, Morrison went on to state:

> To me our mandate was the sense of oppression, physically, that we lived under, the conditions that we lived under and they and they alone justified armed struggle and that was our position. Not this other theological position which a lot of the older people were burdened with.[33]

Radical republicans have continued to reject the impact of changed structural conditions on republican ideology. The contested discourse demonstrates that the issue of legitimacy is entwined with moral rights and the basis from which the morality for actions is derived. As detailed in chapter one, RSF claims that it is the legal and legitimate true Republican Movement. The organisation rejects the Provisionals' claims of legitimacy as the Republican Movement, and similarly rejects assertions from other radical republican groups that claim to be the Republican Movement.[34] In *Dílseacht: The Story of Comdt. General Tom Maguire*, Ruairí Ó Brádaigh outlined the legitimacy of the Second Dáil Éireann and the subsequent delegation of powers which the Second Dáil conferred in 1938 to the IRA's army council. At the first Ruairí Ó Brádaigh summer school in County Roscommon in June 2014, RSF president Des Dalton gave a lecture in which he addressed what he termed 'common misconceptions' regarding RSF's position on the Second Dáil and the subsequent chain of continuity and legitimacy to the present-day RSF organisation. Dalton stated:

> I would like to begin by addressing the most common misconception of the delega-tion of powers by the executive of the Second Dáil which reduces it to a claim that governmental powers were claimed or assumed by one person to be conferred as he wished, namely Commandant-General Tom Maguire. This is false and indeed displays a complete misunderstanding of the process and what it entailed. It also does a complete disservice to Tom Maguire who was punctilious in his duties as a Teachta Dála and conscious in the exercise and preservations of its powers.[35]

Tom Maguire was the last faithful surviving member of the Second Dáil and conferred the legitimacy of the Second Dáil first onto the Provisional IRA in 1969 (in the wake of the split with the Officials) and then onto the RSF Movement in 1986.[36] The Second Dáil was never dissolved and Dalton has described the creation of the Leinster House Assembly as 'a creation of a British Act of Parliament and was not an all-Ireland body'.[37] When Éamon De Valera entered Leinster House in 1927 he claimed that it was not in fact legitimate; rather, he asserted the legitimacy of the Second Dáil and commented on the legitimacy of those outside the Dáil.[38] Therein lies the chain of continuity which is claimed by RSF, upon the conferring of legitimacy to the organisation by Tom Maguire in 1986.[39] RSF have drawn a line of continuity right back to 1916 and have thus rejected the formation of republican groups such as the 32CSM or éirígí and have proclaimed that these organisations are a departure from the true republican mantle.

A spokesperson for the Continuity IRA in North Armagh has stated that the organisation remains active in the contemporary period and has claimed that there is a significant amount of IRA activity taking place which is not reported:

> In this area there's a lot of operations happening but a lot isn't being reported … they deliberately hide them for the fact that if the attacks were reported then people in this area would see that the organisation is active and it generates more support.
> Author: what would be sufficient to produce a ceasefire?
> CIRA: Withdrawal.
> Author: And nothing less?
> CIRA: No.[40]

Later in the interview this Continuity IRA spokesperson stated:

> The IRA want a united Ireland, a full British withdrawal from this country and no British interference. You know, there's nothing else, it's simple. To drive the Brits from Ireland.[41]

In 2007 the last British army patrol departed the streets of Northern Ireland; thus, the context in which republican groups are operating has altered. This spokesperson for the Continuity IRA was asked what constitutes a 'legitimate target' given these changed circumstances, to which he replied:

> Police, British soldiers, prison warders. Commercial targets. In some circumstances British ministers. But security forces would be the main target.[42]

Further, the spokesperson alleged that a number of operations have taken place in Armagh, after which 'they [the PSNI] might've arrested the usual suspects but they weren't even close to the unit that done it'.[43]

Republican Sinn Féin member Brendan Madden (Galway) was a member of the Republican Movement from the late 1950s until his death in 2015. Reflecting on the morality of the armed campaign, he stated:

> I wouldn't kill a bird there on the road but I mean I see no harm in using force to get the British out of our country, out of the six counties and anybody else that invades our country … I've nothing whatsoever against the English people. I have nothing whatsoever against an English soldier but when he's here it's a different story … when he puts on a uniform to stay here you know he's an enemy … and I wouldn't be particularly worried what would happen [to] him here and it's the uniform I'd be against.[44]

Madden went on to comment:

I do agree with the force issue because in every other country it has worked but it is a very very sad thing that it has to be … I'd like to see them gone [England] and I could sleep in comfort.[45]

Peig King, the patron of RSF, has argued 'the Brits will always have plans and promises. They promise the sun, moon and stars but they don't mean one word of it. They were always like that. History tells you that they were always like that.'[46] While Peig King cannot speak for any armed organisation, she has speculated on the campaign:

> You see you don't go to take lives. If you have a cause you're fighting for the cause. In any country there is going to be life lost if they keep their country independent and alive and are proud of their nationality. Now to do that sometimes you have to fight and when you fight there is going to be disaster. But I think too that at times if you don't fight you're trodden on, so you have no life.[47]

1998: Omagh

The Omagh bomb which killed twenty-nine people fundamentally altered the landscape within which militant republican organisations were operating. Public opinion was that the REAL IRA was responsible for the Omagh bomb, and the 32CSM (which shares an ideology with the REAL IRA) experienced a backlash in its aftermath. The honorary president of the 32CSM, Phil O'Donoghue in Kilkenny, has recalled that period:

> There were some very angry meetings after that. Some very angry meetings. It should never have happened. There's some would call it a war crime. A thoughtless act. Or maybe it was deliberate. I am of the opinion that it was deliberate and the reason I say that is this house was raided about four or five hours before the actual bomb went off so they had pre-knowledge of the bomb … I strongly believe that they deliberately allowed that bomb to go off.[48]

O'Donoghue has stated that it was 'the first time I ever considered quitting. But that would be a desertion.'[49] Omagh led to an assessment of the military campaign by the REAL IRA, which announced a cessation of its campaign in 1998.[50] A republican in Derry who is affiliated to the REAL IRA has commented:

> From my point of view the campaign [REAL IRA] was better than the Provos'. When Omagh happened everyone ran for cover. There's no one on this earth that would want that to happen … It's only recovering now from Omagh.[51]

The bombing was received with a level of revulsion which is arguably unprecedented in the recent period and Bowyer Bell has argued 'the REAL IRA with the Omagh bomb merely made the peace process more valid'.[52] In *Legion of the Rearguard*, Frampton cites an interview with radical republican Anthony McIntyre in *The Guardian* in which McIntyre commented on the bomb:

'Omagh should never have happened and when it did, those should have been the last deaths … republicans should have found out by now, armed strategy is the road to disaster.'[53]

Massereene

In 2009 the REAL IRA killed two British soldiers at Massereene Barracks in County Antrim. When asked if the killings achieved anything a senior member of the leadership of the 32CSM has argued:

A strike on the British army. I don't consider it to be counterproductive. No. It showed a ruthlessness there that was necessary. You know we [republicans] are not up against softies when it comes to the SAS or what have you.[54]

The radical republican narrative around 'legitimate targets' as constituting the 'forces of occupation' is no different from the language used by the Provisional IRA into the late 1980s. The Provisional IRA was unambiguous about what constituted a 'legitimate target'. On 2 February 1989 the cover page of *An Phoblacht* was titled 'Thatcher's latest victim' and stated 'Life came to an end for a young British soldier in Belfast on Tuesday night. He died in a war that was not of his making in a country he probably knew little about apart from what his superiors told him. But he dies as soldiers who take up the gun to oppress the people of another country will inevitably die.'[55]

Also in 1998, in March, the Continuity IRA (according to media reports) carried out the murder of PSNI constable Stephen Carroll in Lurgan. Afterwards a press conference took place on the steps of Stormont with then PSNI chief constable Hugh Orde, then first minister Peter Robinson and then deputy first minister Martin McGuinness, during which McGuinness described 'dissident republicans' as 'traitors to Ireland', thus provoking a strong emotional response from republicans.[56] The use of the word 'traitor' by McGuinness was poignant and significant and was greeted with widespread anger among radical republicans. Peig King, the patron of RSF, has commented on McGuinness's statement. King, who knew Martin McGuinness through the Republican Movement prior to the split in 1986, has argued:

He has forgotten that he is Irish, he's forgotten his country. He has forgotten why he became Sinn Féin or a republican, why he went out and risked his life, which he did do. He did his bit the same as everybody else but unfortunately it didn't linger too long with him. Headlines with his name at the top was more important to him.[57]

Interestingly, a senior member of the leadership of the 32CSM in the South of Ireland commented on the killing of PSNI constable Carroll:

I would go so far as to say that there should be no action in the North against any police. Because even at the worst of times there was a fair amount of police in the

North who would give warnings. Decent enough individuals. If they see something being done as something that was wrong they would let you know. If they wouldn't let us know they would let the SDLP know and for that reason I would be cautious about hitting policemen, unless they are really bad individuals. If we look at history we see Collins only singled out particularly obnoxious individuals there who were going out of their way to be obnoxious. So I would have completely different targets than the police.[58]

This individual proceeded to outline 'legitimate' targets as the 'forces of occupation'; therefore, the British army. This is an important revelation from an individual who is part of the leadership, as it represents a departure from the traditional armed republican position and poses the question of whether or not this represents a wider shift in the thinking of republican armed groups regarding what constitutes a 'legitimate target'. This poses a further question regarding the *reason* for the perceived shift: is it reflective of recognition of a more 'localised' nature of policing (which the Patten report intended to bring about)?

The long campaign

Republican groups that continue to advocate an armed campaign have located their actions within the long tradition of armed republicanism. Within this context, advocates of a current campaign have promoted a particular discourse regarding the trajectory which the Provisional Movement has taken. Therefore, views on armed struggle are currently intertwined with views on the previous 'success' or 'failure' of the Provisional IRA's campaign. A common thread of thought throughout radical groups and independents is that the Provisional IRA was 'compromised'. Repeated revelations regarding British agents in the IRA have added weight to this thesis among radical republicans who believe that the campaign itself did not fail; rather, the Provisional leadership failed.[59] The promotion of this narrative throughout radical republican circles illustrates why current groups feel they can succeed where the Provisional campaign failed. Danny Morrison, the former director of publicity for Sinn Féin, has responded to this argument by stating:

Part of their discourse is Gerry Adams and Martin McGuinness must be agents. They ran down the war ... But if it's true of mainstream republicanism, that it is vulnerable to infiltration, then, equally, it is true of dissident republicanism. How do I know that they're not working for MI5, an organisation which was not happy with the peace process, weren't happy to see Martin McGuinness, former commander of the IRA, a leader in government? How do I know that this violence isn't being controlled by agents who work for the British?[60]

A complex discourse exists between the Provisional and 'dissident' worlds which in many respects goes to the heart of current armed republicanism.

Current IRA volunteers believe that they are taking up the gauntlet of previous generations of republicans in the fight against occupation and have argued that the campaign undertaken by the Provisional IRA was one phase in the long trajectory of Irish republicanism, the leadership of which was ultimately compromised. In his work on 'informers' Stephen Hopkins has argued that the 'republican family' has been 'significantly affected by these disclosures in the post-conflict era' and that 'they have become an important element in the contestation between leadership supporters and "dissenters" within contemporary republicanism'.[61] The 'contestation' to which Hopkins refers is in fact evident throughout the entire radical republican discourse, extending beyond the topic of 'informers'. Evidence which has surfaced in recent years regarding the high level of infiltration and informers operating in the PIRA has led to the development of a narrative from so-called 'dissidents' regarding the overall path which the Provisional Movement has taken.[62]

Radical republicans have argued that infiltration at multiple levels within the Provisional Movement must extend to the leadership and have suggested that it is likely that a high-level informer/agent within Provisional Sinn Féin may still be in leadership in the party today. The case of Denis Donaldson is highlighted as an example of high-level infiltration.[63] This belief has subsequently contributed to a narrative promoted by radical republicans that there was an overall plan being pursued by some within the Provisional leadership to wind down the Provisional Movement and to pursue the path which the party is now on, which radical republicans would at best describe as constitutional nationalism.[64]

Stephen Hopkins has argued that the presence of high-level informers in the Provisional Movement meant the state could 'better judge accurately what kind of compromise was necessary and achievable to bring the vast majority of republicans into a future without the IRA. Many so-called dissident republicans would argue that this was also a future without republicanism as an ideology or set of strategic goals.'[65] Gerry McKerr, an independent republican in Lurgan, has traced what he calls the 'mass infiltration' of the IRA to the 1970s and has recalled:

> If you wanted to join the IRA years ago your background was examined. They didn't allow someone in with a criminal record for instance. Okay if you went to daily mass you were sort of in right away. You had to have that standing in society that people could look up to you but unfortunately in later years and particularly in the '70s [they] just took any men, just willy-nilly just to have numbers and unfortunately it degenerated into many touts. I'm not saying they were all touts but they took everybody in for some reason and I think that was the disintegration of the war.[66]

In this respect radical republicans who continue to advocate armed struggle have rejected the dominant narrative that the Provisional IRA reached a stalemate with the British army. A significant portion of interviewees (that were previously

involved with the Provisional IRA at various levels) have stated their belief that the Provisional IRA came close to achieving its objectives. Crucially, this belief sustains arguments that a future phase of the campaign could succeed.

A majority of the interviewees, who were formerly involved with the Provisional Movement, have argued that the campaign waged by the Provisional IRA did not fail; rather, the leadership of the Provisional IRA failed. A dominant theme throughout the radical republican narrative is the distinction which is drawn between the 'volunteers' of the Provisional IRA and the leadership of the organisation, as demonstrated by Lita Campbell of Republican Sinn Féin in Dublin: 'I think that the campaign didn't fail. It was made to fail by the actions of leaders at the time.'[67] Similarly Willie Wong, a CABHAIR prisoner (who was released from Maghaberry in 2016) has commented on the Provisional campaign by stating 'the campaign was weakened by McGuinness and the leadership. They negotiated too early.'[68] Wong's argument echoes those of republicans present and past that 'Irish history was filled with the faithful who had played an endgame too soon, too eagerly, and so were co-opted into a system that they had intended to destroy.'[69]

A belief in the failure of the Provisional leadership (rather than the Provisional campaign) provides an important insight into the motivations of current armed groups. The dominant narrative frequently questions current armed groups on why they feel they can succeed when others did not, including at the height of the Provisional IRA's campaign. However, this conception fails to adequately comprehend the radical republican emphasis on *continuity*. Significantly, current republican armed groups do not distinguish between various IRA 'campaigns' but rather locate their actions as part of one continuous campaign. Radical republicans view the current campaign as the latest phase in a long lineage of republican activists, stretching back to 1916 and indeed reaching further back in history through the various uprisings of the nineteenth century to 1798. Failure to contextualise current armed groups within the long-standing republican campaign fails to understand their raison d'être. When asked why contemporary groups feel they can succeed where others did not, Tony Catney, a former Northern commander of the Provisional IRA, commented:

> With all due respect that is looking at it in the predictable academic fashion. I don't see it as being different campaigns. It's a work in progress as opposed to failed campaigns.[70]

Dan Hoban of Republican Sinn Féin in Co. Mayo has commented:

> The IRA never went away. It was always there and there will always be some sort of an IRA to take on the Brits and to oppose British rule in Ireland. At the moment the position may be weak but we have seen these positions in the past and from a weak position it can only go one way and that's up.[71]

Radical republican discourse on armed struggle is reflective of the narrative presented by the Provisional Movement in the 1970s and 1980s. On 31 October 1975 the front page of *An Phoblacht* contained a section titled 'Steadfast determination' which stated:

> Today Óglaigh na hÉireann are in a very strong position with the ability to win through to final victory – let it be recorded that this is the last phase in Ireland's long fight for freedom – the British have had enough and they know that we can give them much more if they ask for it.[72]

In fact it has been recorded that when a 'call to arms' was issued in 1969, some of the weapons which were provided actually dated back to previous campaigns, including from the 1920s.[73] As stated in chapter three on decommissioning, it is notable that when strategic decisions were taken by the republican leadership to cease fire, arms were placed in secure dumps for the resumption of the campaign at a future date during which conditions would be more favourable.

Commemorations: changed structural conditions

The locating of current armed actions as the 'latest phase' in a historical struggle is not unique to the Irish republican base. Donatella Della Porta has made reference to the Basque social movement for independence by stating that the contemporary is located in the longer struggle spanning over a millennium.[74] As in the Basque context, the culture of commemoration occupies a central role in republican tradition, and reference to past events emphasises the deep-rooted view of one long struggle against British occupation in Ireland; radical republicans view commemorations as remembering and honouring fallen comrades in struggle. When this fact is acknowledged, logic follows that changed structural conditions within the state of Northern Ireland does not impact upon motivation for an armed campaign. The pursuit of sovereignty remains central to current republican actions, as Francie Mackey, chairperson of the 32CSM, has stated:

> I think that in relation to militant republicanism throughout our history, right back to the time of the Fenian men, there will always exist some form of insurgency against the aggressor in the event of the issue of national sovereignty not being dealt with and that's been proven throughout our history.[75]

Levels of activity

The level of armed activity by republican groups in the North of Ireland in the post-1998 period can be gauged through the PSNI chief constable's report. The annual report for 2015–16 reveals that, during this period, the PSNI carried out 8,330 searches and 1,211 arrests as a result of searches.[76] Further, police-recorded

**Table 1. PSNI-recorded security situation statistics
(1 February 2015–31 January 2017)**

	2015–16	2016–17
Bombing incidents	53	30
Casualties of paramilitary-style assaults (non-fatal)	60	68
Casualties of paramilitary-style shootings (non-fatal)	24	23
Firearms found	59	47
Explosives found	2.21 kg	7.91 kg
Rounds of ammunition found	4,445	2,226
Arrests under section 41	153	131
Arrests under section 41 and subsequently charged	19	18

Source: www.psni.police.uk/globalassets/inside-the-psni/our-statistics/security-situation-statistics/2017/january/security-situation-statistics-to-january-2017.pdf. Accessed 23 July 2018.

security situation statistics for the period 1 February 2015–31 January 2017 are shown in table 1. The figures demonstrate a significant amount of armed activity by republican groups. However, the radical republican constituency is not united in its support for armed actions at present. Views range from outright support to outright condemnation. The majority of radical republicans appear to occupy the non-condemnation category. Of the ninety republicans interviewed for this study, the majority stated that they supported the principle of armed struggle but a significant section within that group stated that the conditions or timing was not right at present for an armed campaign. Interestingly, almost all those interviewees who argued against a current campaign did so on the basis that it had 'little chance of success', rather than a moral objection to the use of violence. Individuals who outright condemned the current use of violence infused arguments of morality into their narrative through the rationale that 'little or no chance of success' makes a current campaign lack a moral basis (reflective of the premise of Just War Theory).

Timothy Shanahan has quoted a central premise of Just War Theory: 'for a resort to war to be just, there must be a probability of success. Whether a group is likely to succeed in its aims depends on what those aims are, on the resources available for achieving those aims, and on the resources and resolve of its enemy.'[77] This is the basis on which individuals who were previously members of the Provisional IRA have reconciled their support for that campaign with their opposition to the current campaign waged by groups such as the Continuity, New and REAL IRAs, that is, the low chance of success and the altered conditions in which the armed groups are operating. This group predominantly constitutes individuals within the radical republican world who identify as 'independent'. Commenting on the current armed campaign Ciaran Mulholland, of the James Connolly Society in West Belfast, has argued:

The 'One Ireland One Vote' is something that would take the gun out of Irish politics because you would be able to put it to some of these armed groups to say … you're going to have an all-Ireland referendum so all the people of Ireland can decide where they want to go and at the end of the day you have to respect the majority if they vote in favour of a partitionist country or if they vote for the reunification.[78]

The Continuity IRA has rejected the OIOV campaign which was launched by the 1916 Societies (a single-issue group) in 2009. It has reasserted its allegiance to the all-Ireland Republic as proclaimed in Easter week of 1916 and has argued that Irish sovereignty is not something which can be put to a vote by one generation; it is a fundamental right which already exists.

The meaning of success?

As previously highlighted, there exists a wide spectrum of opinion within the radical republican constituency on the armed campaign and the 'chance of success'. Radical republicans who have asserted their belief that the campaign will ultimately succeed are naturally those who are directly involved in armed struggle (as members of armed groups). The mainstream, particularly within the North of Ireland, has commonly posed the following question: do the 'dissident' organisations believe that they can win? Answering this question involves an examination of what constitutes 'success' for so-called 'dissident' organisations, as relevant to their motivation for continuing with armed actions. As noted by William Gamson in *The Strategy of Social Protest*, 'success is an elusive idea'.[79] Gamson has pointed to 'inclusion' in the form of 'acceptance' as a notable feature of success. However, he has cautioned 'consider, for example, revolutionary groups that have no desire for conventional acceptance by authorities they are attempting to overthrow'.[80] As highlighted in chapter seven, opposition to participation in the partitionist institutions in Ireland is fundamental to radical republican ideology and beliefs. Radical republicans view their continued operation (and existence) outside the system in each state (in the face of repressive legislation) as a form of success.

Armed radical republican groups have referred to the current 'phase' of the campaign as one of rebuilding and reorganising and have been eager to assert that they are equipped to continue the armed campaign, as demonstrated by a spokesperson for the Continuity IRA in North Armagh:

This country is full of guns. That's one sure thing about it. They'll try and make out that organisations now are badly equipped, that they've nothing. This country is an arsenal. Even back in '86 there was guns being moved from one side to the other because people seen what was happening. In '98 when the split in the Provisionals, a lot of weapons shifted hands. There maybe mightn't be some of the up-to-date stuff or there mightn't be as much but there's a lot of material.[81]

Gamson has noted, 'in assessing the achievement of benefits, the group's own perspective and aspirations are the starting point'.[82] Radical republicans who are members of armed groups have referred to the current phase of the campaign as a 'low ebb' (as relevant to the belief that the republican campaign is one continuous campaign, not different campaigns), as noted by a spokesperson for the Continuity IRA:

> Throughout the years there's always been a lull. There's always been a period of quiet but there's always been people willing to step up to the plate. You know you'll get a period of time where there's very little happening but as you've seen this last number of years it's starting to pick up again. It's starting to be revived but again it might take another five, maybe another ten years but it will get back. The strength is growing and it will get back to the full campaign.[83]

Those involved in armed struggle have collectively asserted their ultimate goal of a full British withdrawal from Ireland, as stated by this Continuity IRA spokesperson:

> We're trying to drive the Brits out of Ireland mainly by force. That the political process doesn't work. The British government doesn't reason with anything, only violence, and the only way to rid them out from this country is using force.[84]

However, members of armed groups have also acknowledged the shorter-term goals of the armed campaign. When asked if the armed campaign seeks to stop 'normalisation' of the state of Northern Ireland, this spokesperson for the Continuity IRA stated:

> It's not normal. There's still people that are getting beat on the street by the police. There's still the same brutality from the PSNI as there was from the RUC. There's nothing changed. Provisional Sinn Féin and the DUP can stand on the steps of Stormont and hug each other and make it appear that it's great. There's no difference. Well suppose, if there was nothing happening it would appear normal on the surface but it's not normal and the more that we do the more people will lift their heads and rise, and possibly the more people that will come forward. But if there's nothing going on people are just going to fall into a rut and say well sure there's nobody doing anything, why should we? You know, you have to keep the thing moving. When it slows down you have to keep it going until it picks up and it will pick up.[85]

Further, this spokesperson for the Continuity IRA asserted a belief that the continued campaign will generate support and stated 'as long as it is seen to be kept going. That's what generates support and keeps it alive.'[86] This Continuity spokesperson has also responded to criticism that is often presented from within the radical republican base, that the timing is not right for an armed campaign, by stating:

> I would just say to them when is the time right? When has the time ever been right? Somebody has to take the lead. To me that just sounds like a republican that has lost the will to fight.[87]

This representative concluded: 'the only thing we need to make clear is that an armed campaign will continue until the withdrawal.'[88]

An analysis of the current armed campaign must also take into account a central argument presented by radical republicans, that the armed campaign of the Provisional IRA did not fail, but rather the Provisional leadership failed. The mainstream often criticises 'dissidents' as being obsessional about Sinn Féin. A central point throughout the radical republican narrative is criticism of the institutionalisation of Sinn Féin and the party's subsequent movement away from traditional republican goals. Further, the radical republican narrative has argued that ideological shifts by the Provisional leadership and the 'winding down' of the Provisional IRA campaign have moved the attainment of republican goals further away and have significantly damaged republicanism. Therefore, it is probable that radical republicans view their highlighting of the 'failures' of the Provisional leadership as a form of success in itself. As already asserted, the belief in a failed leadership, rather than failed methods, contributes to our understanding of why radical republican groups continue to pursue their armed campaign.

Prisoners

While the radical republican world consists of a nuanced spectrum from outright support for armed actions to outright condemnation, PSNI statistics provide evidence of sustained military activity by the armed groups.[89] At the time of writing, there are approximately thirty-five republican prisoners in Portlaoise, one in Hydebank, one in Mountjoy Dóchas, one in Limerick and eleven in Maghaberry. Statistics reveal that the majority of prisoners were sentenced for possession of weapons or on membership charges.[90] The heterogeneous spectrum of views on armed struggle within the radical republican base has resulted in some republicans posing the question of whether or not there should be any republican prisoners at present. Phil O'Donoghue, the honorary president of the 32CSM, has argued:

> As far as I'm concerned there should have been no prisoners. What was the role? Why are they in? What did they do? What was their activities? Why did they carry it out? A lot of disjointed thinking at the minute. Even at this late stage.[91]

Arguably, the contemporary period is the first in which this question has been raised within the republican family. Throughout the history of Irish republicanism prisoners have assumed a central role of importance in the Republican Movement. Prisoners were often central to the republican narrative regarding strategy. As demonstrated in chapter one, the leadership of the Provisional

Movement cited the views of prisoners as a reason why the wider movement should support a change of strategy. While Sinn Féin has rejected the legitimacy of armed republican groups, the party has largely accepted current republican prisoners as 'political', as reflected through Sinn Féin delegations which have visited Maghaberry prison to meet with the prisoners. Tonge has argued, 'PIRA former prisoners, most of whom have stayed loyal to the Sinn Féin leadership, are divided over whether the new breed of republican ultra prisoners are "political prisoners".'[92] When asked whether current 'dissident' prisoners are 'political' prisoners, Danny Morrison stated 'Yes. Oh yes. Absolutely.'[93]

Nathan Hastings, a current republican prisoner in Maghaberry prison, who is affiliated to Saoradh, has stated:

> My legitimacy comes from the illegitimacy of the British occupation in Ireland … as long as the British occupy Ireland there will be men and women who will resist them. It doesn't matter what I think. This will be the case.[94]

When asked what would produce a ceasefire, Hastings stressed that he could not speak for armed groups but stated:

> Conditions would have to change. If the British gave a declaration of withdrawal then what would be the point in continuing an armed campaign?[95]

Gabriel Mackle, a current CABHAIR (RSF) prisoner in Maghaberry, has reasserted traditional republican ideology and has argued:

> This is not what Bobby Sands died for … You have to be committed. It's either jail or death and so if fellas aren't committed to that then they shouldn't be in it … Yes it's absolutely worth it … as long as the Six Counties are occupied by the British forces.[96]

Martin Corey, a high-profile republican prisoner (under 'guest' status in Maghaberry prison between April 2010 and January 2014[97]), was also previously a republican prisoner in Long Kesh.[98] When comparing the two experiences Corey has argued that in the contemporary context, in Maghaberry, 'a lot of people don't know what they're in for'.[99] However, Fra Halligan of the RSM in Belfast has stated that the same was true in Long Kesh:

> The cages of Long Kesh were full of young sixteen- to twenty-one-year-olds with long hair who then hadn't a clue what they were doing there. They followed friends, followed relatives.[100]

This fact has clearly been noted by republican groups whose activities include educational seminars and public events such as summer schools. In 2016 Na Fianna Éireann member Calvin McDonnell from Dublin addressed the RSF Ruairí Ó Brádaigh autumn school in Roscommon about the importance for republicans to understand 'why they are doing what they are doing'. McDonnell spoke about the ideological continuity of the organisation and where the

Republican Movement derives legitimacy from. This seminar is reflective of educational seminars which are taking place throughout the republican base regarding the nature of the republican campaign. Francie McGuigan, an independent in Belfast, has stated:

> Now we were taught the army constitution backwards. We were taught Irish history and before you were accepted you were questioned on the constitution of the IRA. What it was about and how it was formed and what happens in this situation and what do you do in this situation.[101]

No support

> I believe that it's a waste of time unless you can get the people behind you. Well, the only way you can get the people behind you is through Sinn Féin; through educating the people to Republican principles, and the ideals of Republicanism. And the fact is, we think it is for the ultimate good of the whole Irish nation that Republicanism should succeed. With the support of Sinn Féin, the Army [IRA] can do things.
>
> Liam Hannaway[102]

Existing literature has acknowledged the 'glass ceiling' on support for Sinn Féin while an IRA campaign was taking place. Arguably, there has never been mass support for an armed campaign in Ireland.[103] The 1916 Rising drew minimal support at the time and as the insurgents were captured and marched through the streets of Dublin, it is reported that they were jeered and spat upon.[104] In fact it was only after the execution of the leaders of the Rising that public support began to follow suit. The radical republican discourse has emphasised a rejection of the dominant narrative which states that the Provisional campaign had mass support. Pádraic MacCoitir of éirígí in Belfast has stated:

> I mean the IRA was a ruthless organisation. It killed a lot of people and unfortunately killed a lot of civilians and obviously a lot of people didn't support them. A lot of people in this area did not support the IRA even though now the revisionists are saying 'oh they had massive support', that's not true. Sinn Féin had massive support and Sinn Féin grew because people wanted an end to the campaign.[105]

In *The Provisional IRA: From Insurrection to Parliament*, Tommy McKearney has noted that 'by the end of the 1970s, the IRA was finding it more difficult to win supporters in the Republic of Ireland'.[106] Sinn Féin's 'armalite and ballot box' maintained a glass ceiling on support for the party which could only be removed through the ending of the Provisionals' armed campaign.[107] While militant republicanism has never enjoyed widespread popular support, it is undeniable that in the post-GFA context, where the Southern state of the Republic of Ireland has removed its territorial claim to the North (articles 2 and 3), radical republicans are operating in an environment of arguably unprecedented popular hostility.[108]

Tonge has commented, 'even by previous standards, the dissident IRAs appear particularly bereft of support'.[109] The radical republican base remains divided on the significance of popular support as the armed groups assert their legitimacy as located in historical determinism. A spokesperson for the Continuity IRA in North Armagh has argued:

> When you join up you know it's not a game ... The outcome would be you'll either be very successful at what you do or you'll go to jail or worse be killed ... nobody wants war. Nobody wants death but it happens. You know at the same time, throughout the years, even with the Provisionals they never had the full public support ... You'll never get the full support of your community because not everybody wants to see people shot. That's the reality of it. That's the reality of war.[110]

However, independent radical republican Gregory Creaney in Lurgan has argued 'you can't have an armed struggle without popular support because – should you be doing it without popular support? What would give me the right to go out and fight if nobody wanted me to?'[111]

The cyclical nature of Irish republicanism

The issues which have arisen in the current discourse on armed republicanism are issues which have been prominent throughout its history. The armed campaign waged by so-called 'dissident' groups cannot be viewed in a vacuum. Rather, the radical republican campaign is the latest phase in a long tradition of armed republicanism, throughout which the same issues arise cyclically. It is worth illustrating historical junctures at which the republican leadership took the decision to cease fire or dump arms, due to the cyclical nature of Irish republicanism and the fact that the same questions and issues have arisen regarding the armed campaign at pivotal junctures.[112] Debates which were taking place in the army council in 1923 centred around the chance of success. The order to 'cease fire and dump arms' was issued on 24 May and De Valera issued a proclamation which stated 'further sacrifice on your part would now be in vain and continuance of the struggle in arms unwise in the national interest'.[113] At that time republican Mary MacSwiney was vocal in her opposition to the decision to enter into negotiations, to which De Valera argued:

> You speak as if we were dictating terms and talk ... of a military situation. There is no military situation. The situation now is that we have to shepherd the remnant of our forces out of this fight so as not to destroy whatever hope remains in the future by allowing the fight to peter out ignominiously.[114]

Despite the ceasefire, there was no change on political and constitutional issues; as stated by Hopkinson, 'the civil war therefore, ended without any negotiated peace'.[115] Crucially, those who were calling for a ceasefire were not saying that they were opposed to fighting the Free State forces; rather, their support for a ceasefire was based on practical conditions of sustainability.

De Valera's comments to MacSwiney clearly illustrate the importance of strategic considerations which proved paramount in the decision to temporarily 'dump arms'. Similarly, Aiken talked about the necessity of civilian support and the fact that the weapons were outdated.[116] In fact, by the time the ceasefire was called, republican activity had already largely ceased in most areas, therefore leading Hopkinson to argue that the orders were 'a rubber stamping of the fact that republican arms had failed'.[117] Themes which have surfaced in contemporary debates within the radical republican family – that is, the utility of violence, chance of success, levels of public support as relevant to moral justification, and ethics – have arguably surfaced at every major juncture throughout the history of Irish republicanism where a ceasefire or 'dump arms' order was issued.

In 1962 the army council of the IRA was faced with ethical and moral questions concerning the utility of the continuation of Operation Harvest, amid a failed campaign which was petering out.[118] Internal discussions which ensued centred around the utility of the campaign, as well as the ethical implications of continuing with a campaign which was deemed unsustainable.[119] On 26 February 1962 a formal announcement was made, largely penned by Ó Brádaigh, which marked an end to the IRA's 1956–62 campaign. Yet again, amid poor morale, low public support and a campaign which could not be sustained, the republican leadership took the decision to temporarily cease fire and dump arms for a future generation to resume the campaign when the conditions would prove more favourable.

Conclusion

On 27 March 2017 the newest radical republican group Saoradh released a statement on its website titled 'We hit Crown Forces with explosively formed projectile claim IRA–Saoradh Nuacht.'[120] This statement made reference to an incident which took place in Tyrone in March 2017 when a PSNI patrol in Strabane encountered an explosion which took place on Townsend Street. Saoradh stated 'in the days after the attack, the Crown forces moved in and raided the homes of a number of Saoradh activists in Newtonstewart and Strabane, two members of Saoradh were taken to Musgrave Barracks for interrogation.'[121] In the contemporary setting such armed incidents appear infrequent and the radical republican armed campaign can be characterised as occasional activity rather than sustained military activity.

Less than one month after this incident, on 17 April Óglaigh na hÉireann (viewed as the military wing of RNU) gave an Easter address in Ardoyne in Belfast during which it signalled a shift in strategy and the possible ending of the ONH armed campaign.[122] It has been recorded in the *Irish News* that

RNU is undertaking a 'process of modernisation' and ONH has stated that it is engaged in a 'wide ranging discussion about tactics, strategy and the future of the republican struggle'.[123] Further, the article quotes a source close to ONH as stating that, while no announcement has been made, a 'de facto' ceasefire is in place while internal discussions take place.[124] Evidently, a strategic rethink has taken place within RNU and ONH; it is probable that the utility of an armed campaign in present circumstances was central to the debate. In contrast, Easter addresses delivered by the Continuity and New IRAs throughout the North and South of Ireland reaffirmed their commitment to continue the armed struggle.[125] Interestingly (while he cannot speak for armed groups) Andy Martin from RNU has speculated 'I can't see a ceasefire because I don't see that the British have anything to offer republicans, anything that is in their gift that we want.'[126] Martin has also commented:

> Weapons aren't being used that often for a ceasefire to be a primary goal of the Brits. It would be different if the war was happening every day. It's happening now and again. It's not happening enough for that to be an issue anyway so I don't think it is an issue. I don't think there will be a ceasefire.[127]

However, following a period of speculation regarding ONH's armed campaign, the organisation sent a statement to the *Irish News* on 22 January 2018 which announced:

> At this time the environment is not right for armed conflict … therefore the leadership of Óglaigh na hÉireann are announcing that with immediate effect we will suspend all armed actions against the British state … the leadership of ÓNH remain unbowed and unbroken. We will continue to protect our membership and base as we move forward in a spirit of united determination to achieve our political aims.[128]

The *Irish News* article further stated that sources had denied that any negotiations had taken place between the organisation and the British government around the ceasefire. It is notable that the statement referred to the environment not being right for armed conflict, therefore suggesting that the armed campaign could be resumed at a future date in altered conditions.

The current radical republican world can be largely characterised as one of disparate groupings who view themselves as being in a period of rebuilding and reorganisation and who are aiming to, at a minimum, keep the flame burning. Dan Hoban of RSF in Mayo has speculated:

> I see the Republican Movement in the mould of being rebuilt to come back to where it was before. That would be the way I would be looking at it. [They're] not throwing in the towel like. What I believed in forty years ago I believe in today. I don't make any bones about that.[129]

However, Hoban, who joined the Republican Movement in the 1950s, has commented 'I don't think at the moment that an armed campaign could be sustained.'[130] He has argued that there exists a legacy from the Provisional Movement which is impacting on current support and has stated that:

> An awful lot of abuse of houses by people in the Provisional Movement has left an awful lot of people very suspicious of republicanism. The heart has gone out of people I think in a lot of cases and it will take a bit of rebuilding.[131]

Hoban's narrative is reflective of the wider radical republican constituency which has highlighted the aim of 'passing on the torch', as compatible with the republican assertion that a future generation will take up the gauntlet. While Hoban has emphasised that he cannot speak on behalf of any armed group, he has commented:

> Maybe it won't happen in my time but if we had something left to pass on to the next generation that's something to build on. As a republican that's the way you have to think and leave something to the generation that is coming up … look we've fought the Brits for 800 years and we might have to fight them for another 800 but there's no surrender. As they say, Tiocfaidh ar la.[132]

Notes

1 MacSwiney, *Principles of Freedom*, p. 1.
2 Gerard Hodgins, interview with the author, Belfast, 13 September 2012.
3 Regan, *Irish Counter-revolution*, p. 70. In October 1922, as a prisoner in Kildare, Sinn Féin propagandist and anti-treatyite Aodh de Blacam wrote 'my attitude was the same since last June. I held the attack on the Four Courts to be unjustified and unauthorised, and so considered that the men who resisted had right on their side. I would not have thought them justified if the Dáil had authorised the attack. While, therefore they were fighting an unjustified attack I would not publicly repudiate them, tho' I still abstained from co-operation that might implicate me in the shedding of one drop of blood.'
4 The 1923 'dump arms' order marked the end of military engagement in the Irish Civil War, and in February 1962 the IRA used the republican paper the *United Irishman* to announce the end of what was the 1956–62 campaign.
5 *Éire: The Irish Nation*, Vol. 1, No. 33 (1 September 1923). A letter by Frank Aiken was carried on the front page: 'We'll keep our arms because we believe, with Davis, that "No nation, whether enslaved or free, has the right to abjure the principle of defending its existence by arms if need be".'
6 For an assessment of the Provisional IRA campaign within Just War Theory, see T. Shanahan, *The Provisional Irish Republican Army and the Morality of Terrorism* (Edinburgh, Edinburgh University Press, 2009). For an assessment of 1916 within Just War Theory and 'democratic standards', see Murphy, 'Easter ethics'.
7 Murphy, 'Easter ethics', p. 392.
8 *Ibid.*, p. 330.
9 *Ibid.*, p. 330.
10 Shanahan, *The Provisional Irish Republican Army*, p. 105.

11 *Ibid.*, p. 105.

12 Anthony McIntyre, interview with the author, Dublin, 3 April 2013.

13 Tommy McCourt, interview with the author, Derry, 21 August 2013.

14 Shanahan, *The Provisional Irish Republican Army*, p. 145.

15 H. Khatchadourian, 'Terrorism and morality', *Journal of Applied Philosophy*, 5:2 (1988), pp. 131–9.

16 Anthony McIntyre, interview with the author, Dublin, 3 April 2013.

17 Doherty and Keogh *1916*, p. 335.

18 Francie Mackey, interview with the author, Omagh, 8 February 2013.

19 Jim McCrystal, interview with the author, Lurgan, 22 August 2013.

20 Documentary titled *To Die for Ireland*, interview with Dáithí Ó Connaill. The interview can be viewed on YouTube: https://youtu.be/PTHrBzxjyCE. Accessed 13 March 2018.

21 Anthony McIntyre, interview with the author, Dublin, 3 April 2013. See Shanahan, *The Provisional Irish Republican Army*, p. 105.

22 Documentary titled *To Die for Ireland*.

23 Continuity IRA spokesperson, interview with the author, North Armagh, 2014.

24 Tony Catney, interview with the author, Belfast, 14 September 2012.

25 Shanahan, *The Provisional Irish Republican Army*, p. 109.

26 Bowyer Bell, *The IRA 1968–2000*, p. 59.

27 See English, *Armed Struggle* (2003), pp. 213–14.

28 See M. Dillon, *The Dirty War* (London, Arrow, 1991). Also see S. Hopkins, 'The "informer" and the political and organisational culture of the Irish republican movement: old and new interpretations', *Irish Studies Review*, 25:1 (2016), p. 5.

29 Spokespersons for the Continuity IRA, interviews with the author, North Armagh, 2014.

30 O'Brien, *The Long War*, p. 351.

31 English, *Armed Struggle (2003)*, pp. 213–14.

32 Danny Morrison, interview with the author, Belfast, 7 May 2014.

33 *Ibid.*

34 Whiting, *Spoiling the Peace?*.

35 Des Dalton, lecture to the first Ruairí Ó Brádaigh summer school, Abbey Hotel, Roscommon, June 2014. Attended by the author.

36 It has been claimed that Gearoid O'Sullivan, who was elected to the Second Dáil for the Carlow-Kilkenny constituency, survived Tom Maguire by two years. This is incorrect – O'Sullivan in fact died in 1948. Born in 1891, he was a native of Skibbereen in Co. Cork. He took part in the 1916 Rising as a member of the GPO garrison. During the War of Independence of 1919–21 he was adjutant-general of the IRA. He was a professor of languages at Carlow College during this period. See *Irish Times* (26 March 1948); also see P. O'Farrell, *Who's Who in the Irish War of Independence and Civil War: 1916–1923* (Dublin, The Lilliput Press, 1997), p. 85.

37 Des Dalton, lecture to the first Ruairí Ó Brádaigh summer school (2014). Attended by the author.

38 Bowyer Bell, *The Secret Army* (1997), p. 76.

39 Ó Brádaigh, *The Story of Comdt. General Tom Maguire*. Also see Dalton, lecture to the first Ruairí Ó Brádaigh summer school (2014).

40 Continuity IRA, interview with the author, North Armagh, 2014.

41 *Ibid.*

42 *Ibid.*

43 *Ibid.*

44 Brendan Madden, interview with the author, Galway, 4 June 2013.

45 *Ibid.*

46 Peig King, interview with the author, Dublin, 26 July 2016.

47 *Ibid.*

48 Phil O' Donoghue, interview with the author, Kilkenny, 4 November 2013.

49 *Ibid.*

50 Frampton, *Legion of the Rearguard*, pp. 106–7.

51 Derry republican, interview with the author, Derry, January 2014. This individual joined the Republican Movement in 1986.

52 Bowyer Bell, *The IRA 1968–2000*, p. 70.

53 Frampton, *Legion of the Rearguard*, p. 162.

54 Member of the 32CSM leadership, South of Ireland, interview with the author, 2013.

55 'Thatcher's latest victim', *An Phoblacht* (2 February 1989).

56 'McGuinness traitor remark "extraordinary" – Hugh Orde' (22 March 2017). www.bbc.co.uk/news/uk-northern-ireland-39352346. Accessed 23 July 2018.

57 Peig King, interview with the author, Dublin, 26 July 2016.

58 Member of the 32CSM leadership, South of Ireland, interview with the author, 2013.

59 For information on Provisional IRA infiltration see G. Bradley and B. Feeney, *Insider: Gerry Bradley's Life in the IRA* (Dublin, O'Brien Press, 2009); R. Gilmour, *Infiltrating the IRA: Dead Ground* (London, Little, Brown & Company, 1998); M. Ingram and G. Harkin, *Stakeknife: Britain's Secret Agents in Ireland* (Dublin, O'Brien Press, 2004); M. McGartland, *Fifty Dead Men Walking: The Heroic True Story of a British Secret Agent Inside the IRA* (London, John Blake Publishing Ltd, 2009); S. O'Callaghan, *The Informer* (London, Bantam, 1998); E. Collins with M. McGovern, *Killing Rage* (London, Granta Books, 1998).

60 Danny Morrison, interview with the author, Belfast, 7 May 2014.

61 Hopkins, 'The "Informer" ', p. 1.

62 See Frampton, *Legion of the Rearguard.*

63 Denis Donaldson was a senior member of Sinn Féin and the Provisional IRA. A former republican prisoner in Long Kesh, he was a friend of Hunger Striker Bobby Sands. In the post-1998 period he was Sinn Féin's senior administrator at Stormont. In a press conference in December 2005, Donaldson revealed that he was recruited by the RUC Special Branch in the 1980s and since then had been a paid informer for British intelligence. He was expelled from Sinn Féin and moved from Belfast to a rural part of Donegal, where a journalist tracked him down in 2006 and published the story in the *Sunday World*. Weeks later Donaldson was shot dead at the cottage. The Provisional Movement denied responsibility for the killing. See White, *Out of*

the Ashes, p. 360. Also see http://news.bbc.co.uk/1/hi/northern_ireland/4877516. stm. Accessed 22 July 2018.

64 See Moloney, *Secret History of the IRA*.

65 Hopkins, 'The "informer"', p. 3. Also see McIntyre, *Good Friday*, pp. 177–93.

66 Gerry McKerr, interview with the author, Lurgan, 22 August 2013.

67 Lita Campbell, interview with the author, Dublin, 21 October 2013.

68 Willie Wong, interview with the author, Maghaberry prison, 9 January 2014.

69 Bowyer Bell, *The IRA 1968–2000*, p. 301.

70 Tony Catney, interview with the author, Belfast, 14 September 2012.

71 Dan Hoban, interview with the author, Dublin, 3 November 2013.

72 *An Phoblacht*, Vol. 6, No. 44 (31 October 1975), p. 1.

73 J. Bowyer Bell, *The Gun in Politics: An Analysis of Irish Political Conflict, 1916–1986* (New Brunswick, Transaction Publishers, 1987), p. 33; Bowyer Bell, *The IRA 1968–2000*, p. 182; J. Bowyer Bell, *The Irish Troubles: A Generation of Violence, 1967–1992* (Dublin, Gill & Macmillan, 1993), p. 170.

74 See Della Porta, *Clandestine Political Violence*, p. 219.

75 Francie Mackey, interview with the author, Omagh, 9 February 2013.

76 Annual PSNI chief constable's report 2015–2016. 'Police and Criminal Evidence (PACE) Order – Article 5 Persons and Vehicles Searched 2015-16'. www.psni. police.uk/globalassets/inside-the-psni/our-departments/finance-and-support-ser vices/documents/AnnualStatementofaccounts15-16. Accessed 23 July 2018.

77 Shanahan, *The Provisional Irish Republican Army*, p. 102.

78 Ciaran Mulholland, interview with the author, Belfast, 5 May 2014.

79 W. Gamson, *The Strategy of Social Protest* (Belmont, CA, Wadsworth Publishing, 1990), p. 28.

80 *Ibid.*, p. 32.

81 Continuity IRA, interview with the author, North Armagh, 2014.

82 Gamson, *Strategy of Social Protest*, p. 34.

83 Continuity IRA, interview with the author, North Armagh, 2014.

84 *Ibid.*

85 *Ibid.*

86 *Ibid.*

87 *Ibid.*

88 *Ibid.*

89 www.psni.police.uk/inside-psni/Statistics/security-situation-statistics/. Accessed 23 July 2018.

90 For information on persons arrested and charged in the post-1998 period see Horgan, *Divided We Stand*.

91 Phil O' Donoghue, interview with the author, Kilkenny, 4 November 2013.

92 Tonge, 'An enduring tradition or the last gasp of physical force republicanism?', p. 113.

93 Danny Morrison, interview with the author, Belfast, 7 May 2014.

94 Nathan Hastings, interview with the author, Maghaberry prison, 8 March 2017.

95 *Ibid.*

96 Gabriel Mackle, interview with the author, Maghaberry prison, 27 September 2016.

97 The prison landings which house republican prisoners are generally designated by organisational affiliation. On occasion a prisoner who is not a member of the organisation will be granted 'guest status' on that organisation's landing.

98 Martin Corey was never successfully charged with any offence. The court was told that Corey, as a life sentence prisoner, could be returned to jail due to his continued association with 'proscribed organisations'. The Crown stated that they had recordings of Corey meeting 'certain people'; however, no evidence of this nature was disclosed to the defence or the judge. For further information see 'Double IRA murderer Martin Corey loses Supreme Court bid for prison release', *Belfast Telegraph* (4 December 2013) and *The Pensive Quill* online blog: 'Martin Corey – Irish political prisoner held without charge, Trial' (2 July 2013). http://thepensivequill.am/2013/07/martin-corey-irish-political-prisoner.html. Accessed 23 July 2018. Also see, 'Martin Corey appeal rejected by London Court', *Irish Times* (4 December 2013). www.irishtimes.com/news/crime-and-law/martin-corey-appeal-rejected-by-london-court-1.1616743. Accessed 23 July 2018.

99 Martin Corey, interview with the author, Maghaberry prison, 30 August 2013.

100 Fra Halligan, interview with the author, Belfast, 19 November 2013.

101 Francie McGuigan, interview with the author, Belfast, 24 July 2013.

102 Quoted in O'Sullivan, *Patriot Graves*, p. 62.

103 Murray and Tonge, *Sinn Féin and the SDLP*.

104 See K. Griffith and T. O'Grady, *Curious Journey: An Oral History of Ireland's Unfinished Revolution* (Cork, Mercier Press, 1998), pp. 77–9.

105 Pádraic MacCoitir, interview with the author, Belfast, 4 October 2012.

106 McKearney, *The Provisional IRA*, p. 146.

107 See Tonge, 'An enduring tradition or the last gasp of physical force republicanism?', p. 100.

108 In the South of Ireland 94 per cent of voters supported changing the Irish constitution to drop articles 2 and 3. This referendum in the South of Ireland saw a 56 per cent turnout.

109 Tonge, '"No-one likes us; we don't care"', p. 222.

110 Continuity IRA spokesperson, interview with the author, North Armagh, 2014.

111 Gregory Creaney, interview with the author, Lurgan, 22 August 2013.

112 For information on the 1923 'dump arms' order see Hopkinson, *Green Against Green*.

113 *Ibid.*, p. 257.

114 *Ibid.*, p. 258.

115 *Ibid.*, p. 258.

116 Frank Aiken was chief of staff of the IRA from 1923–5. He was a founder member of Fianna Fáil in 1926.

117 *Ibid.*, p. 259.

118 Commenting on Operation Harvest', Richard English has stated 'Cronin had drawn this up at the start of 1956, and it outlined a scheme for attacking military installations, communications and public property in the north with a view to paralysing the place'. English, *Armed Struggle* (2012), p. 73; Bowyer Bell, *The Secret Army* (1990), p. 332–4.

119 See White, *Out of the Ashes*, p. 40.

120 The full text of this article is available on the Saoradh website: http://saoradh.ie/we-hit-crown-forces-with-explosively-formed-projectile-claim-ira-saoradh-nuacht/. Accessed 23 July 2018.

121 *Ibid.*

122 'Óglaigh na hÉireann may be preparing to end its military campaign', *Irish News* (17 April 2017).

123 C. Young. 'Hard-line republican group to step up process of modernisation', *Irish News* (15 November 2017).

124 *Ibid.*

125 See Continuity IRA Easter statement, 'The voice of the republican movement', *Saoirse: Irish Freedom* (April 2017). Also see New IRA Easter statement: 'Uncompromising Easter statement from IRA', *Irish News* (18 April 2017).

126 Andy Martin, interview with the author, Newry, 6 February 2013.

127 *Ibid.*

128 A. Morris, 'ÓNH announces immediate ceasefire; Dissident group suspends all armed actions against British State', *Irish News* (23 January 2018).

129 Dan Hoban, interview with the author, Dublin, 3 November 2013.

130 *Ibid.*

131 *Ibid.*

132 *Ibid.*

6

2007: policing – a step too far

There would be people from those areas [Derry] who would have joined the security forces. They couldn't walk among the community.

Derry republican, interview with the author, Derry, 10 January 2014

There's a lot of republicans who went through it all who would still come round and tell you the PSNI are just the RUC in a different uniform ... they will not communicate with them at all. If there's a burglary in this estate they would come to us before they'd go to them.

Continuity IRA spokesperson, interview with the author,
North Armagh, 2014

Introduction

The issue of policing provides an insight into the contested narratives between the mainstream and radical republican arenas regarding the normalisation of the state of Northern Ireland. Sinn Féin engaged in attempts to keep its base united on this issue; the party emphasised its changed stance as 'tactical' in a post-Patten context. In contrast, radical republicans have rejected the significance of the change from the RUC to the PSNI and have propagated a narrative which rejects the PSNI as a different force which is more localised in nature.

The contested narratives around policing provide a significant lens on the fundamental issue of reform within the state of Northern Ireland; in this regard radical republicans have argued that Sinn Féin's acceptance of the PSNI is acquiescing in the normalisation agenda. Radical republicans have emphasised 'the legacy' of the RUC and have rooted their rejection of the PSNI in claims of collusion and mistrust. The insights provided by interviewees are particularly useful, given the fact that in the contemporary period radical republican discourse is largely dominated by references to negative interaction with the police, particularly in the North of Ireland. Radical republicans have engaged in 'community policing' as a result of their rejection of the PSNI; however, a nuanced spectrum of opinion exists *within* the radical republican world on 'IRA policing' regarding anti-social behaviour.

Eamon Cairns: a personal testimony

The radical republican narrative which rejects policing and the security services extends beyond immediate contact with the police to include the narrative that the police prove an obstacle to achieving redress regarding the past. One powerful testimony is that of Eamon Cairns in Lurgan, who is not a member of any organisation. In 1993, while Eamon and his wife were at an Irish language class in Lurgan town, gunmen entered his home and killed his two sons, Gerard and Rory, aged twenty-two and eighteen. Eamon Cairns has described arriving back at their house that night as 'unbearable'. He has stated:

> I could see the red and white tapes floating in the wind. I knew that, the thing just fell over me … The cars of the loyalists, [name withheld] and them, had been on this road the previous fortnight … when the UDR invade your home. Now I know. Nobody knows better than me that they organised the killing and were part of it. So they were gloating in it. They were enjoying the scene … when I looked in the back door I could see Rory sitting in the chair with his head over to the side but I couldn't see Gerard. Gerard was actually lying there.[1]

Cairns has argued that he never got justice for the death of his sons. Cairns met with police ombudsman Nuala O'Loan on multiple occasions and has argued:

> In our circumstances here in the North I would say there's an awful lot of people on both sides of the divide struggling big time with hate because they never got redress.[2]

Cairns described the murder of his sons as 'collusion' and has stated:

> A loyalist car couldn't have come down the Clare road because there was a road check there at such and such a time. [name of loyalist withheld] was standing talking to police at the crossroads at twenty minutes to eight … and a whole lot of stuff like that.[3]

In an interview lasting several hours, Cairns detailed all the points which he feels proves it was collusion and commented:

> [name withheld] … is the first person I would stand against the wall, without a shadow of a doubt … the families that she told lies, compounded the lies. Put a nice face on the lies of the RUC and the investigation into everybody's case … collusion was in our case the whole way through. So a sense of justice? No, not in the least.[4]

Eamon Cairns's personal testimony is an important illustration of the level of rejection which radical republicans feel towards the RUC and latterly the PSNI, as well as the accompanying structures such as the Police Ombudsman. Republican hostility towards the police in the North is deeply rooted amid claims of collusion and distrust regarding the RUC, which has been carried over into attitudes towards the PSNI as republicans reject the claim that the PSNI is a new force.[5]

Patten

In 1999 the landscape of policing in the North of Ireland was transformed through the emergence of the Patten report.[6] Against a backdrop of unionist opposition, the Royal Ulster Constabulary became the Police Service of Northern Ireland, with a new policing board, a new oath, a police ombudsman, a new badge and symbols, and a new dark green uniform. Further, the Patten report resulted in implementation of a fifty:fifty recruitment policy over a ten-year period of Protestant and Catholic recruits. Simultaneously, the report's recommendations increased the number of women in the PSNI through the implementation of a gender quota. The increased number of Catholic recruits transformed the nature of the organisation into a more 'localised' force in relation to the Catholic community. One of the report's recommendations stated that 'police stations built from now on should have, so far as possible, the appearance of ordinary buildings'.[7] The altered police force (and even the deliberate use of the word 'service' rather than 'force') was reflective of the 'normalisation' agenda regarding the state of Northern Ireland in the post-Good Friday Agreement period. Against this backdrop, Sinn Féin's transformation into a constitutional nationalist party saw the organisation increasingly incorporated into the structures of the state of Northern Ireland, and the party's anti-police stance became increasingly incompatible with its reformist agenda.

Sinn Féin's continued rejection of the legitimacy of the police proved a major point of contention in relations with unionists in the lead-up to the St Andrew's Agreement. During that period republicans were active in Community Restorative Justice Schemes such as CRJ located in Andersonstown in West Belfast.[8] Sinn Féin and CRJ argued that community-based Restorative Justice Schemes were a viable alternative to the expulsions and so-called 'punishment attacks' meted out by paramilitary groups. The scheme attracted criticism, which was led by the SDLP. In 2006 Alex Attwood from the SDLP (then MLA for West Belfast) argued that 'there have been groups of people who have been self-appointed who have run secret organisations and have assumed onto themselves authority in communities'.[9] Similarly, SDLP adviser Brian Barrington commented 'we want proper accountability. We want to ensure it's appropriate people doing this that don't have a reputation or background in punishment beatings or attacks on young people.'[10]

This was the context in which policing (in relation to Sinn Féin) was firmly on the agenda in the lead-up to the St Andrew's Agreement in 2007. Jonathan Powell, Tony Blair's chief of staff, has recalled that period: 'what time we had, we spent working with Sinn Féin on policing'.[11] In 2007 the party held a special Ard Fheis at which Sinn Féin members were advised to accept the PSNI and, of potentially more significance, to 'co-operate' with the police service. By extension the party would also be accepting the judicial structures within the North.

On the altar of Clonard

Anathema to the traditional republican position, acceptance of a six-county police service was a major step for Sinn Féin and evidently the leadership was resolute that the issue would not split the organisation. Therefore, during 2007 Sinn Féin held public meetings throughout the North of Ireland at which prominent party members spoke of the need to accept the PSNI.[12] Tommy McKearney has argued:

> Finally, the Provisional IRA had to give its public support to policing. This was brought about by having the Sinn Féin leadership tour the country, convening meetings in order to convince its membership of the value of supporting Northern Ireland's police force. The party did not distinguish between different forms of policing and refused to differentiate between the type that helps old ladies and gentlemen across the road and the kind that defends the state or arrests trade unionists for unofficial picketing.[13]

The author attended one of these meetings which was held in the Sinn Féin heartland of West Belfast. The meeting took place in Clonard Monastery, a significant setting for the historic meeting given its role as a venue for peace talks in the 1980s and 1990s as well as the Hume–Adams talks (at the behest of Father Alec Reid who played a central role in the peace process).[14] The meeting took place in the church of the monastery and a sense that history was being made was evident as prominent Sinn Féin representatives stood on the actual altar as they addressed the packed church. It appeared that the priests and brothers of Clonard were not in the main church at this time. The assembled crowd, which comprised local people from West Belfast, were told the importance of accepting the legitimacy of the PSNI. The Sinn Féin speakers on the altar couched their message amid language of 'tactics' and 'strategy', during which shouts emerged from the back of the church as different individuals expressed their rejection of the PSNI. The author witnessed emotional outbursts from individuals who stated that their family members had not died for this. Clear lines were being drawn in the sand and some individuals and families exited Clonard Monastery at that point while the Sinn Féin members continued to argue their case from the pulpit.

Proving a step too far, for some republicans this became a significant 'departure point' from the Provisional Movement. To radical republicans, through its acceptance of a partitionist police force Sinn Féin had done the unthinkable. As noted by Bean, 'the Provisionals' endorsement of the PSNI would be "its most neuralgic decision of the peace process" and would "mark the end of the ideological road for republicans and render the IRA defunct"'.[15] Significantly, a section of the republican constituency had remained within Sinn Féin or the Provisional Movement throughout the ceasefires of the 1990s and subsequently through PIRA decommissioning in 2005 to then depart at this point, such was the level of rejection of the new Sinn Féin position on policing. Radical republicans have rejected the Provisional narrative which emphasises the significance of 'reform' of the police and have asserted the traditional republican position that the state of Northern Ireland and its associated structures are un-reformable. Radical republicans have propagated the argument that the PSNI is simply the RUC in a different uniform and have rejected Sinn Féin's assertion that the post-Patten reform has resulted in a new police force.

For groups such as RSF, the 32CSM, Saoradh and éirígí, protests against the PSNI form a significant portion of their visibility within the North. At such protests republicans carry banners which state 'Disband the RUC' or 'RUC–PSNI: Different name, same aim'. Similarly, the IRSP has produced a poster which shows a police land rover and states 'PSNI: Don't be fooled! Reject the "New" RUC!'. The current rhetoric from radical republicans is starkly similar to the message propagated by Sinn Féin in the early 2000s. On 8 November 2001 an article appeared in *An Phoblacht* titled 'Different name, same bigots: RUC replaced by PSNI', which stated 'Those officers who colluded in the killings of nationalists and republicans have not been suddenly transformed into determined upholders of human rights and seekers of justice.'[16] It further stated: 'Sunday was the day when the British state thought it would be able to fob off the nationalist community in the Six Counties with the old force in new clothes. Only it can't.'[17] Such rhetoric would sit comfortably within statements from radical republicans today. Radical republican Kevin Hannaway in Belfast has argued 'prior to them [the PSNI] coming about it was the RIC which became the RUC and the RUC is now the PSNI and they are still doing the same thing. They're still raiding homes. They are still arresting people.'[18]

Republican rejection of a six-county police force is historically and deeply rooted in ideology, tradition and symbolism. Ciaran Mulholland, a member of the James Connolly Society in West Belfast, has argued:

> The legacy which the RIC and thereafter the RUC has left in Ireland and particularly the Six Counties is horrendous … Patten comes out with a report in terms of how he views progressing policing within the North of Ireland and it's not implemented … McGuiness has come out and acknowledged that there is a dark side to policing. You can only say that after Adams has been arrested.[19] People have been saying that for years.[20]

Further, Mulholland has called for a 'civic' police and has criticised accountability within the PSNI, arguing that:

> Those [Special Branch] agents within the PSNI work at the pleasure of the secretary of state and MI5. You have an MI5 basically securocrat cabal of policing still operating in the Six Counties … that is something that is completely and utterly wrong and irrespective of your political persuasion as a human rights activist it's something that needs to be changed and it needs to be changed urgently.[21]

Radical republican rejection of the PSNI can be located within the attitudes of the wider nationalist community in the North of Ireland towards the PSNI. In 2001 an independent recruiting agency which processes applications to the PSNI revealed that, from approximately 7,700 people who had applied to join the PSNI, only 35 per cent were from the Catholic community.[22] More recently, a more positive picture has been painted by The Northern Ireland Omnibus Survey, which was conducted by the Northern Ireland Statistics and Research Agency in April 2017. This revealed that 74 per cent of respondents 'indicated that the police were doing a very/fairly good job in their area' and 90 per cent of respondents 'indicated either total, a lot, or some confidence in the PSNI's ability to provide an ordinary day-to-day service for all the people of Northern Ireland'.[23] However, despite this, PSNI statistics reveal that 78.21 per cent of police staff are 'perceived Protestant' compared with 19.46 per cent 'perceived Roman Catholic'. Regarding police officers, 66.61 per cent are 'perceived Protestant' and 32.10 per cent are 'perceived Roman Catholic'.[24]

In November 2017, in the *Irish News*, commentator Brian Feeney stated 'let's be clear about this. No-one wanted a reliable, impartial, effective, representative police service more than Northern Nationalists. They've never had one. They still haven't.'[25] Commenting on the PSNI recruitment figures, Feeney highlighted the fact that the PSNI is not representative of society in the North of Ireland, stating 'all indications are the PSNI isn't going to become representative of society, isn't on track to be and because of that hasn't managed to treat nationalists or manifestations of nationalism impartially.'[26] Feeney described the 'biggest blow' to preventing a representative police service emerging as being the 'success of the unionists in stopping 50:50 recruitment'.[27] The article highlights the fact that approximately 1 per cent of the PSNI of the rank of inspector or above is Catholic. Commenting on the figures Feeney stated 'what's being done about this disparity? Nothing. Sinn Féin silent.'[28] Therefore it must be acknowledged that the radical republican position on policing sits within a degree of continuing hostility from the wider nationalist community towards the PSNI. Independent republican (formerly of éirígí) Máire Óg Drumm in Belfast has argued that the feeling of hostility towards the PSNI in the local West Belfast area exists to such an extent that:

> Very few of them [Catholic recruits] will let on because I accidentally heard just lately about someone who had joined and they actually told relations of their own that they joined the fire-brigade. So I mean does that not tell you something when they're not willing to say to their own family?[29]

Regarding radical republican hostility towards the PSNI, Joe Dillon of the 32CSM in Skerries, outside Dublin, has stated:

> I believe if an Irishman sees a foreign force being forced on him such as the PSNI their natural reaction will be to … resist him. In that context, whether it's necessary or whether it was inevitable, it's the same fight continued after the latest betrayal …

PSNI man says 'I've been sent over from Essex to head the police force' – violation of the sovereignty.[30]

In 2009, after the killing of PSNI constable Stephen Carroll by the REAL IRA, Martin McGuinness stood on the steps of Stormont alongside PSNI chief constable Hugh Orde calling 'dissident' republicans 'traitors to Ireland', thus marking the culmination of Sinn Féin's transformed position regarding policing. The symbolism of Martin McGuinness next to the PSNI chief constable on the steps of Stormont was not lost on radical republicans. Republicans have highlighted Sinn Féin members assuming positions on policing boards and have argued that Sinn Féin is supporting a police service which arrests and imprisons republicans, including former comrades. Republicans such as Marian Price and Martin Corey have been imprisoned for up to four years in Maghaberry prison without trial, leading radical republicans to argue that, far from being relegated to the past, 'internment' is still in use against republicans who fall beyond the status quo. Francie Mackey of the 32CSM in Omagh has stated:

> We've had a Tyrone man serve over twelve months on a falsified charge which the PSNI said they had the evidence that he could be connected to materials and bomb-making materials … the IRA. He was over a year on remand in Maghaberry. When the papers were issued for the case to begin – there wasn't one shred of evidence and when it went to court the prosecution withdrew the charges. That was internment of this young man from his family and from his children for over a year.[31]

Where are the Catholic recruits?

Paul Nolan, the former head of the Community Relations Council in the North of Ireland, has outlined six short-term objectives of 'dissident' republicans, one being 'to drive Catholics out of the PSNI and convert it back to a Protestant dominated force'.[32] Mainstream literature has highlighted the fact that Stephen Carroll and Ronan Kerr, PSNI officers who were killed by republicans, were Catholics and Kerr was a member of the GAA. The *Irish Times* stated 'the symbolism was lost on no one, of the GAA's declaration, that the murder of Ronan Kerr last Saturday was also an attack on the GAA'.[33] The issue was also cited in the 2012 'Northern Ireland Peace Monitoring Report: Number One', which stated : 'the funeral of the PSNI officer Ronan Kerr, killed by dissidents in April 2011 marked a rallying point, bringing the political, security, religious and sporting elites together in a symbolic show of unity.'[34] However, reductionism regarding the role of 'religion' disregards the fact that radical republicans claim they do not target officers because they are Catholic: radical republicans have claimed that they have targeted the PSNI 'as they are the front line of the British state apparatus in Northern Ireland.' As highlighted by Tonge, the REAL IRA's 2010 New Year statement declared that the PSNI 'are the first line of defence for the British government'.[35]

Radical republicans view the PSNI as enforcing British rule in Ireland and have rejected any localised nature to the service, as demonstrated by Francie Mackey: 'British rule can only survive in this country through special courts, special policing and special justice acts that allow a British government to intern people and [allow] an abuse of their human and civil rights.'[36] The killing of PSNI member Ronan Kerr resulted in competing narratives from the mainstream and 'dissident' constituencies, the themes of which proved similar to narratives produced at the time of the Irish War of Independence when the targeting of local police officers assumed a central place in debate. On 21 January 1919 the Soloheadbeg ambush in Tipperary marked the beginning of the War of Independence during which two RIC men were killed by the IRA, both of whom were Catholic. One was a native Irish speaker from County Mayo. Republicans at the time were definite in their assertions that 'the killing was irrespective of religion or language; they were killed as members of the RIC, a British police force in Ireland.'[37]

In the aftermath of the killing of Constable Ronan Kerr, the bitterly contested narratives between nationalist and 'dissident' arenas struck to the heart of the fundamentally opposed positions regarding 'reform' versus 'radical change'. Republicans have proven keen to emphasise that, in the footsteps of the Protestant father of modern-day republicanism Theobold Wolfe Tone, republicanism is not sectarian but seeks to unite Protestant, Catholic and Dissenter.[38] However, the killing of Catholics such as Constable Ronan Kerr and Stephen Carroll within the North has caused division even within the radical republican constituency, as stated by Gerard Hodgins in Belfast:

> The only people that the 'dissidents' have killed in Belfast is three Catholics. So it's hard to accept that they are genuinely at war with anybody. I think the leaderships of those organisations, any decent people who are in those leaderships, should look seriously at what is being done on the ground in their name.[39]

Co-operation with the PSNI: the unthinkable has happened

A central argument in the radical republican rejection of the PSNI concerns the passing of information to the police. Sinn Féin's acceptance of the legitimacy of the PSNI has culminated in the party calling on members of the nationalist community to co-operate with the PSNI and to report crimes to the police. Given the history of the Republican Movement, this call from Sinn Féin has proven a step too far for radical republicans, as demonstrated by Fra Halligan of the RSM in Belfast:

> Young lads were put in their grave for things like that. So that's a hard thing to swallow if your brother or sister was executed as an informer and the very people are saying inform on your neighbour.[40]

The depth of feeling was compounded by Geraldine Taylor in Belfast:

> You see the worst scenario there is that our biggest enemy now is the Provos for they have called on their people to become informers and tout on as they call dissidents, to give information to the police. So this is supposed to be republicans telling people to inform on other people to the police. Informants were shot years ago. Now they're the biggest informants of all.[41]

In February 2017 the West Belfast Taxi Association (a public transport service in the area) came under criticism from prominent radical republicans regarding an advertisement for 'crime stoppers' which was carried on some of the Black Taxis.[42] A statement by radical republican Alex McCrory was published on the Saoradh website on 11 February 2017:

> Is it now to be the case that the people's taxis are to be used to promote the very agency that colluded in the murder of many of its employees? Lest it be forgotten, the PSNI incorporates the trained killers and directors of terrorism of the RUC … Have we forgotten so much that we are prepared to abandon the proud history of the West Belfast Taxi Association? Surely not.[43]

The depth of criticism of the PSNI was evident in this dispute: the Black Taxis' advertising for crime stoppers struck at the heart of something fundamental to radical republicanism, that is, rejection of a six-county police force which it views as still the RUC (in a different uniform) with its accompanying legacy.

Redress of the past

Republicans have rejected the police on the basis that they are 'the apparatus of the state' as well as in relation to legacy issues. 'Dealing with the past' and 'legacy issues' have occupied a central position in the contemporary political landscape of the North: significantly, no consensus has been reached around such issues. A prominent point of contention was the Northern Ireland Offences Bill, or 'on-the-runs legislation' as it is commonly known, which was introduced in November 2005. As was the case regarding restorative justice schemes, the SDLP was at the forefront of criticism of the 'on-the-runs' bill. SDLP leader Mark Durkan argued that the bill amounted to 'the worst piece of Irish legislation ever presented to the British parliament'.[44] The 'on-the-runs' legislation proved a point of significant contention in the Northern Ireland Assembly between the unionist and nationalist blocs, as it made provision for those who have been 'on the run' since before 1998 to face a special tribunal after which the individual might be released on licence. Debate surrounding the legislation demonstrated a deeply divided society which has reached no consensus regarding how to deal with the past.

In 2010 the conclusions of the Saville inquiry into Bloody Sunday resulted in heightened republican calls for the prosecution of British soldiers of the First

Battalion of the Parachute Regiment that was present in Derry on 30 January 1972 when thirteen unarmed civilians were shot dead during a civil rights march.[45] To date there have been no prosecutions. Calls for redress of past events including Bloody Sunday and 'Ballymurphy' 1971 (known locally as 'the Ballymurphy massacre' when eleven civilians were killed by the same parachute regiment that was present on Bloody Sunday) have assumed a central position in the republican narrative.

In November 2017 it emerged that an amendment has been proposed to the 2014 Stormont House Agreement regarding 'legacy' which calls for the application of a 'statute of limitations' regarding prosecutions of the security forces, leading Sinn Féin president Gerry Adams to reject the proposal as an 'amnesty' for the security forces. During a protest outside Stormont, which was led by victims' families, Sinn Féin's Gerry Kelly stated 'they [families] want the truth and state forces acted with impunity. It's a slap in the face to those who have lost loved ones over a long period.'[46] DUP leader Arlene Foster responded by warning against moves that could lead to a wider amnesty.[47] The significance of unionist concerns about 'redress' was reflected in an all-party report produced by the Dáil in August 2017. This report stated that retribution for acts by the security services is a dominant point of unionist concern which must be addressed when looking at Irish unity.[48] It remains to be seen how issues around 'dealing with the past' will be dealt with in the state of Northern Ireland and whether reconciliation processes, such as those applied in South Africa, will be drawn upon.

IRA policing

The increasing normalisation of the state of Northern Ireland and the departure of the Provisional IRA from republican areas have led some commentators to argue that the Provisionals left behind a vacuum regarding dealing with anti-social behaviour and drug-dealing.[49] Jonathan Powell has stated that in the lead-up to the St Andrew's Agreement in 2007 'it was clear the vacuum left in Catholic working-class areas by the end of punishment beatings was serious. Crimes were going undeterred and the community was getting increasingly restive. The IRA had to bring off the difficult trick of frightening the dissident republicans out of filling the vacuum themselves without being able to use violence.'[50] A decade later in February 2017 the *Belfast Telegraph* quoted a PSNI source:

> People are being told to call the police in emergencies but in many cases when they do they're not getting quick and efficient help … These dissidents are going out and dealing with things when the police aren't there in time … The PSNI is losing control of North and West Belfast and dissident groups are filling that space.[51]

Armed groups such as the Continuity IRA, REAL IRA, New IRA and ONH have engaged in the 'policing' of areas regarding anti-social behaviour and drugs.

Republican Action Against Drugs (an armed group which was formed in 2008 in Derry) has been particularly active in its punishment of 'drug-dealers' and anti-social behaviour in Derry and Tyrone.[52] RAAD has emphasised its rejection of the legitimacy of the PSNI and has targeted the PSNI through armed attacks.

The role which radical republican groups have assumed in relation to 'policing communities' is unsurprising given the historical role which the IRA assumed in this regard. Throughout the 1980s and 1990s the Provisional IRA engaged in a high level of community 'policing' of anti-social behaviour, particularly in the North of Ireland. In *A Secret History of the IRA*, Ed Moloney has alleged that the IRA, using the name 'Direct Action Against Drugs', shot dead a notorious drug-dealer called Micky Mooney in Belfast in 1995.[53] Moloney has also recorded alleged continuing IRA activity against a drug-dealer in Lurgan in 1996.[54] Throughout the 1980s the Sinn Féin newspaper *An Phoblacht* carried IRA statements regarding action taken against individuals engaged in anti-social behaviour and drugs. On 5 January 1989 *An Phoblacht* published an article titled 'RPG hit on Land Rover ':

> Belfast Brigade has claimed responsibility for actions against named criminals in South Belfast and has warned a criminal gang operating out of the Divis flats complex to end its activities and its talk of taking on the IRA in an armed confrontation.
>
> A criminal who had taken advantage of an IRA amnesty but re-involved himself in anti-social behaviour activities was shot and wounded on December 28th.[55]

Later that year, on 3 August, *An Phoblacht* published an article titled 'British "justice" under attack' which referred to a 'family of thugs and bullies who also have a record of involvement in drugs and fencing stolen property'.[56] The statement claimed that the family had received several warnings from the IRA following approaches from residents who wanted the family removed from the area. The IRA statement recorded, 'South Down command Óglaigh na hÉireann have issued a statement giving a man from Carnaget who has ignored previous warnings seven days to leave the country … If he does not comply he will be executed. There will be no more warnings.'[57]

Community control

Historically Sinn Féin and the wider Republican Movement have embedded within nationalist communities at a local level, including assuming positions on residents' committees or other such local initiatives.[58] Through the policing of areas the Provisional Movement exercised a tight control on nationalist communities throughout the North.[59] English has argued that 'part of the Provos' concern about policing lay in the fact that the RUC tried to recruit informers from among petty criminals in Catholic areas'.[60] It is unsurprising that radical republican groups have continued 'policing communities', given that most 'dissident groups' were the result of splits in the Provisional Movement. Community policing by republicans has included kneecapping, punishment shootings, punishment beatings and the expulsion of individuals from residential areas for drug-dealing and anti-social behaviour. Radical republicans have been particularly active in community policing in Belfast, Dublin and Derry. Independent republican Veronica Ryan in West Belfast has argued:

> If you took a poll and asked people do you think that the hoods or rapists should be shot they would say yes. You have to remember people in these areas are living at the mercy of these thugs. You know so they [Provisionals] just walked out of our areas and left us to it.[61]

When the author asked a spokesperson for the Continuity IRA in North Armagh about the large electoral mandate possessed by Sinn Féin, the interviewee acknowledged that Provisional Sinn Féin are performing well electorally in the North of Ireland but stated 'at the minute they don't hold the same sway as they would have. People see what they're doing as a failure.'[62] The North Armagh republican went on to argue:

> Our strength is growing … if there was a problem in an estate, where in recent years they'd have run to the Provisionals, they'll now come to us because they know they'll do nothing … the support is coming our way and regardless of whether they like to say it or not … an awful lot of people come to us regarding anti-social behaviour and drugs issues.[63]

However, while radical republicans are united in their condemnation of the PSNI, they remain divided on whether or not 'policing communities' is a legitimate function of armed republicanism. Independent republican Anthony McIntyre in Drogheda (originally from West Belfast) has rejected the role which some radical republicans have assumed in dealing with anti-social behaviour:

> Republicans should not be going in and violating people's human rights by mutilating them. Shooting them in the legs or shooting them dead. Because that undermines the call for human rights.[64]

Further, Phil O'Donoghue, honorary president of the 32CSM, has argued:

> As far as some of us are concerned, the drug-dealing, that's a police matter. It should be a police matter. We shouldn't interfere one way or another. We should keep as far a distance from that as possible.[65]

Community policing: 'this is not the answer boys'

The Rosemount Centre, which is located in Derry, facilitates local community workers and is predominantly used by local radical republicans. Within the Rosemount Centre radical republicans from various republican groups (as well as independents) are informally co-operating through their community work. Gary Donnelly is a member of the 32CSM in Derry and is an elected councillor for Derry and Strabane. Donnelly is active in the Rosemount Centre and engages in community and youth work. During a focus group held in the Rosemount Centre, comprising independents and members of the 32CSM, radical republicans highlighted local activity in which they are involved regarding their activism in tackling anti-social behaviour. Members of the focus group were critical of punishment shootings and punishment beatings performed by republican armed groups. One republican commented: 'the use of violence [in the form of punishment beatings and shootings] in itself is not the only answer to this. There are other ways this can be dealt with like prevention programmes, training programmes, counselling support.'[66] A stated aim of the centre is to act as an intermediary between perpetrators of anti-social behaviour and militant groups which are carrying out punishment shootings. An independent republican stated:

> When we talk to these other groups we say this is not the answer boys. There are other ways of doing this. You are alienating your own community … I'm not saying that major drug-dealers shouldn't be dealt with but young people, they are at the bottom of the ladder and maybe because of peer pressure they tried this or maybe because of unemployment. They can't get jobs, so they'll make a quick few bob this way.[67]

Republicans in the Rosemount Centre have criticised Sinn Féin's method of referring individuals to the police (resulting in that individual acquiring a criminal record) and have argued that this could be dealt with another way.[68] Similar work has been undertaken at a community level by Conflict Resolution Services Ireland in Belfast, which is run by Republican Network for Unity, the office of which is located on the Falls road in West Belfast. The work of Conflict Resolution Services includes mediation when a young person is 'under threat' of a punishment beating or shooting, benefit inquiries, housing inquiries and student inquiries. While radical republican groups are engaging in similar work at a community level, there is no official co-operation on this basis between groups; rather, geographical location has assumed significance.

Conclusion

The devolution of policing and justice powers to Northern Ireland in 2010 further transformed the political landscape in relation to policing. Sinn Féin has emphasised the significance of the devolution of powers, which took place after a decade of protracted debate within the mainstream. Since the devolution of policing, radical republicans have remained steadfast in their rejection of the PSNI: the highlighting of negative interaction with the police remains a central component of the 'dissident' message. This is reflective of Della Porta's findings on social movements that 'activists react to a more proximate dimension: the policing of protest, that is the police handling of protest events – what protestors usually refer to as "repression" and the state characterises as law and order.'[69] Della Porta has argued that 'protest policing has a direct impact on social movements, being a sort of barometer for the available political opportunities'.[70] Radical republican literature remains infused with references to negative interaction with police (particularly in relation to republican events such as protests, commemorations and marches) which they argue evidences suppression of those who fall beyond the status quo.[71] A more detailed discussion of radical republicanism in relation to perceived 'political opportunities' and navigation of the political system (in the context of rejecting the 'slippery slope' to constitutionalism) is provided in chapter four.

Radical republicans frequently come into conflict with the PSNI or An Garda Síochána – as the first line of defence of the state. Attendance at radical republican events (even as a spectator) is sure to result in your name and address being taken by Special Branch officers North and South, and a researcher in this area is likely to experience 'stop and search' by the PSNI. Tactics employed by radical republicans reflect their aim of disrupting the 'normalisation process' in the state of Northern Ireland. All radical republican groups conduct on-going anti-police campaigns to highlight alleged 'PSNI harassment' of republican activists. A central aim throughout such campaigns is to highlight the abnormal nature of policing in the North of Ireland and to dispel the notion that the PSNI is a new 'normal' police service which is rooted in the community. A telling exchange took place during the Waterfront debate in 2012 between Sinn Féin's Jim McVeigh and RNU's Ciaran Cunningham. The contrasting narratives regarding the police in the North of Ireland were starkly evident as Cunningham directed the following comment to McVeigh:

> I'm very happy that your children aren't afraid of the Crown Forces because my children are terrified. They are the people that smash up my house and bring me to Antrim.[72]

Sinn Féin's absorption into the structures of the state of Northern Ireland is evidenced through the party's acceptance of the PSNI and the roles which party members have assumed on policing boards. As with other significant ideological shifts, Sinn Féin has couched its acceptance of the PSNI in language which emphasises 'tactics' and 'strategy'. In contrast, radical republicans have rejected 'reform' of the police and have continued to assert their pursuit of revolutionary change and their rejection of a six-county police force.

Notes

1 Eamon Cairns, interview with the author, Lurgan, 23 August 2013. See his *Our Sons – Our Brothers: An Account of the Murders of Gerard and Rory Cairns* (self-published).
2 Eamon Cairns, interview with the author, Lurgan, 23 August 2013.
3 *Ibid.*
4 *Ibid.*
5 English, *Armed Struggle* (2012), p. 267: 'The Pat Finucane killing began a long argument (and ultimately an inquiry) concerning alleged collusion by the security forces in his death.' (p. 267).
6 The Patten report on policing is available at www.cain.ulst.ac.uk. Accessed 23 July 2018.
7 *Ibid.*
8 The loyalist-based restorative justice scheme, namely 'Alternatives', had its office on the Shankill road in West Belfast.
9 Alex Attwood, interview with the author, Belfast, 7 August 2006.
10 Brian Barrington, interview with the author, Belfast, 21 December 2005.
11 Powell, *Great Hatred, Little Room*, p. 279.
12 McKearney has made reference to such meetings in *The Provisional IRA*, p. 181.
13 *Ibid.*, p. 181.
14 Along with Rev. Harold Good, Fr Alec Reid witnessed the process of IRA decommissioning in 2005.
15 Bean, *New Politics of Sinn Féin*, p. 122. Bean is quoting F. Millar, 'Will a pragmatic Paisley finish his career by "doing the deal"?', *Irish Times* (11 November 2006).
16 F. Lane. 'Different name, same bigots: RUC replaced by PSNI', *An Phoblacht* (8 November 2001).
17 *Ibid.*
18 Kevin Hannaway, interview with the author, Belfast, 24 July 2013.
19 On 30 April 2014, after presenting himself for interview at Antrim police station, Gerry Adams was arrested by the PSNI; he was released after four days. The arrest followed the PSNI gaining access (through court cases) to some of the tapes from the Boston College Project; particularly the Brendan Hughes interview. Adams was questioned in relation to the killing of Jean McConville in December 1972 by the IRA. McConville was one of 'the disappeared'; her body was secretly buried. In 2003 her body was found on a beach in Louth. Adams has denied any involvement in the killing and has stated 'I believe that the killing of Jean McConville and the secret burial of her body was wrong and a grievous injustice to her and her family.' See bbc.co.uk/news/uk-northern-ireland-27233712. Accessed 23 July 2018.
20 Ciaran Mulholland, interview with the author, Belfast, 8 May 2014.
21 *Ibid.*
22 'Nationalists reject policing figures' (14 June 2001). http://news.bbc.co.uk/1/hi/northern_ireland/1387831.stm. Accessed 23 July 2018.
23 OMNIBUS survey, 'Public perceptions of the police, PCSPs and the Northern Ireland policing Board', published by the Northern Ireland policing board (April 2017). www.nipolicingboard.org.uk/surveys. Accessed 23 July 2018.

24 PSNI, 'Workforce composition statistics'. Information is correct as of 1 July 2018. www.psni.police.uk/inside-psni/Statistics/workforce-composition-statistics/. Accessed 24 July 2018.

25 B. Feeney, 'PSNI not representative of society – and that's a big problem', *Irish News* (8 November 2017).

26 *Ibid.*

27 *Ibid.*

28 *Ibid.* Feeney also highlighted the fact that in 2015 there were 500 new PSNI recruits, seventy-seven of whom were Catholic.

29 Máire Óg Drumm, interview with the author, Belfast, 6 March 2014.

30 Joe Dillon, interview with the author, Skerries, 19 March 2013.

31 Francie Mackey, interview with the author, Omagh, 8 February 2013.

32 Nolan, 'Long, long war'. .

33 D. Fahy, 'Ronan Kerr, policeman and GAA player', *Irish Times* (9 April 2009).

34 P. Nolan, 'Northern Ireland Peace Monitoring Report: Number One' (February 2012). http://cain.ulst.ac.uk/events/peace/docs/nipmr_2012-02.pdf. Accessed 24 July 2018.

35 Tonge, 'An enduring tradition or the last gasp of physical force republicanism?'.

36 Francie Mackey, interview with the author, Omagh, 8 February 2013.

37 M. Hopkinson, *The Irish War of Independence* (Dublin, Gill & Macmillan, 2002), p. 115. On the shooting of the two RIC men, Hopkinson writes: 'Both the men appear to have been popular in the locality and the action was widely criticised in pulpits and Press' (p. 115). See also J. Ambrose, *Dan Breen and the IRA* (Cork, Mercier Press, 2006), pp. 58–9. Dan Breen used his witness statement to the Irish Bureau of Military History to set out the motivation behind the Soloheadbeg ambush: 'I would like to make this point clear and state here without any equivocation that we took this action deliberately having thought the matter over and talked it over between us. [Sean] Treacy had stated to me that the only way of starting a war was to kill someone and we wanted to start a war, so we intended to kill some of the police whom we looked upon as the foremost and most important branch of the enemy forces which were holding our country in subjection. The moral aspect of such a decision has been talked about since and we have been branded as murderers, both by the enemy and even by some of our own people, but I want it to be understood that the pros and cons were thoroughly weighed up in discussions between Treacy and myself and, to put it in a nutshell, we felt that we were merely continuing the active war for the establishment of the Irish Republic that had begun on Easter Monday, 1916.'

38 *The Writings of Theobald Wolfe Tone, 1763–98, Volume II: America, France and Bantry Bay, August 1795 to December 1796*, ed. T.W. Moody, R.B. McDowell and C.J. Woods (Oxford, Clarendon Press, 2009), p. 301.

39 Gerard Hodgins, interview with the author, Belfast, 13 September 2012.

40 Fra Halligan, interview with the author, Belfast, 19 November 2013.

41 Geraldine Taylor, interview with the author, Belfast, 14 October 2012.

42 The West Belfast Black Taxi Association has been in operation since the 1970s and is unique in nature, given that a significant number of the drivers are former IRA prisoners. It was formed as a community service at a time when buses and public

transport would regularly be stopped due to 'security situations'. The Association is an integral part of the fabric of West Belfast and provides low-cost transport from the city centre to the Falls road and the surrounding housing areas of Poleglass, Lagmore, Twinbrook, Ladybrook, Whiterock the Glen road and Andersonstown. There is also a service to Ardoyne. The taxis also undertake internationally recognised tours of the murals and sights of political interest.

43 Saoradh, 'West Belfast Black Taxi's – from revolutionary to reformist – Alex McCrory Op-Ed – Saoradh Nuacht' (11 February 2017). http://saoradh.ie/west-belfast-black-taxis-from-revolutionary-to-reformist-alex-mccrory-op-ed-saoradh-nu acht/. Accessed 24 July 2018.

44 *Irish Times* (26 December 2005).

45 A fourteenth person later died as a result of their injuries.

46 S. Fenton, 'Families protest over proposed amnesty for security forces Troubles killings', *Irish News* (28 November 2017).

47 M. Devenport, 'Arlene Foster "concerned" over security force amnesty', BBC (24 November 2017). www.bbc.co.uk/news/uk-northern-ireland-42114814. Accessed 24 July 2018.

48 Joint Committee on the Implementation of the Good Friday Agreement, *Brexit and the Future of Ireland: Uniting Ireland and its People in Peace and Prosperity* (August 2017). http://data.oireachtas.ie/ie/oireachtas/committee/dail/32/joint_co mmittee_on_the_implementation_of_the_good_friday_agreement/reports/2017/ 2017–08–02_brexit-and-the-future-of-ireland-uniting-ireland-and-its-people-in-pe ace-and-prosperity_en.pdf. Accessed 23 July 2018.

49 See Bean, *New Politics of Sinn Féin*, pp. 110–11 regarding concerns of the nationalist community about the 'growth of a hood [hooligan] culture' and crime in a 'normal-ised Northern Ireland'.

50 Powell, *Great Hatred, Little Room*, p. 279.

51 C. O'Boyle, 'Belfast Officer says crime victims turn to dissidents for help as police "lose control in parts of city"', *Belfast Telegraph* (7 February 2017).

52 In 2012 RAAD merged with the REAL IRA to form the New IRA.

53 Moloney, *Secret History of the IRA*, p. 437.

54 *Ibid.*, p. 440. Regarding the killing of drug-dealers by the IRA at this time, Moloney has stated 'starting on December 8 the IRA killed four times, and the killing contin-ued into the New Year. A fifth drug dealer was shot dead in January 1996 in Lurgan, where the local IRA leader was also a critic of the Adams strategy. The DAAD killings were a barometer of rank-and-file unease and a measure of the current weakness of the peace camp in the IRA leadership' (p. 440).

55 'RPG hit on Land Rover', *An Phoblacht*, Vol. 10, No. 52 (5 January 1989), p. 3.

56 'British "justice" under attack', subsection: 'IRA Warnings', *An Phoblacht* (3 August 1989), p. 2.

57 *Ibid.*

58 For an assessment of the Provisional Movement's organic links see K. Cassidy, 'Organic intellectuals and the committed community: Irish Republicanism and Sinn Féin in the North', *Irish Political Studies*, 20:3 (2007), 341–56.

59 See English, *Armed Struggle* (2012), p. 275. ' … republicans apparently carrying out

1,228 punishment shootings between 1973 and 1997, and a further 755 beatings during 1982–97.'

60 *Ibid.*, p. 275.

61 Veronica Ryan, interview with the author, Belfast, 8 January 2014. In reference to the PSNI, Veronica Ryan has commented 'I don't care if my house was ransacked tomorrow I would not lift the phone to phone them. No I would never invite them to come into my house. They've been in it a few times but they weren't invited.'

62 CIRA spokesperson, North Armagh, interview with the author (conducted in North Armagh), 2014.

63 *Ibid.*

64 Anthony McIntyre, interview with the author, Dublin, 3 April 2013.

65 Phil O'Donoghue, interview with the author, Kilkenny, 4 November 2013.

66 Member of Focus Group with the author, Derry, 21 August 2013.

67 *Ibid.*

68 Over 300 cases have been dealt with by the Rosemount Centre. Approximately 290 were resolved without violence. Statistics provided by the Rosemount Centre.

69 Della Porta, *Clandestine Political Violence*, p. 35.

70 *Ibid.*, p. 35.

71 See White, 'From state terrorism to petty harassment', pp. 45–64.

72 Public debate, Waterfront Hall, Belfast, February 2012. Attended by the author.

7

Legitimacy and mandates

It has been said that democracy is the worst form of government, except all the others that have been tried.

Winston Churchill, speech in the House of Commons, 11 November 1947

I don't think you can judge Sinn Féin by what electoral strength we have. You have to judge Sinn Féin on how we use it. If I was asked how I would judge the party it would have to be in what changes we have been able to bring about or what changes we were part of bringing about, the positive changes for the best and that's the way to judge a party like Sinn Féin – is how we have succeeded in our agenda.

Gerry Adams, interview with the author, Belfast, 5 March 2009

There was a parade that came through that estate two years ago and there was over 4,000 people at it. You know for a microscopic organisation that's some amount of people.

Continuity IRA spokesperson, North Armagh, interview with the author (conducted in North Armagh), 2014

Introduction: political status

Throughout Irish history, terminology has played a significant role in 'defining' those who fall beyond the status quo. The concept of political legitimacy (and where it derives from) has remained a dominant theme throughout Irish republicanism. Contested narratives within the republican family have predominantly revolved around the issue of 'legitimacy' and who constitutes the legitimate Republican Movement. Historical determinism is a constant throughout radical republicanism, as evidenced by assertions from republican groups that their lineage stretches back to 1916. The Hunger Strike period of the early 1980s demonstrated the significance of legitimacy in the republican world, as republican prisoners embarked on Hunger Strikes for political status; 'special category status' had been removed from the prisoners in 1976. Current republican prisoners in Maghaberry, located outside Lisburn in the North of Ireland, are not housed among the criminal population, but are housed in Roes three and four; however, the prisoners are not granted freedom of association or movement on their landings (demands which were asserted during the Blanket protests and Hunger Strikes of the late 1970s and early 1980s). Sinn Féin has proven divided on the classification of current republican prisoners as political.

Terminology: 'dissident' republicanism

In the post-Good Friday Agreement context, the mainstream narrative in the North and South of Ireland has seized upon the word 'dissident' (mainly propagated by Sinn Féin) in an attempt to delegitimise republicans who fall beyond the mainstream. The word 'dissident' is commonly used with the implication that republican 'dissidents' are a recent phenomenon on the political stage, or are embarking on something new – contrary to the reality that many individuals involved in radical republicanism have been involved with the Republican Movement since the pre-1969 period. The radical republican discourse has emphasised loyalty to traditional republican ideology, and, significantly, republicans have professed their allegiance to the same Republican Movement which they joined many years ago, in many cases decades ago. In this respect radical republicans have rejected Provisional Sinn Féin as the true Republican Movement. The minority status (numerically) of non-mainstream republicans coupled with a lack of popular support has allowed the term 'dissident' to dominate the mainstream narrative.

The history of republicanism is littered with references to irregulars, anti-treatyites, trucileers and dissidents. In fact the term 'dissident' first entered mainstream usage in the 1920s. Language has played a significant role in the contested narratives of the mainstream and non-mainstream, and has been used by both in attempts to delegitimise the other. The terms 'constitutional nationalist Sinn Féin' and 'Mainstream Sinn Féin' are evident throughout radical republican literature in an attempt to delegitimise Sinn Féin as the true Sinn Féin Republican Movement. RSF continues to condemn Provisional Sinn Féin for using the name 'Sinn Féin', and individuals who have left the Provisional Movement in the more recent period (post-1998) have also rejected Sinn Féin as the true Republican Movement. Nuala Perry, who left Sinn Féin in 2000, has argued 'we see ourselves as the Provisionals and we didn't see how they could ride off into the sunset carrying that label and I'll always be sad when I hear people referring to them as the Provos because, well who were we?'[1]

Radical republicans have rejected the mainstream narrative that Sinn Féin holds the brand of republicanism. At an event titled 'the burning of Long Kesh', hosted by the 1916 Societies in Tyrone on 16 October 2013, a self-confessed Sinn Féin supporter in the audience announced that he was 'on board with the peace process' and that he had joined the IRA at the age of fifteen. In response, prominent radical republican Kevin Hannaway pointedly stated 'I joined the same movement as you'. At one point during the heated exchange the Sinn Féin speaker from the floor argued that it is 'our history too'.[2] Exchanges such as these reflect a contestation which is taking place regarding republican history and specific events. Albert Allen, an independent republican in Clonard in Belfast, has argued that the Provisional Movement are attempting to retain events such as the Hunger Strikes, the burning of Long Kesh and the H-Block escape of 1983 as 'their' history and part of the Provisional Sinn Féin narrative: 'they're definitely trying to keep that in [the Provisional Sinn Féin Movement] because they see it as holding on to what gels republicans.'[3]

A common theme that runs throughout the radical republican narrative, among former members of the Provisional Movement (or members of RSF who were in the movement prior to the 1986 split), states that Provisional Sinn Féin were 'brought along' by people who now fall outside of the party and are labelled 'dissidents'. The common theme of resentment, in this respect, was evidenced throughout the interviews. Significantly, radical republicans fuse ideological assertion with personal testimony. Peig King of RSF and Cumann na mBan in Dublin has commented on women who have claimed allegiance to Cumann na mBan but who are not members:

> We know that at times there has been people walking up the Falls road in uniform who should not be in uniform … I know some of them even got their uniform out of the dramatic clubs … the only conclusion that I can come to is that they haven't got the strength of commitment to be seen. They feel it, they want it but they haven't got the courage or commitment to walk out on that street, down that street to put a hat or a badge on and to hell with everybody looking at you.[4]

Irregulars, trucileers and dissidents

During the Civil War of the 1920s the issue of legitimacy was of central importance and was bitterly contested. The newly formed Free State claimed that it was the legitimate Irish Republican Movement. In contrast anti-treaty forces asserted their legitimacy as the true Republican Movement. The Free Staters' use of the word 'irregulars' was an attempt to de-legitimise the anti-treaty forces. As documented by J. Bowyer Bell, the six months following the 1921 Truce saw the IRA maintain its structures above ground.[5] The newly formed Provisional government, which went unrecognised by anti-treaty republicans, set up a Ministry of Defence under the direction of Richard Mulcahy. Bowyer Bell states: 'to the disgust and alarm of the IRA, the Free State was building up an alternative army and police, while the Free State cabinet was deeply concerned at indications that the radical wing of the IRA was one step from declaring a military dictatorship.'[6] Bowyer Bell goes on to state that 'the members of the Free State Cabinet felt that the activities of the IRA were illegal, immoral, and undemocratic. The Dáil had spoken. Everyone admitted the people favoured the Treaty. The Republicans offered nothing but renewed war as a programme.'[7]

In *The Singing Flame* (1978) Ernie O'Malley documented continued hostility from the newspapers towards the 'anti-treatyites'. He referenced a document which was intercepted by the IRA that had been distributed to censors and editors. The document included 'censorial instructions' which stated that 'Irregular leaders are not to be referred to as of any rank, such as "commandant", etc, or are not to be called officers.'[8] Subsequently it stated: 'They [censors] may, however, propose to substitute words or phrases, such as "irregulars" for "republicans", "fired at" for "attacked", "seized" for "commandeered", "kidnapped" for "arrested", "enrolled" for "enlisted".'[9] The document, which was by order of the army publicity department at Beggars Bush Barracks in Dublin, illustrates an attempt by the state to control the popular narrative and to de-legitimise anti-treaty republicans. In *Green Against Green: The Irish Civil War* Michael Hopkinson states that Cosgrave's government in 1922 put a heavy stress on its 'authority': 'circulars to the press ordered that the government should be referred to as "the National government" and not "the Provisional government", and that the Republican opposition of all shades, should be known as irregulars.'[10]

In the contemporary period, non-mainstream republicans have located their actions within a long continuum of republican struggle. Radical republican discourse has emphasised attempts by both states to 'delegitimise, de-politicise and criminalise' non-mainstream republicans. Republicans have drawn a line of continuity throughout the 'long struggle' and have highlighted 'repression' as a constant throughout. In this regard, radical republicans (who have emphasised the current period as the 'latest phase' in the long struggle) have argued that the repression they face in the contemporary period is demonstrative of the historical 'repression' of republicans who existed beyond the status quo.

Criminalisation

Mainstream 'criminalisation' of non-mainstream republicans is not a uniquely contemporary phenomenon. In the post-treaty period those in opposition to the treaty were labelled anti-treatyites, and John M. Regan has stated in *The Irish Counter-revolution* that:

> Criminalisation of anti-treatyites had been the policy of the treatyite Government since the beginning of the war. The denial of prisoner-of-war status and the suspension of habeas corpus in July attempted to deprive the IRA of any claim to political legitimacy while facilitating the processing of large numbers of anti-treaty prisoners taken in Dublin … In the midst of fratricidal conflict, bitter and frustrated, the treatyite elite dismissed completely the ideological basis of the IRA campaign, and anti-treatyite criminality ceased to be an expedient and became the defining motive for the treatyites' prosecution of the war.[11]

Regan has cited Kevin O'Higgins's comment to Richard Mulcahy on 1 September 1922: 'the fighting seems to have reached a stage when major military operations are almost at an end. In three fourths of our area it is becoming less and less a question of war and more and more a question of armed crime.'[12] In the contemporary period, the biggest threat to radical republicanism is the 'criminalisation' of republicanism by the mainstream. Pádraig Garvey of RSF in Cahersiveen in Co. Kerry was an RSF candidate in the 2014 local council election for the South and West Kerry constituency.[13] Garvey, who joined RSF in 2000, has argued 'sometimes I think republicanism has this kind of cloak and dagger image and I think it's taking on an image of kind of feeling involved in criminality.'[14] Similarly, Anthony Ryan of the 32CSM in Dublin has argued:

> I mean nobody can label me as a criminal. I don't speak to criminals. I despise drug-pushing and I wouldn't even say hello to a drug-pusher and I think that the issues of republicanism and criminality are black and white. You know, either you despise criminality or you're not a republican.[15]

Radical republican discourse has emphasised the danger which is posed to the survival of republicanism, if in the public mind radical republicanism becomes synonymous with criminality. While republicanism has never possessed a popular mandate, it has been widely documented that the republican campaign in the historical period, and in the more recent period from 1969, has been sustained through the provision of safe houses and support from the public.

The Sinn Féin electoral mandate

Sinn Féin has emphasised its strong electoral mandate in the North of Ireland and its strengthened electoral mandate in the South as a provider of legitimacy.[16] The current narrative of Sinn Féin is dominated by references to the party's electoral mandate alongside the centrality of the Good Friday Agreement to the political process. Sinn Féin has frequently cited the lack of an electoral mandate possessed by 'dissidents'. However, the radical republican narrative does not equate popular support with legitimacy. Significantly, radical republicans do not derive 'legitimacy' from the polls. Therefore personal testimonies gathered have proven valuable in determining where republicans take their legitimacy from.

This chapter also explores the electoral fortunes of radical republicans to date, many of whom have contested local elections as 'independent' candidates. Further, an analysis is provided of Sinn Féin's engagement with the electoral system prior to the 'ballot-box and armalite' strategy propagated by Danny Morrison in 1981, thus challenging the common perception that this signalled a significant shift in the strategy of Sinn Féin (given the party's engagement with the electoral process prior to this period).[17]

Within the republican world, legitimacy has never been solely drawn from the ballot box. When Danny Morrison made his famous 'ballot box and armalite' speech at the Sinn Féin Ard Fheis in 1981, the ballot box was presented as one part of an overall strategy which included an armed campaign. However, by the early 1990s it was apparent that there was a glass ceiling on electoral support for Sinn Féin while the IRA campaign continued.[18] The party had also struggled to make significant electoral gains in the South of Ireland – as noted by Tommy McKearney, 'any lingering doubt about the southerners' views were dispelled in 1981 when, at the height of the long and agonising hunger strike in the H-Blocks, only two IRA candidates were elected to the Republic's parliament.'[19] Significantly, Sinn Féin's vote in the South of Ireland did not rise above 2 per cent in the 1980s.[20]

1981: the ballot box and armalite

During the 1981 Sinn Féin Ard Fheis, Danny Morrison and Jimmy Drumm (on behalf of the Sinn Féin Ard Chomhairle) spoke in opposition to contesting local government elections. Ruairí Ó Brádaigh had advocated contesting the 1981 local elections in the North but was defeated by the Ard Chomhairle. However, Morrison has argued:

> But when you saw the vote that Bobby Sands got we realised it was a mood change. We realised that it had been a mistake not to put forward local government candidates in May 1981. So we began changing the policy.[21]

In 1981 two 'People's Democracy' candidates were elected to Belfast City Council, two members of the IRSP were elected, and Pat Fahey was elected in Omagh for the Irish Independence Party. Danny Morrison has argued:

> So we had missed the boat. We realised the value of elections even from a propaganda point of view. Thatcher had been saying 'how can I talk to you, you don't have a mandate'. But when Bobby Sands had a mandate she still wouldn't talk! But the international publicity around the election of Bobby Sands and the Hunger Strike, and, of course, the death of Bobby Sands was massively damaging to the British.[22]

Morrison has further commented:

> We also saw elections and the opening up of advice centres across the North as a way of giving back something to the people because, I mean, throughout the struggle the republican call was 'lend me your car, can we use your house, would you give us some money'… this was now an opportunity to give something back to the people by having elected representatives who could fight for them and that was what was behind it.[23]

A mood change had taken place within Sinn Féin which recognised that an opportunity had been missed. It was within this context that the party's 1981 Ard Fheis took place; the clár for the Ard Fheis contained a motion which would empower the incoming Ard Chomhairle to make a decision about contesting future elections. The motion was hotly contested and Danny Morrison has recalled that Adams said to him 'you better get up here and speak to this motion', which resulted in Morrison joining the long queue of those wishing to speak on the motion. Morrison has recalled 'I wasn't sure what I was going to say and it was only when I stepped up to the platform that I used the expression about armalite and ballot box. "You know, we can do both together," was the message I was trying to get across. In a sense I was playing to the gallery, and we won. We got support to contest elections.'[24]

The mainstream narrative has portrayed the 1981 Hunger Strike period as the Republican Movement's first venture into electoral politics. This is not the case and in fact misrepresents the Republican Movement's engagement with the electoral arena prior to this period. Notable examples include four candidates put forward by the Republican Movement in the November 1933 Westminster election, during which Paddy McLogan was elected for South Armagh with 4,803 votes.[25] On 26 May 1955 Sinn Féin had two candidates elected to Westminster on an abstentionist basis: Tom Mitchell (Mid-Ulster) and Philip Clarke (Fermanagh and South Tyrone); at the time both were prisoners in Crumlin Road jail in Belfast. On 5 March 1957 Sinn Féin won 65,640 votes in the Dáil elections, thus electing four TDs including Ruairí Ó Brádaigh (Longford-Westmeath), John-Joe Rice (South Kerry), Éighneachán O'Hanlon (Monaghan) and John-Joe McGirl (Sligo-Leitrim).[26] Further, Sinn Féin councillors were elected in the 1960s and 1970s.[27] The party had fielded Ruairí Ó Brádaigh as a candidate in Fermanagh-South Tyrone in 1966. Bobby Sands's significant candidature in 1981 did mark the beginning of a new era for the organisation; however, it did not mark the beginning of engagement with the electoral process.

Bobby Sands: the contested narrative

What took place in the lead-up to Bobby Sands standing as a candidate in 1981 has proven a central point of contestation between the mainstream and 'dissident' narratives. It has assumed a point of significance, as radical republicans have rejected the portrayal of 'dissidents' as 'hawks' and as anti-elections. Understanding this contested narrative provides an insight into radical republican thinking. According to Gerry Adams, in *Before the Dawn*, Jim Gibney suggested that Bobby Sands should contest the by-election for Frank Maguire's seat.[28] However, in *Out of the Ashes: An Oral History of the Provisional Irish Republican Movement*, Robert W. White states that Cathleen Knowles,[29] who was then general secretary of Sinn Féin, argued that it was in fact Dáithí Ó Conaill who proposed that Sands contest the election, which was met with opposition from the Belfast members.[30] Knowles has claimed that the issue came to the Coiste Seasta and was then referred to the Ard Chomhairle. She has stated that 'the Belfast people' had to be convinced that it was a good idea to put

Sands forward as a candidate and has recalled 'so Dave [Dáithí Ó Conaill] had to convince them that – he went back to Terence Mac Swiney's death and what happened after his hunger strike in 1920.'[31]

Lita Campbell of RSF in Dublin was a member of the Sinn Féin Ard Chomhairle in the early 1980s and has recalled:

> Dave O'Connell came to an Ard Chomhairle meeting and he proposed, I think it was seconded by Richard Behal, that we stand Bobby Sands. And I thought Gerry Adams would have a heart attack. He said we wouldn't be elected. We'd have no support … Dave O'Connell – now he said, if we lose it we lose it. But he said this is a chance of going places. Anyway the Ard Chomhairle backed him very narrowly because the Northern people were totally against it and they did their best to sabotage it.[32]

It is somewhat ironic that, in the contemporary narrative, elections are central to the position of Provisional Sinn Féin, while Ó Brádaigh's party is associated with a lack of enthusiasm for contesting elections. Historically, Sinn Féin's relationship with elections is more nuanced than is often portrayed. The fact that the Hunger Strike period has assumed a central point in the radical republican narrative (through O'Rawe's assertions in *Blanketmen* and the contested narrative over the candidacy of Bobby Sands) is unsurprising given the centrality of the Hunger Strike period to Irish republicanism.

A republican mandate?

A predominant theme throughout the radical republican discourse has been the rejection of the Provisional Sinn Féin mandate. This has centred around the fact that Sinn Féin has altered its course and stance. As Sinn Féin moderated its message and standpoint, the party reaped electoral dividends.[33] Through the acceptance of the consent principle the message of Sinn Féin has moved closer to that of the SDLP. Radical republicans have stressed the fact that Sinn Féin did not possess a strong electoral mandate when articulating a 'pure' ideological republican position. Radical republicans have further argued that republicanism has never possessed (nor sought) a strong electoral mandate. While radical republicans continue to profess an allegiance to traditional republican principles, Sinn Féin has continued to emphasise its position as the true Republican Movement (and has denied any departure from republican principles), while simultaneously emphasising its changed message and stance as 'tactical'.

Radical republicans have argued that Sinn Féin has gained its electoral mandate by 'saying one thing and then going on to do something else'. This is an argument which has also been used by radical republicans in the South of Ireland against Fianna Fáil, Fine Gael and Labour, as demonstrated by Louise Minihan of éirígí in Dublin:

Even in the last elections them two parties Fine Gael and Labour – they put out a mandate of what they were going to government for. They haven't kept one of them … so I don't know, especially when your country is occupied, that is your mandate.[34]

Similarly, in Belfast Angela Nelson has argued:

It's all very well to turn around and say 'this is our mandate and this is what we'll do', but the proof of the pudding is in the eating you know. You can promise the sun and the moon and the stars but you know, you have to deliver and none of them are delivering.[35]

Central to the radical republican discourse is the argument that at some point Sinn Féin ceased to be republican; the point at which this happened forms a central component of the radical republican message and in fact explains why so-called 'dissident' republicanism is so fragmented.

In May 2016, during the Assembly elections, outside the polling station at Good Shepherd primary school in West Belfast, the ground was littered with Sinn Féin mock ballot papers.[36] It proved a notable site in the Sinn Féin heartland in West Belfast, and posed a question regarding whether or not Sinn Féin had commanded the unwavering electoral loyalty that it had previously assumed in the area. The mood change was confirmed when the election results were announced and Gerry Carroll from 'People Before Profit' was elected and in fact topped the poll.[37] It appeared that 'People Before Profit' were tapping into an appetite for change. Eamonn McCann was also elected for the party in Foyle in Derry. However, Sinn Féin regained its poll position in the constituency in the 2017 elections. Significantly, disaffection with Sinn Féin has not translated into electoral support for radical republican candidates, whose vote has remained minor.

Where 'dissidents' take their legitimacy from

Traditionally, republican legitimacy has not been sought at the electoral polls, nor has it been drawn from popular support. In 1982 Martin McGuinness, when talking to the media, stated 'We don't believe that winning elections and winning any amount of votes will bring freedom in to Ireland. At the end of the day it will be the cutting edge of the IRA which will bring freedom.'[38] Generations of Irish republicans have cited Emmet's Proclamation of 1803, the Fenian Proclamation of 1867 and the 1916 Proclamation as providers of republican legitimacy and mandate. The Proclamation of 1916, which is quoted almost universally at Irish republican commemorations, states:

We declare the right of the people of Ireland to the ownership of Ireland and to the unfettered control of Irish destinies, to be sovereign and indefeasible. The long usurpation of that right by a foreign people and government has not extinguished the right, nor can it ever be extinguished except by the destruction of the Irish people. In every generation the Irish people have asserted their right to national freedom and sovereignty; six times during the past three hundred years they have asserted it in arms.

Each year in June, republican groups assemble in Bodenstown in County Kildare to invoke the message of Theobold Wolfe Tone of the 1798 United Irishmen, who is commonly referred to as the father of modern-day Irish republicanism. Significantly, it is not exclusively radical republicans who make the annual journey to Wolfe Tone's grave. The commemorative practice is also undertaken by Fianna Fáil, Provisional Sinn Féin and the Workers' Party, among others. Speeches undertaken at the graveside commonly invoke 200 years of Irish republican history and emphasise continuity, legitimacy and lineage. Wolfe Tone's grave is one of many republican sites at which a variety of organisations gather for commemorations. Edentubber and the Charlie Kerins monument in Tralee are other places at which Sinn Féin and RSF each gather annually for a commemorative ceremony.

RSF: To capture the enemy's post

In 1921 Terence MacSwiney referred to taking places on local councils:

> We take these posts as places conceded in the fight and avail of them to strengthen, develop and uplift the country and prepare her to carry the last post. Surely this is adequate. On a field of battle it is always to the credit of a general to capture an enemy's post and use it for the final victory.[39]

However, MacSwiney asserted that taking places in the councils is as close to the 'enemy' as republicans should be prepared to go. At the 1986 Sinn Féin Ard Fheis, Ruairí Ó Brádaigh echoed the argument of MacSwiney: 'with regards to Councils, Sinn Féin has always been in the councils and that is as near to the enemy system that we dare to go.'[40] In the state of Northern Ireland RSF do not presently contest council elections due to the 'test oath'. The declaration against terrorism, which is part of the Elected Authorities (Northern Ireland Act 1989), states:

> Part 1
> Form for inclusion in consent to nomination
> I declare that, if elected, I will not by word or deed express support for or approval of:
> (a) any organisation that is for the time being a proscribed organisation specified in [F1 Schedule 2 to the Terrorism Act 2000]; or
> (b) acts of terrorism (that is to say, violence for political ends) connected with the affairs of Northern Ireland.[41]

In 2011 a number of RSF members put themselves forward as candidates in the local council elections, including Geraldine Taylor in Belfast who commented 'they wouldn't accept our papers because we refused to sign the test oath'.[42] The organisation maintains its abstentionist policy in relation to Stormont and Leinster House. RSF member Mickey McGonigle was first elected as a councillor for Sinn Féin in 1983. McGonigle opposed the dropping of abstentionism in 1986 and was one of the founding members of RSF. He was a sitting councillor at the time of his resignation from Sinn Féin and has recalled:

> Now I got fair stick. They gave me wild stick. And I said, well now I'm not accepting Leinster House … and it's a thing that Dáithí Ó Conaill once said – any republican who goes into Leinster House, he goes in green, he turns yellow and he comes out rotten. But you see the ones that went into Stormont, they were rotten before they went into it.[43]

RSF do not have any elected councillors in Northern Ireland; however, they do have an elected councillor in the South, in Galway, namely Tomás Ó Curraoin. In the 2009 elections Ó Curraoin secured 1,387 first preference votes (8.42 per cent) of the vote in the Connemara constituency in Galway.[44] In the wake of the election the organisation's newspaper, *Saoirse* carried coverage of the victory and quoted Ó Curraoin:

> I will stand for the people. I will stand for their rights. I am a member of Republican Sinn Féin and as a result I am a 32-County man, but I will represent everyone, be it Catholic, Protestant or Dissenter, as Wolfe Tone said. I plan on representing everyone.[45]

In 2014 he went on to win 1,072 first preference votes (6.36 per cent) of the total vote.[46] Throughout his election campaigns in Galway, it has been very clear that Ó Curraoin is an RSF candidate. The ballot papers did not have 'RSF' alongside Ó Curraoin's name as the organisation does not recognise Leinster House and consequently is not registered as a political party in the South of Ireland, thereby its name cannot appear on the ballot papers. However, throughout his campaigns, Ó Curraoin consistently made reference to himself as an RSF candidate on local and national media, as well as in his election literature. It would therefore be untrue to the spirit of the campaign to suggest that he contested as an independent candidate, as some literature has suggested. In fact in 2011 a journalist advised Ó Curraoin that he should stand as an independent candidate as he would surely be elected, to which Ó Curraoin replied that he had no interest in contesting as anything other than a Republican Sinn Féin candidate. He has argued 'my role as a councillor, I suppose was to keep the name of Republican Sinn Féin on the agenda.'[47]

Ó Curraoin has acknowledged that not all those who voted for him are republicans. As a popular figure in Galway he has gained votes on a personal basis as well as from people who he has worked for on the ground. Ó Curraoin is prominent in GAA circles, being involved in his junior hurling club in the west of the county, to the present day. Ó Curraoin's independent affiliation on the ballot paper is in keeping with the traditional Sinn Féin position; prior to 1986 Sinn Féin candidates contested elections without the party name appearing on the ballot paper. The RSF message is dominated by references to continuity of the Sinn Féin organisation and claims that Provisional Sinn Féin should not use the name 'Sinn Féin'. Paramount in the party's narrative is an assertion of continuity with the pre-1986 organisation. It is therefore unsurprising that Ó Curraoin contested the election without the Republican Sinn Féin name appearing on the ballot paper. It is simply consistent with Sinn Féin practice pre-1986.

The broadcasting ban of 1988–94 in the North of Ireland and section 31 of the Broadcasting Act in the South from 1971–94 resulted in Sinn Féin's exclusion from media such as RTÉ. As recorded by Robert W. White in his biography of Ruairí Ó Brádaigh, 1974 was the first time after the outbreak of the latest phase of conflict in 1969, that Sinn Féin was able to gauge support in the South of Ireland through elections.[48] After distributing 100,000 copies of its election manifesto, Sinn Féin successfully grew its representation from twelve representatives in the nine counties to twenty-six representatives in fourteen counties (local government elections).[49] In this election the candidates could not be formally labelled as Sinn Féin on the ballot paper; however, there was no mistaking the fact that they were Sinn Féin candidates. Commenting on the election result, then Sinn Féin president Ruairí Ó Brádaigh stated 'I look forward to seeing the Sinn Féin councillors putting the Éire Nua policies before the people. I regard their achievements as a victory for the small man over the all-consumer society of big business and the gigantic forces of the E.E.C.'[50] The candidates were not permitted to contest on the ballot paper as 'Sinn Féin' due to the 1963 Electoral Act, which allowed only political parties registered with Leinster House to appear on the ballot paper. This requirement remained unchanged in the 1992 Electoral Act.[51]

Local elections: 'carrying the trenches of the enemy' (Terence MacSwiney, 1921)[52]

In the 2014 local council elections in Northern Ireland Sinn Féin gained 152,573 votes, which translated into 24.3 per cent of the total vote. The radical republican vote was minor in comparison. However, radical republicans did have some successes. While standing on an independent platform, Gary Donnelly, a prominent member of the 32CSM, topped the poll in the Derry and Strabane constituency with 1,154 votes. Also, in Mid-Ulster Barry Monteith, an independent republican candidate, received 1,458 first preference votes and was duly elected.[53] In Newry Mourne and Down, independent Davy Hyland, a former Sinn Féin MLA, secured 1,045 first preference votes and was elected. In Fermanagh and Omagh independent republican Bernice Swift secured 1,195 first preference votes and was also elected. In contrast, RNU and éirígí failed to get their candidates elected. RNU received 0.08 per cent of the vote and éirígí received 0.28 per cent. The Workers' Party received 0.16 per cent of the vote. Éirígí's election result was particularly disappointing for the party, which had fielded prominent candidates such as Pádraic MacCoitir and Máire Óg Drumm in West Belfast, both of whom were eliminated. [54] Dee Fennell, a prominent independent republican in Ardoyne in Belfast, was also eliminated.

Radical republicans have failed to make a significant dent in the Sinn Féin vote even at council level. However, Pádraic MacCoitir, who also contested the 2011 local elections for éirígí, has highlighted the tactical use of elections. He has argued that it is 'OK to have some stunts' and 'they show you are still there. Those éirígí ones, what are they doing?'[55] MacCoitir has stated that he and John McCusker (the éirígí candidate for the Lower Falls) felt that they had a good chance of winning at least one seat, possibly two, due to the feedback that they were getting on the ground. He has stated:

> I also believed that by standing in that election it would make people aware that this was an alternative to the status quo in our local areas, whether it be SDLP or Sinn Féin. And we achieved a fair bit of that even though we weren't elected of course. And that was one clear way in which we were able to measure our support.[56]

Éirígí attempted to gather support and to promote the organisation's stance through Easter commemorations, its website and periodicals which the party delivered throughout West Belfast, as well as articles in the *Andersonstown News*. However, MacCoitir has expressed the difficulty which éirígí faced regarding being labelled alongside other organisations as 'dissident' by the mainstream and the associated negative connotations. He has commented:

> The other thing that puts people off, at least publicly supporting us, is that there is fear among people which has been manifested over the past few years – the so-called dissident groups – you know, that éirígí is one of them. You used to have Sinn Féin spokespeople coming on and would have talked about different groups like the Continuity IRA, the REAL IRA and RNU, and the Societies and éirígí. They would always lump us in. Some media latched on and done the same … But then they don't mention us now in the same breath as they used to because they realise themselves, they were shooting themselves in the foot, that people did support us … people weren't lumping us in – with all due respect – to these so-called dissident groups.[57]

MacCoitir has referred to the public perception (which is propagated by the mainstream) as difficult but not something that the organisation 'lost any sleep over'. Similarly, Gary Donnelly of the 32CSM in Derry has commented on his election campaign:

We are being followed 24/7 by the PSNI in armoured land rovers with a rifle hanging out. So you picture – you are knocking at a door asking somebody to give you their vote and there's a land rover following the candidate. They don't want to be seen talking to you because their name goes down in a notebook and when they get out or go into their car to go to work or go down the shop they are pulled in and stopped.[58]

During his election campaign in 2011 Gary Donnelly was arrested on two occasions. His election agent was also arrested, as was his son. Under such conditions Donnelly deemed 10 per cent of the vote a success and stated 'you had all that, you had media censorship, but we still received 10 per cent'.[59]

Saoradh

In the 2016 Stormont Assembly elections the newly formed Saoradh articulated an abstentionist position and called on the electorate to boycott the election. At the organisation's first Ard Fheis in Newry in October 2016 party chairperson Davy Jordan stated 'Our history is littered with the failures of successive ventures into constitutional nationalism, as they were subsumed into the very systems they set out to overthrow.'[60] The Saoradh position stated that participation in Stormont elections would serve to legitimise an illegitimate parliament. However, the party's boycott of the election resulted in the status quo remaining unchallenged electorally, which may have contributed to party member (and current prisoner in Maghaberry) Nathan Hastings subsequently stating 'I think it would have been better if we'd just said nothing instead of telling people not to vote. People are going to vote because these people are making decisions which affect their lives.'[61] Therein lies the problem for radical republicans who promote an abstentionist position.

Independents

While radical republicans have achieved a small degree of electoral success, many have contested elections on an independent platform rather than as a stated member of their organisation. This has led Danny Morrison to state:

I mean I've always stood on a Sinn Féin ticket. So why wouldn't they stand on a Thirty-Two County Sovereignty Movement ticket? Why? Because they would be afraid of a poor vote or that dissident activity would hurt their vote. So they can't even publicly stand for what they stand for.[62]

The fact that individuals such as Donnelly have contested elections as independent candidates begs the question: are groups such as the 32CSM internally divided on electoral strategy? Or is it simply the case that candidates fear a low vote would reflect badly on their organisation? The honorary president of the

32CSM Phil O'Donoghue has provided an insight into this issue when commenting on Gary Donnelly's candidacy in Derry in 2011:

> We were not in agreement with him going forward. But as an individual he can go forward, but he would get no support from the Sovereign Thirty-Twos. We wouldn't be foolish enough to go forward as an election group because right now we would be battered into the ground and give our enemies all the ammunition they want. We have no intention of ever becoming a political party. Now an awful lot of people have done their damndest to get the name changed, to go into politics. Now these people are working to someone else's agenda. That's the way we look at it. But it's not going to happen.[63]

O'Donoghue has emphasised his personal support for Gary Donnelly; however, his candid remarks reflect the age-old internal divisions within republicanism regarding the tactical use of elections. Nathan Hastings, a former spokesperson of the 32CSM in Derry, has stated:

> In the 32s in Derry – Gonzo [Gary Donnelly] – there were discussions and a lot of people opposed him running. The word republican wasn't even on the ballot paper.[64]

RSF has also proven internally divided regarding the contesting of elections, as evidenced at the organisation's 2013 Ard Fheis during which a motion regarding contesting elections in the North of Ireland was present on the clár. As the speakers took to the podium on the issue, the organisation's president Des Dalton stated 'I ask you not to tie the hands of the Ard Chomhairle on elections.'[65] However, the 'slippery slope' argument was advanced at the podium in opposition to contesting future local elections in the North and the motion was defeated.

The republican mandate

Despite the election of radical republican candidates, republicans have continued to strongly assert the fact that the republican mandate does not come from the ballot box, as demonstrated by Dee Fennell in Ardoyne in North Belfast:

> I mean Tom Williams didn't have electoral strength behind him in the 1940s. The border campaign didn't have electoral strength. The IRA in the 1930s when they were being executed didn't have electoral strength. But their cause was no less legitimate.[66]

In an interview during his election campaign in 2013 Fennell commented:

> What I think I can do at a council level is give a voice and make the lives of people in this area, and New Lodge, Ligoniel, the Bone and the Cliftonville, make their lives better by actually impacting on facilities and things that do affect their lives, rather than Stormont which is really just a talking shop and throws money at problems

but doesn't actually be on the ground solving anything. And rather than actually Westminster which is obviously a foreign government and shouldn't even be in our country. … But I don't see legitimacy being based on electoral strength. Not by any stretch of the imagination.[67]

Reflecting the dominant sentiment around elections throughout radical republican circles, prominent Belfast republican Gerard Hodgins has stated 'Adolf Hitler was democratically elected. He got a mandate. So what?'[68] An alternative view has been presented by Anthony McIntyre:

Ultimately mandates have to matter. How else do you decide? … There are serious limitations but mandates must matter because in the absence of mandates, what do you get? Group decisions made by groups? Self-appointed groups? Where do they get their mandate from? Why do we even talk in terms of mandates if mandates don't matter?[69]

However, McIntyre has qualified his comments by stating that the issue must not be reduced to simple majoritarianism 'otherwise the majority will crush the minority'.[70]

The on-the-ground operation of radical republican groups has been determined by geography. As Kevin Cassidy's 'Organic intellectuals' states, Sinn Féin was adept at operating effectively at a local community level throughout the North of Ireland.[71] Cassidy has argued that the 'organic' quality in terms of providing individuals with roots in the community is what allows them to exercise leadership in that community. Cassidy has further argued that this culture, which is shared by community workers and Sinn Féin party activists, helps to generate legitimacy and electoral support for Sinn Féin. When considering the operation of non-mainstream republicanism (at a local level), it is evident that radical republicans are struggling to fulfil the traditional republican ethos of assuming community roles such as positions on residents' associations or other such bodies, due to the fact that Sinn Féin members are already ingrained throughout those positions. While radical republicans appear to have experienced a greater degree of success in this regard in locations such as Tyrone and Lurgan, Sinn Féin strongholds such as West Belfast have proven more difficult.

The ingrained position of Sinn Féin throughout republican and nationalist areas is a direct legacy of the historical nature of the relationship between those areas and the state; Sinn Féin often undertook roles which would be provided by the state in a normal society, the legacy of which has a direct impact on the organisation of radical republicans who fall beyond the mainstream. Radical republican Nuala Perry has commented on 'attempts to organise' in the Clonard area of West Belfast:

Clonard is nailed down. Nothing happens round here without the say so of Sinn Féin. Everything in this area is controlled by Sinn Féin. How people work and where people work in this area is controlled by Sinn Féin.[72]

Perry has claimed that businesses and taxi ranks in the area are aligned to Sinn Féin. Consequently, radical republicans are operating outside the mainstream institutions of the state in Northern Ireland, while simultaneously failing to take root at the local community level.

Bereft of support?

There is very limited survey evidence regarding support for radical republicans; however, the 2010 Economic and Social Research Council general election survey conducted by Jonathan Tonge revealed that 12 per cent of respondents from a nationalist community background declared support for RSF or the 32CSM.[73] Tonge has compared this level to two BBC Hearts and Minds polls which were conducted in 2002 and 2006, which indicated that those two organisations were supported by 7 per cent of nationalists.[74] As noted by Whiting, survey results tend to under-represent views which are deemed 'socially unacceptable'.[75] However, the surveys provide some indication for such groups, in the absence of further survey evidence. A further indication of support for republican groups is attendance at commemorations and public events organised by the groups. The RSF 1916 centenary commemoration took place in Dublin on 23 April 2016. The parade assembled at the garden of remembrance in Parnell Square and proceeded along O'Connell Street to the GPO. The *Irish Times* recorded attendance at the commemoration as up to 2,000 people.[76] It is contested whether attendance at commemorations can be an accurate indicator of support; however, the president of RSF, Des Dalton has argued that this large attendance demonstrated that 'people connected with it, not the pageantry' which was evident in the official state commemorations.[77] The assembled crowd largely stayed for the duration of the commemoration, including throughout the speeches which were given by John Joe McCusker, John Hunt and Des Dalton.[78]

A new Ireland

Interestingly, the chairperson of éirígí, Brian Leeson in Dublin, has offered an analysis on republicanism and internal flaws, regarding gathering support:

> In socialist republicanism … we believe revolutionary struggle has at least four distinct spheres of activity or four distinct areas in the form of the political, the cultural, the economic and the social; and what has tended to happen within republicanism is the focus is on one which is the political, and even narrows that down simply to the national element of political, and that [means] we have tremendous weaknesses within republicanism … You gather very little strength if you organise around a single issue and it's ignoring the fact that the struggle against imperialism is the struggle against capitalism.[79]

Leeson has warned 'the larger republican movements in the North seem to be maybe focused on the national question and you know we think that's a fundamental flaw.'[80] In contrast, the éirígí discourse has focused on present structural conditions and a rejection of capitalist conditions. Leeson has described history as 'just that. It's history.'[81] RNU and the RSM are closer in message to éirígí; in contrast to RSF and the 32CSM, which present a more nationalistic outlook. The éirígí message has encompassed the argument that there must be a 're-conquest of the cultural sphere'.[82] In this regard, éirígí has stated that the struggle for women's rights, language rights and against racism are all part of the same struggle.[83] The éirígí position has argued that a prioritising of socialist principles will prove inviting to the unionist position and Leeson has stated 'if the unionist population no longer receives a material benefit for supporting British rule. If the jobs in the shipyards are no longer there – possibly within that community there will be a bit of a rethink, possibly.'[84]

Radical republicans are keen to dispel the popular misconception that republicanism aims simply to unite the North with the South in its current form.[85] The radical republican narrative stresses the traditional republican position that a united Ireland would constitute a new configuration. Until 1983 Sinn Féin held the Éire Nua policy which was chiefly authored by Dáithí Ó Conaill and Ruairí Ó Brádaigh. The Éire Nua policy remains a prominent policy position of RSF and outlines a federalist configuration with each of the four provinces of Ireland possessing a level of autonomy. The policy would see the dissolution of the Republic of Ireland. Billy McKee in Belfast has argued:

> You see the way there's more corruption in the twenty-six counties than there is in any other part of the world … the whole country needs overhauled with honest men and I don't know where you're going to get them.[86]

The late Brendan Madden of RSF in Galway has recalled an incident from his childhood:

> Back when I was about twelve years of age when Seán South and Feargal O'Hanlon was shot in an ambush in the Six Counties and my mother always bought the republicans' paper – so that was the time that I started reading about Tone and Pearse and Connolly and all those people … But there's a bit more to it. It's the way your country is being ran and it's the way it's being regarded.[87]

Madden has argued 'we have the richest offshore territory in the world and we have given it away.'[88] Until his death in 2015 Brendan Madden was a prominent figure in his community in Galway as chairman of the gun club and a member of the local parish council. Madden was also known for his activism around turf rights. The EU laws around turf-cutting changed in the South of Ireland in 2013 and Madden has argued:

> The real issue is taking your property and without consulting you and that to me is like invading your country again. It's the same thing as what the British done when

they took our land. Now our own crowd are doing the exact same thing. But at least the British fought their way in. It was done this time by Irish.[89]

The mainstream narrative has frequently misinterpreted the republican desire for Irish unity as tantamount to simply joining the North and South of Ireland under one Dublin administration. Republicans reject the Southern state and Leinster House in the same manner in which they reject Stormont and the Northern state, both states being products of partition in 1921 under the Government of Ireland Act 1920. RSF councillor Tomás Ó Curraoin has stated:

> [In the twenty-six counties] we are under the lashes of the Free State but we always have the feeling here that you have it a bit easier than they have it in the Six Counties and hopefully someday they'll be all together in a united and free Ireland.[90]

The 32CSM (which shares the goals of RSF) has also asserted its opposition to the twenty-six-county state of the Republic of Ireland and has questioned the legality of the partition of Ireland, as evidenced through the legal challenge which the organisation took to the United Nations in 1998 (and then in 2001) which declared that Britain's sovereignty over the state of Northern Ireland is illegal. Joe Dillon in Skerries has commented 'in other words we are challenging the legitimacy of the Dublin government's constituted position as well'.[91]

Conclusion

At each juncture throughout Irish history, ideological shifts and moves within the Republican Movement have been accompanied by the cultivating of new terrain for support. Sinn Féin is targeting a much wider electoral constituency than its previous focus on the republican constituency. As recorded by John M. Regan, this was also the case with the treatyites in the 1920s. Cultivation of the non-Sinn Féin constituency was evident both electorally and 'in the process of manning the new institutions of the Provisional government'.[92] In the post-1998 period, Sinn Féin's incorporation into the mainstream institutions within Northern Ireland begs the question: will they eventually take their seats in Westminster, thus ending the long-held policy of abstentionism? When asked if this is a possibility Danny Morrison has stated 'I wouldn't support that. I would publicly condemn that. How can we argue that the Brits have no right to be in Ireland and then tell them how to run their country? There's nothing to be gained in it.'[93] Speculation is rife throughout the radical republican discourse that Sinn Féin will ultimately take its seats in Westminster.

As the centenary of 1916 approached multiple commemorations were planned throughout Ireland by various groups, including a group in Dublin called the 1916–21 Club, a veterans' group established in the 1940s. One of its founding aims was to bring together veterans from both sides of the Civil War divide. In the lead-up to the 1916 centenary, the dominant narrative of the Dáil was one which expressed concern that the official commemoration of 1916 should not emphasise the military aspect. Francie McGuigan, a prominent republican in Belfast, was present at a meeting of the 1916–21 Club in the planning stage of the commemoration, during which a member of the Club spoke about wearing the Easter Lilly, to which another member replied 'you can't do that because the Easter Lilly is associated with men of violence.'[94] Francie McGuigan has recalled that he stood up and stated:

> I think we are here to commemorate 1916 and if I'm not mistaken what the fuck was Connolly and Pearse at? You know it wasn't snowballs that they were throwing.[95]

McGuigan has stated, 'they don't want to have anything associated with republicanism you see. Today you are either Sinn Féin or a dissident.'[96]

Murphy has argued that 'Irish governments have been keen enough to celebrate the Easter Rising, without examining too closely what it represents.'[97] In the run-up to 2016 the Dublin government invoked history as a provider of legitimacy and a battle ensued between the various shades of green in Ireland regarding who are the legitimate inheritors of the flame. This decade of centenaries (of significant events in Irish history) is witnessing a contestation of ownership of the past and of the republican mantle. Speeches at republican commemorations throughout Ireland are reflecting this battle, as demonstrated at the RNU commemoration in Dundalk at Easter 2014 when the speaker addressing the crowd stated:

> Let us celebrate the fact that we and others have kept the faith and like our fathers before them, have not only regrouped and gathered here, but have gathered with increasing confidence and vigour, willing and capable of reclaiming and rebuilding revolutionary republicanism, promising to practice its principles and realising its full potential.[98]

RSF has argued that it possesses the true republican mantle, as demonstrated by the direct lineage to the Second Dáil Éireann, and is dismissive of claims by other groups that they are legitimate republican movements. During an 'education session' at the 2016 RSF Ard Fheis, Thomas Clarke, a member of RSF in Dublin stated 'no individual can survive without their memories. Without them we don't know who or what we are.'[99]

Notes

1 Nuala Perry, interview with the author, Belfast, 15 August 2013. When stating 'we' Nuala Perry is referring to individuals who have departed the Provisional Movement.
2 Event attended by the author.
3 Albert Allen, interview with the author, Belfast, 17 October 2013.

4 Peig King, interview with the author, Dublin, 26 July 2016.

5 Bowyer Bell, *The Secret Army* (1990), p. 31.

6 *Ibid.*, p. 32.

7 *Ibid.*, p. 33.

8 E. O' Malley, *The Singing Flame* (Dublin, Anvil Books Ltd, 1978), p. 177.

9 *Ibid.*, p. 177.

10 Hopkinson, *Green Against Green*, p. 180.

11 Regan, *Irish Counter-revolution*, pp. 103–4.

12 *Ibid.*, pp. 103–4.

13 Garvey secured 489 first preference votes and was not elected.

14 Pádraig Garvey, interview with the author, Killarney, 30 October 2013.

15 Anthony Ryan, interview with the author, Dublin, 5 May 2013. Anthony Ryan is the brother of Alan Ryan, who was a member of the 32CSM and was killed in September 2012 in Dublin. Anthony Ryan and the wider 32CSM have rejected what they call the 'demonisation' of Alan Ryan in the media.

16 In the 2014 council elections in Northern Ireland Sinn Féin received 152,573 first preference votes (24.3 per cent). In the 2017 Westminster election Sinn Féin secured 29.4 per cent of the vote (up 4.9 per cent on the previous election). In the 2016 general election in the South of Ireland Sinn Féin secured 13.8 per cent of the vote (twenty-three seats).

17 In *An Phoblacht* (31 October 1975) the following was printed regarding the role of Sinn Féin: 'The role of Sinn Féin is to assist that spearhead [Republican Movement], to back it on every occasion; whether it be as a protest movement in the streets or a political movement in the council, chamber, or assisting in a financial drive for the prisoners dependants, its role is to assist and inspire others to assist.'

18 Murray and Tonge, *Sinn Féin and the SDLP*.

19 McKearney, *The Provisional IRA*, p. 147.

20 Tonge, '"No-one likes us; we don't care"'.

21 Danny Morrison, interview with the author, Belfast, 7 May 2014.

22 *Ibid.*

23 *Ibid.*

24 *Ibid.*

25 B. Hanley, *The IRA: 1926–1936* (Dublin, Four Courts Press, 2002), pp. 153–5.

26 Bowyer Bell, *The Secret Army* (1990), p. 303; also see White, *Ruairí Ó Brádaigh*, p. 75.

27 White, *Out of the Ashes*. Also see White, *Ruairí Ó Brádaigh*.

28 Cited in White, *Out of the Ashes*, p. 177.

29 Cathleen Knowles was general secretary of Sinn Féin from 1980 until 1983, when she resigned along with Dáithí Ó Conaill and Ruairí Ó Brádaigh. She was general secretary of RSF from 1987 until 1993 and vice-president from 2006 to 2008. See *Saoirse: Irish Freedom*, No. 236 (December 2006), and *Saoirse: Irish Freedom*, No. 260 (December 2008). Also see White, *Ruairí Ó Brádaigh*, pp. 275, 292–3.

30 White, *Out of the Ashes*, p. 177.

31 *Ibid.*, p. 178.

32 Lita Campbell, interview with the author, Dublin, 21 October 2013.

33 Murray and Tonge, *Sinn Féin and the SDLP*.

34 Louise Minihan, interview with the author, Dublin, 1 February 2013.

35 Angela Nelson, interview with the author, Belfast, 17 September 2012.

36 In some constituencies in the North of Ireland Sinn Féin members stand outside polling stations handing mock ballot papers to voters. The mock ballot paper is an exact replica of the ballot paper which contains the numbers which Sinn Féin voters should put beside each candidate in order to maximise the Sinn Féin vote. For example, in the West Belfast constituency voters on the Lower Falls would be instructed to give their preferences to Sinn Féin candidates in a different order from voters in the Poleglass or Twinbrook areas. Consequently, under the Proportional Representation system Sinn Féin maximises the number of Sinn Féin candidates elected.

37 S. Doyle, 'West Belfast: Gerry Carroll tops the poll', *Irish News* (6 May 2016).

38 See footage at www.YouTube.com/watch?v=nzvpMlHuIrs. Accessed 24 July 2018.

39 MacSwiney, *Principles of Freedom*, p. 52.

40 Speech by Ruairí Ó Brádaigh opposing the motion on abstentionism (resolution 162), Sinn Féin Ard Fheis, Dublin (2 November 1986). https://youtu.be/QjXVJoUMVVc. Accessed 27 July 2018.

41 www.legislation.gov.uk. Accessed 24 July 2018.

42 Geraldine Taylor, interview with the author, Belfast, 14 October 2012.

43 Mickey McGonigle, interview with the author, Derry, 18 August 2013.

44 www.electionsireland.org. Accessed 24 July 2018.

45 'Victory in Galway', *Saoirse: Irish Freedom*, No. 267 (July 2009).

46 www.electionsireland.org. Accessed 24 July 2018.

47 Tomás Ó Curraoin, interview with the author, Galway, 4 June 2013. Similarly, in 2009 a journalist advised RSF president Des Dalton to contest the upcoming council election as an independent, to which Dalton replied that he would not contest as anything other than RSF (interview with the author, Dublin, 15 February 2013).

48 White, *Ruairí Ó Brádaigh*, p. 216.

49 *Ibid.*, p. 216. White has stated 'Sinn Féin distributed 100,000 copies of an election manifesto that called for a national housing fund to finance home purchases, comprehensive free medical service, and more local control over educational facilities. The manifesto called for self-government for the Gaeltacht.'

50 *Ibid.*, p. 216.

51 The 1963 Electoral Act stated: '(b) where a candidate is not the candidate of a political party registered in the Register of Political Parties, he shall be entitled to enter after his name on the nomination paper the expression "non-party" and, if he does so, the returning officer shall cause a statement of that expression to be specified in relation to the candidate on all the ballot papers and on notices.' Section 9, point 3(b). www.irishstatutebook.ie/eli/1963/act/19/enacted/en/print#sec6. Accessed 24 July 2018.

52 MacSwiney, *Principles of Freedom*.

53 In 2011 Monteith topped the poll.

54 Máire Óg Drumm is the daughter of prominent republican Máire Drumm. In 1975 Máire Óg Drumm was arrested and subsequently imprisoned for eight years

for possession of a revolver with intent. Due to political status, Drumm served four years.

55 Pádraic MacCoitir, interview with the author, Belfast, 4 October 2012.
56 *Ibid.*
57 *Ibid.*
58 Gary Donnelly, interview with the author, Derry, 21 August 2013.
59 *Ibid.*
60 Saoradh Ard Fheis, Newry, September 2016. See www.facebook.com/Saoradh/videos/334441560235968/. Accessed 20 July 2018.
61 Nathan Hastings, interview with the author, Maghaberry prison, 8 March 2017.
62 Danny Morrison, interview with the author, Belfast, 7 May 2014.
63 Phil O' Donoghue, interview with the author, Kilkenny, 4 November 2013.
64 Nathan Hastings, interview with the author, Maghaberry prison, 8 March 2017.
65 RSF Ard Fheis, Wynn's Hotel, Dublin, 2 November 2013. Attended by the author.
66 Dee Fennell, interview with the author, Belfast, 28 November 2013.
67 *Ibid.*
68 Gerard Hodgins, interview with the author, Belfast, 13 September 2012.
69 Anthony McIntyre, interview with the author, Dublin, 3 April 2013.
70 *Ibid.*
71 Cassidy, 'Organic intellectuals', pp. 341–56.
72 Nuala Perry, interview with the author, Belfast, 15 August 2013.
73 Tonge, '"No-one likes us; we don't care"'.
74 *Ibid.* The ESRC survey in 2010 was based upon a weighted representative sample of 1,200 face-to-face interviews.
75 Whiting, *Spoiling the Peace?*, p. 110.
76 P. Smyth, 'Dissident republicans mark 1916 Rising outside GPO', *Irish Times* (23 April 2016). www.irishtimes.com/news/ireland/irish-news/dissident-republicans-mark-1916-rising-outside-gpo-1.2622441?mode=sample&auth-failed=1&pw-origin=https%3A%2F%2Fwww.irishtimes.com%2Fnews%2Fireland%2Firish-news%2Fdissident-republicans-mark-1916-rising-outside-gpo-1.2622441. Accessed 24 July 2018.
77 Des Dalton, Ruairí Ó Brádaigh autumn school, Abbey Hotel, Co Roscommon, 23 September 2017. Attended by the author.
78 M. McGlinchey, 'Unbroken continuity', *Village Magazine* (July 2016).
79 Brian Leeson, interview with the author, Dublin, 1 February 2013.
80 *Ibid.*
81 *Ibid.*
82 *Ibid.*
83 *Ibid.*
84 *Ibid.*
85 During the Feakle talks in 1974 the republican representatives emphasised this point to the Protestant clergy. See White, *Out of the Ashes*, p. 119.
86 Billy McKee, interview with the author, Belfast, 8 August 2013.
87 Brendan Madden, interview with the author, Galway, 4 June 2013.
88 *Ibid.*

89 *Ibid.*
90 Tomás Ó Curraoin, interview with the author, Galway, 4 June 2013.
91 Joe Dillon, interview with the author, Skerries, 19 March 2013.
92 Regan, *Irish Counter-revolution*, p. 55.
93 Danny Morrison, interview with the author, Belfast, 7 May 2014.
94 This incident was recalled by Francie McGuigan, interview with the author, Belfast, 24 July 2013.
95 *Ibid.*
96 *Ibid.*
97 Murphy, 'Easter ethics', p. 343.
98 RNU speech at Easter commemoration, 26 April 2014.
99 RSF Ard Fheis, education session, 12 November 2016. Attended by the author.

Conclusion

Some of these centenaries are very inconvenient for the political establishment, particularly 1916. It reminds them, and it reminds people more importantly, of how far we've gone off track, how far we're removed from those high ideals and the kind of Republic that Pearse and Connolly spoke about and the kind of Republic that the Proclamation talks about. I mean for this state to even describe itself in the same terms I think is a travesty really and if you want to hold up a mirror, I think the comparison with this state and that Republic is a far from flattering one.
-Des Dalton, interview with the author, Dublin, 15 February 2013

So the onus is on you if you're a dissident or a critic, the onus is on you to say how it can be done differently and what are you going to do, because if you read the bulk of dissident publications on Twitter or on Facebook it is obsessional, 90 per cent of it is about Sinn Féin.
-Danny Morrison, interview with the author, Belfast, 7 May 2014

Introduction

This book offers an analysis of the ideology, tactics and motivations of what is commonly referred to as 'dissident republicanism'. Based on ninety interviews throughout Ireland with non-mainstream republicans, this work has attempted to enter the psyche of republicans, through their own words. This work rejects the term 'dissident' as inaccurate and unhelpful; rather, it locates republicans within the long trajectory of Irish republicanism and has adopted the term 'radical republican' to refer to the group of individuals and organisations which reject the status quo in Ireland and fall beyond the dominant 'mainstream'. The wide spectrum of interviewees is reflective of the heterogeneous nature of radical republicanism and reflects differences in location, age, gender, occupation and group membership (or independent status). The large body of interview material amassed has allowed for the extraction of a cohesive 'radical republican' narrative which has emphasised the following themes: a belief in 'betrayal' by the Provisional leadership; a rejection of the authoritarian nature of the Provisional Movement (specifically an inability to express dissenting views from within); a rejection of Provisional Sinn Féin's journey into constitutionalism (and away from republican ideology); a rejection of the post-ceasefire development of Sinn Féin politics; the assertion of traditional republican ideology; a rejection of electoral mandates; the assertion of legitimacy rooted in 1916 and 1798; and a rejection of the mainstream normalisation agenda in Northern Ireland.

1986: the emergence of modern-day 'dissidents'

When Ruairí Ó Brádaigh led a walkout from the Sinn Féin Ard Fheis in 1986 (and subsequently formed RSF) it signalled the beginning of what the mainstream has termed 'dissident republicanism'. Radical republicans who were active in the Republican Movement prior to the split have documented that period as complex and 'messy'. During the period leading to the 1986 split, the issue of prisoners had assumed a central role, predominantly through the 1980–81 Hunger Strikes.

When referring to that period, contemporary radical republican discourse has emphasised a contested narrative regarding prisoners; non-mainstream republicans have developed a discourse which suggests that prisoners were 'used' at various points to convince the general membership of the movement to accept a fundamental change in position. The late Gerry McKerr, who was a prominent member of the Provisional Movement in Lurgan, has recalled an incident from 1986 when he attended a football match in Davitt Park:

> When a guy came in and said, I knew who he was, I had an idea why he was there and he tapped me on the shoulder and whispered 'Are you with us or against us?' I said 'Explain to me what you're talking about.' I had a fair idea what was happening and he said 'All the prisoners have agreed that we enter Leinster House.' Says I, 'That's the thin edge of the wedge.'[1]

When the man reiterated that the prisoners supported it, McKerr replied 'but what about those who are still operational? Is their opinion asked?'[2] McKerr continued 'the reason the prisoners were only asked – they were told – Sinn Féin went into them with "if you support this we'll have you released."'[3]

McKerr's recollections are reflective of the wider discourse propagated by former members of the Provisional Movement who are now radical republicans. They have expressed frustration regarding the intolerance of dissenting views within the Provisional Movement. McKerr, who had occupied a senior position within the movement, was aggrieved that his opinion was not sought. Further, he expressed resentment that he was not at the 1986 Ard Fheis, claiming that he was not permitted delegate status. McKerr has stated that he did not 'associate' with Ó Brádaigh after the 1986 Ard Fheis, stating that:

> When the division came there was a meeting called. All the Sinn Féin cumainn would have come along and where I disagreed with Ó Brádaigh and Dáithí Ó

Conaill and those guys was that they decided to walk out. I maintain you should have stayed in and fought your corner because the Ard Fheis then was loaded. There were people asked who had just formed cumainn and they were asked to send delegates and there were others who disagreed [with the Adams–McGuinness position on the dropping of abstentionism] who were not asked.[4]

For this reason, McKerr remained independent after his departure from the Provisional Movement until his death in 2015.

A nuanced description of the 1986 period is also provided by members of the 32CSM who have stated that they fundamentally objected to the ending of abstentionism; however, they remained within the Provisional Movement for tactical reasons, including the large arsenal of weapons which had been procured by the Provisional IRA. This begs the question of why, upon their departure from the Provisional Movement, these members went on to form the 32CSM rather than joining RSF. Between 2010 and 2013 the leadership of the 32CSM made approaches to the RSF leadership in an attempt to establish a working relationship; however, these approaches proved unsuccessful. While RSF and the 32CSM share the same goal of sovereignty, there is clear ideological water between the two organisations, which is particularly evident through RSF's absolutist rejection of any engagement with the state. Further, the RSF code of conduct and a resolution passed at the 2006 Ard Fheis prohibit any links with other organisations claiming to be the Republican Movement.

RSF and the 32CSM have continued to assert the traditional ideological republican position, drawing their legitimacy from 1916 and 1798. The more recently formed éirígí and RNU have rooted their legitimacy in more contemporary events and look less to 1916 and 1798. They have rejected such historical determinism in favour of republicanism which is grounded within contemporary structural conditions, that is, a rejection of capitalism and neo-liberalism.

All radical republican groups and independents are united around the 'right' to Irish sovereignty. However, division has surfaced regarding how that right should be exercised. Therefore, the radical republican discourse is interspersed with competing conceptualisations of how to express 'dissent'. This in part was reflected in the nature of the various departure points during which individuals broke from the Provisional Movement.

Independents: the suppression of dissent

Individuals who have left the Provisionals in more recent years (after the formation of RSF and latterly the 32CSM) have centred their opposition to the Provisional Movement on a rejection of the authoritarian nature of the movement; this is particularly evident among individuals who are classed as independent republicans. Prominent radical republicans, such as the late Tony Catney, have highlighted their experience within the Provisional IRA regarding the suppression of dissent

as the main reason for their departure, rather than ideological objections. This is
a significant revelation which aims to contribute to an understanding of the body
of radical republicans which has emerged in the post-1998 period (after major
ideological changes). It contributes to our understanding of why individuals who
are now prominent radical republicans stayed with the Provisional Movement
or Sinn Féin throughout significant shifts in position, such as acceptance of the
ending of abstentionism, the ceasefires, the Mitchell Principles, the Good Friday
Agreement and acceptance of the PSNI. This phenomenon is particularly evident
among radical republicans who were supportive of the PIRA ceasefires in the
1990s, only to depart the movement or party at a later date.

Tommy McKearney, who is critical of a current armed campaign, has framed
his criticism of Sinn Féin around what happened within the movement in the
post-ceasefire period and has argued 'it was at that stage that I would tend to
differ with the politics of and analysis of the Provisional Movement, Sinn Féin
movement. My differences are around the distance and the drift and the charac-
ter of the response from the Sinn Féin party thereafter.'[5] Therefore the often simplistic definition of republican 'dissidents' as anti-peace process or supportive of
an armed campaign is an over-simplification which does not capture the reality
or the complexity of the radical republican world. McKearney has noted, 'what
I do argue is the Provisionals smashed the Orange state.'[6] He has also described
the ending of the PIRA campaign as a 'rational decision' and has argued that they
'didn't really have any other option'; however, 'the question then became how to
manage the situation around that and after that'.[7] McKearney has summed up
his rejection of Sinn Féin by stating that they 'have now come to be the representatives of the Catholic population'[8] and has stated that this is anathema to the
republican philosophy of uniting 'Protestant, Catholic and Dissenter' as stated
by Wolfe Tone, the founding father of Irish republicanism.

It has emerged that many republicans remained within the wider Provisional
Movement out of a sense of loyalty and camaraderie that is present throughout
social movements. In the Provisional Movement, individuals were operating
within a highly authoritarian structure where there was an expectation to toe the
party line. Anthony McIntyre, a former member of the Provisional Movement
in Belfast, has stated:

> I felt that what we had in the Republican Movement, both the army and the party,
> were vertical structures of communication and that we could only speak up and
> they could speak down and that what we needed was something else, a mechanism
> whereby we could be able to speak to everyone, the whole grassroots, the horizontal
> structures of the organisation, which they denied because they knew that the vertical
> structures were the means of controlling thought on the ground.[9]

Since 2015 a number of Sinn Féin councillors have resigned from the party, crit-
icising the culture of the organisation. In September 2017 the *Limerick Leader*

published an article titled 'Limerick councillor resigns from "toxic and hostile" Sinn Féin', which detailed the resignation of Lisa Marie Sheehy from the party and quotes Sheehy as stating 'I cannot stand behind a party that does not take its membership's valid concerns seriously.'[10] Radical republicans have highlighted these resignations as further proof of the authoritarian culture of Sinn Féin and the continued inability to express individual opinions.

The winding down of the IRA

Former Provisionals such as Anthony McIntyre have asserted their opposition to the direction in which the Provisional leadership has led the movement. Since 2005 a body of literature has begun to emerge from radical republicans, including McIntyre, O'Rawe and McKearney. The literature has presented a contested narrative regarding the raison d'être for the Provisionals' campaign – a position which has proven central to the radical republican discourse. Consequently, contested narratives regarding this period have produced diametrically opposed interpretations of the significance of altered structural conditions within the state of Northern Ireland. The Sinn Féin narrative is presently dominated by the significance of such change. Sinn Féin has emphasised the end of discrimination which saw Catholics as second-class citizens and continues to highlight the enshrinement of 'parity of esteem' in the Good Friday Agreement.

The Sinn Féin discourse has argued that the raison d'être for continuing an armed campaign has been removed due to the ability to pursue republican objectives through different means. Radical republican discourse has rejected Sinn Féin's justification for the PIRA armed campaign and consequently argues that altered structural conditions within the state of Northern Ireland do not impact upon the republican project. Rejection of the Sinn Féin position regarding the IRA campaign proved a central theme throughout the interviews. Largely, interviewees expressed anger at any suggestion that the PIRA campaign was waged for anything less than sovereignty.

A further point of contention between the Provisional and radical republican narratives is the question of an overall strategy hatched by the Provisional leadership to wind down the IRA campaign. While denied by Sinn Féin, the radical republican narrative is permeated with the line of thought that there was a deliberate direction in which the leadership were steering the movement. Such thought is evidenced throughout literature produced by radical republicans such as Richard O'Rawe's *Blanketmen* and *Afterlives* and Anthony McIntyre's *Good Friday: The Death of Irish Republicanism.*[11] In McIntyre's book he recalls the Anne Kennedy memorial lecture delivered by Ed Moloney in 2008 at the Cuirt International Festival of Literature in Galway: 'the packed town hall was told that Gerry Adams' alternative to the armed struggle had been in place for years, even when others were racking their brains trying to escalate the war.'[12]

Provisional Sinn Féin and commentators such as Danny Morrison have vehemently rejected suggestions from radical republicans that an overall plan was in place from the 1980s; and contestation of this fact has dominated much of the debate between the Provisional and radical republican arenas. Morrison, the former director of publicity for Sinn Féin, has argued:

> If you had asked me in 1981 that in 2001 Sinn Féin would be sitting in the power-sharing administration I wouldn't have believed you. I mean back then I saw the electoral strategy as being one in support of armed struggle … people who ascribe to us this Machiavellian plan, or this was part of a bigger plan to go down that particular road – that is not true.[13]

The slippery slope

The organising principles (and culture) of republican groups have been influenced by the perceived problems and failings of the Provisional Movement and Sinn Féin. Individual experiences within the Provisional Movement have resulted in the adoption of absolutist positions in an attempt to avoid the 'slippery slope' to constitutionalism. The RSF constitution states that the organisation can only recognise Leinster House or Stormont on the basis of 100 per cent of the vote at an Ard Fheis in favour of such a change, as stated by Geraldine Taylor:

> You know you'll never get 100 per cent of people. There's always somebody will vote against it. But we have that embedded … so people can trust us to say we will never ever recognise Leinster House, Stormont and Westminster because it's there in black and white in our constitution that we can't.[14]

This protection embedded within the RSF constitution is arguably a reaction to the experience of individuals within the Sinn Féin and IRA movement prior to the 1986 split. Radical republicans continue to warn against reformism and compromise of the republican position. However, there exists a danger of everything being elevated to the level of 'principle'. Within this context there exists such a disparate range of views within radical republicanism that there is no coherent policy or strategy regarding a way forward.

Within RSF this absolutist strain of thought has played out regarding republican parades, as demonstrated in chapter two. The RSF organisation has also placed significant emphasis on 'due process' being afforded to any members who have complaints about the organisation. It is clear that some of the groups spend a significant amount of time dealing with internal matters such as conflict between members; it appears that groups are affording such time and energy in this area as a reaction to experiences within the Provisionals where (it is argued by radical republicans) dissenting views were not tolerated, often resulting in an absence of 'due process'. However, it may be asked, are radical groups getting so bogged down in internal conflict, inquiries and complaints that it is inhibiting moving forward?

While RSF has a rigid organisational structure, Brian Leeson, the chairperson of éirígí, has emphasised the flat structure of éirígí which is a rejection of the authoritarian nature of the Provisional Movement. Leeson has stated 'I suppose our organisational model has been influenced by the sort of libertarian thinking, or our analysis of how organisations can be corrupted by small cliques at the top, so we put in a number of safeguards which to my knowledge no republican organisation has, or certainly didn't at the time we organised.'[15] Similarly, Saoradh has stated that it will rotate its leadership. At the party's second Ard Fheis in November 2017, the chairperson, Davy Jordan, announced that he would stand down at the next Ard Fheis and Nuala Perry has stood down as vice-chair. It is probable that Saoradh have introduced this rotation policy to avoid the 'cult of the personality' which has formed a central thread throughout criticism of the Provisional Movement. The radical republican narrative around 'betrayal by the Provisional leadership' places an emphasis on specific personalities at the top of the organisation.

The high number of 'independents' in radical republicanism can also be explained through a rejection of the authoritarian nature of the Provisional Movement. Numerous independents have cited their experience within the Provisional IRA or in Sinn Féin as discouraging them from joining any organisation. Many independents have emphasised the value they place on their freedom to operate outside organisational structures in terms of writing or expressing views.

Legitimacy

The current message of Sinn Féin places an emphasis on the party's strong electoral mandate, particularly within the North of Ireland. In contrast, republican groups (collectively) do not seek an electoral mandate, nor do they draw their legitimacy at the polls. Rather, groups have taken their legitimacy from the 'illegal occupation' of the North of Ireland and have drawn their lineage back to 1916. The most recently formed group, Saoradh, announced that it will not be contesting elections. In February 2017 *The Pensive Quill* published an interview by Martin Galvin with Saoradh member Packy Carty during which Carty stated 'we're taking an approach from outside of the British institutions and we're asking people not to vote. We're asking people to vote with their feet and stay at home.'[16] The Saoradh position has rejected the significance of electoral mandates and has stated that voting in elections simply serves to legitimise the partitionist institutions of Stormont and Leinster House. Carty's reference to 'voting with their feet by staying at home' is a pointed statement which illustrates the party's rejection of elections (to the illegitimate institution of Stormont) as a 'democratic process'.

As illustrated in chapter four the radical republican narrative does not view republicanism and liberal democratic values as incompatible. Radical republicans often claim to act on 'behalf of the people'; however, the low level of public support for radical republican groups proves problematic in this respect. Sinn Féin has maintained an electoral grip on the nationalist community throughout the North of Ireland, which is largely fearful of any return to violence; public perception has largely viewed 'dissident' republicanism as synonymous with armed violence. Independent republican Tommy McKearney has argued that:

> With a resumption of armed struggle deeply unpopular among a majority of republicans, advocates of physical force are in practice, diverting attention from the failures of Sinn Féin to make meaningful progress through its engagement in the Assembly and in the context of economic catastrophe for tens of thousands of working people as neo-liberalism runs aground.[17]

McKearney's analysis is reflective of a current throughout radical republicanism which focuses criticism of Sinn Féin on how the party has developed in the post-1998 period and what it has achieved, as the largest representative of the nationalist community in the North of Ireland (since 2001).

Gerard Hodgins, an independent republican in Belfast, has stated that he is not opposed to Provisional Sinn Féin's entering Stormont or signing up to the policing board, and has argued:

> Once you go into a political system and you have your political power you are going to have to do them things. My criticism of them would be that they are not delivering anything. Whenever they go into Stormont, whenever we have an election and they meet in Stormont, there is brilliant co-operation between them in divvying up the best-paid jobs with the best pensions and the best fringe benefits, and then after that the co-operation ends and it's back to the trenches.[18]

Arguments presented by republicans such as McKearney and Hodgins have highlighted a recurrent argument throughout Irish republicanism regarding 'reform' versus revolutionary or radical change, which in essence sums up a fundamental division between the Provisional and so-called 'dissident' worlds. McKearney has argued:

> They have bought into the settlement. As it stands they are bound by the prevailing winds from London … their economic strategy is merely the administration of, at best the tinkering with, the decisions of London.[19]

Radical republicans reject the dominant narrative which suggests that revolutionary change is not realisable. Republicans have highlighted the fact that there has yet to be a Bill of Rights. They have also proven critical of policing, arguing that the PSNI is 'more of the same' and they have expressed opposition to what they describe as the internment in Maghaberry and Portlaoise prisons of republicans who fall beyond the status quo. Hodgins has argued:

They are now acquiescing in, I would call it internment and persecution of republicans simply because they don't sing off the same Sinn Féin hymn sheet. I mean
Martin Corey and Marian Price are not a threat to state security in any shape or
form … they know these people are not a threat. Yet they're keeping them in prison
as a warning to everybody. And Sinn Féin acquiesces in that.[20]

Martin Óg Meehan, formerly of RNU in Belfast, voted yes for the Good Friday
Agreement. Meehan was a member of Sinn Féin from 1984. He has argued
that the Provisional Movement compromised core principles, not regarding the
armed campaign but regarding its 'socialist economic principles', and has stated:

I was deluded into believing that it [the GFA] was a transitional arrangement and
that there would be a massive peace dividend for working-class communities in the
Six Counties, and based on that I voted yes for the Good Friday Agreement because
it was an army order at the time to do so and I just followed orders.[21]

England's difficulty is Ireland's opportunity: Brexit

Currently, republicanism is experiencing a 'low ebb' which radical republicans
have compared to other periods throughout Irish history, such as the 1950s
border campaign after which everything changed from 1969. McIntyre has commented 'I think things will change if there's a cataclysmic event, which is unforeseen at the minute … we can only predict the trajectories from what we can see,
and the trajectories do not take us to a crisis of transformative potential.'[22] It is
unlikely that there will be another 'Bloody Sunday' or large-scale internment
which would radically alter the context in which radical republicans are operating. Radical republicans have failed to gather public momentum around the issue
of Irish sovereignty and are heavily reliant on ideologically motivated republicanism. However, in an interview with the author in 2010 Séamus Mallon, the
former deputy first minister of Northern Ireland, quoted Harold Macmillan:
'events dear boy, events'.[23] As asserted by Mallon, unforeseen events can radically
alter the political landscape, which is what happened in June 2016 when 51.9
per cent of the electorate in the 'UK and Gibraltar' voted in favour of leaving the
European Union (Brexit). Brexit has significantly altered the landscape in which
radical republicans are operating and has brought a contemporary relevance to
the radical republican message. Brexit has provided a much needed 'shot in the
arm' for republicanism and has put the issue of the Irish border and sovereignty
back into mainstream debate. When commenting on the significance of Brexit
RSF patron Peig King has stated: 'This is the time. It's the best chance we've had
since 1916.'[24]

A central part of the normalisation agenda in the post-Good Friday
Agreement period was the removal of the hard border between the North and
South of Ireland. Brexit has reopened the question of a hard border and has

served as a stark reminder that the border is constitutionally still there: as stated by Saoradh's chairperson Davy Jordan at the organisation's second Ard Fheis in November 2017, 'there is a generation of young people who don't remember the physical manifestation. With a hard border you can see that the island is partitioned, so on that point of view we would very much see it as something to exploit.'[25]

Contested narratives on Brexit

On 28 August 2016 a debate took place in the Royal College of Surgeons in Dublin which was organised by the 1916 Clubs.[26] The debate was titled 'Brexit – what does this mean for the North?'[27] Participants in the debate were Des Dalton from RSF, Neal Richmond from Fine Gael, Darragh O'Brien from Fianna Fáil and Matt Carthy from Sinn Féin. The debate provided an insight into the contested narrative around Brexit between radical republicanism and the mainstream parties in the South of Ireland. Significantly, during the debate the Fine Gael representative asked 'would the world really stop spinning if we were to re-join the Commonwealth? We can't afford a united Ireland.'[28] Fianna Fáil's Darragh O'Brien described Sinn Féin's call for a border poll as a 'publicity stunt' and stated 'a referendum should be called when it is clear a vote will pass. There is no evidence this would pass.' Matt Carthy, an MEP for Sinn Féin, described Brexit as 'the most important political issue facing the people on the island of Ireland today … Brexit has changed everything.' Matt Carthy also called for the Irish government to provide a Green Paper on Irish unity, stating 'constitutional change is now in the hands of the people in the North and South'.

Interestingly, the speakers from Sinn Féin and RSF couched their positions within democratic principles. Carthy argued, 'I've spent my life hearing you must respect the democratic wishes of the people of the North. I say that right back. We must now uphold that.' The RSF president Des Dalton argued 'what democracy is about is breaking the connection with England. The British system is highly centralised and the EU was a further extension of that.'[29] Dalton framed his arguments on Brexit around the sovereignty and independence of Ireland and stated that Brexit 'highlighted the fundamental highly undemocratic nature of the UK'. The fact that the majority of people in the North voted 'remain' (56 per cent) is irrelevant to the wider UK vote which voted 'leave'.

The rare debate proved significant as it demonstrated how the radical republican organisation RSF frames and conceptualises the issues of Brexit, sovereignty and the nation state, in contrast to the mainstream parties.[30] Interaction between the speakers on the platform demonstrated arguments which strike to the heart of what democracy means and how republican arguments relate to democratic values; a theme which is explored in chapters four, five and seven in relation to the work of Irvin, Shanahan and Murphy. Dalton's emphasis on the 'consent principle' as a 'unionist veto' struck to the heart of the fundamental contestation between the Provisional and radical republican positions. Brexit has catapulted the issue of the Irish border to prominence throughout Ireland and the UK as the mainstream grapples with questions around the nature of the border.

UK election 2017

The political landscape of the North of Ireland was further altered in the wake of the UK Westminster election which took place on 8 June 2017. The Conservative Party under the leadership of Theresa May failed to secure an overall majority; consequently talks began between the Conservative Party and the DUP on 9 June 2017 regarding forming a government. On 26 June a 'confidence and supply' deal was reached between the two parties where it is understood that the DUP will support the Conservatives in major votes in Westminster; an arrangement which included a promise of an extra £1 billion to the North of Ireland. With the DUP now in government in Westminster, the political landscape was radically altered for Sinn Féin, whose narrative has emphasised the party's all-Ireland representation including seats in Dáil Éireann. Danny Morrison has stated 'you have to ask why Sinn Féin would go back into an executive when the DUP has a disproportionate influence on the British government.'[31] A fundamental principle of the Good Friday Agreement is the position of the British government as 'neutral' in the context of the consent principle. As Morrison has pointed out, the DUP–Conservative pact calls this aspect into question.[32]

2017: the collapse of Stormont

On 10 January 2017, in an emotional interview with the media, Martin McGuinness resigned as the deputy first minister of the state of Northern Ireland, thus collapsing the power-sharing administration at Stormont. McGuinness cited the DUP's conduct regarding the controversy around the Renewable Heat Incentive (RHI) scheme as the main reason for his resignation. Other critical issues highlighted were funding for inquests into killings during the recent conflict and the decision to end funding for an Irish-language project.[33] Tellingly, McGuinness's resignation letter stated 'At times I have stretched and challenged republicans and nationalists in my determination to reach out to our unionist neighbours. It is a source of deep personal frustration that those efforts have not always been reciprocated by unionist leaders … The equality, mutual respect and all-Ireland approaches enshrined in the Good Friday Agreement have never been fully embraced by the DUP.'[34] Interestingly McGuinness also wrote 'over this period successive British governments have undermined the process of change by refusing to honour agreements, refusing to resolve the issues of the past while imposing austerity and Brexit against the wishes and best interests of the people here.'[35]

Since the collapse of the Assembly in January 2017, the Sinn Féin narrative has been dominated by references to the need to 'protect the Good Friday Agreement', which it argues has been undermined. Commenting on McGuinness's resignation interview, Jim Gibney has stated 'in his last interview, before his illness overwhelmed him, he left behind the most telling of all comments which is now a watchword for republicans – There will be no return to the status quo.'[36] At the time of writing, a public inquiry into the RHI scheme is on-going; however, the particulars of this 'scandal' are not as relevant as the fact that the Assembly has collapsed and what this illustrates about the nature of the working relationship between the DUP and Sinn Féin. The Sinn Féin message has argued that the DUP are not respecting the equality of nationalists, as McGuinness's resignation letter demonstrates. In August 2017 Danny Morrison, a former director of publicity for Sinn Féin, argued that 'Sinn Féin's support base had become disillusioned with power-sharing because unionists failed to reciprocate outreach gestures from the likes of former Deputy First Minister Martin McGuinness.'[37] Morrison also stated 'it appeared to me, even at that stage [RHI], that Sinn Féin was still trying to preserve things but I believe the base had shifted.'[38] Morrison's assessment leads to the question: are Sinn Féin coming under pressure from the traditionally republican base on the ground? Undoubtedly, radical republicans will cite the Assembly's collapse (yet again) as evidence that Northern Ireland is a failed political entity.

While united in their rejection of power-sharing at Stormont, radical republicans have failed to articulate a coherent strategy regarding the significant number of unionists within the North of Ireland who will not concede to Irish unity. RSF have put forward their Éire Nua programme which encompasses a federalist approach where the four provinces of Ireland would each have a level of autonomy, therefore providing unionists in Ulster with a level of power at a local provincial level. However, unionists appear presently unresponsive to the Éire Nua policy and also significantly reject any vote on Irish unity which would take place on a thirty-two-county basis; the unit of determination (the thirty-two counties) is a fundamental rock on which the radical republican position rests. The unit of determination has proven a dominant point of contention between radical republicans and Sinn Féin, whose current strategy prioritises unionist persuasion (namely unionist outreach) and a border poll on unity.

Criminality

Arguably, the most significant challenge to contemporary radical republicanism is the mainstream narrative which links so-called 'dissident' republican groups to criminality. Some groups have rejected membership applications on the basis of the individual being connected to criminality, or even connected to someone involved in criminal behaviour. Groups recognise the fundamental threat posed to republicanism of 'dissident groups' becoming synonymous with 'criminality' in the public perception.

Historically the IRA campaign has not received mass support; however, crucially it has found doors open to volunteers from individuals or families who were not necessarily republican. History is littered with instances of Fine Gael, Fianna Fáil and SDLP homes sheltering republicans. An illustration of this fact was demonstrated recently in the story of Dermot McNally from Lurgan in County Armagh, who in 1983 escaped from Long Kesh prison.[39] After escaping, McNally went to Sligo, where he was sheltered by local people for several years and has recalled 'some of these people would have been very wealthy people, business people, some of them Fine Gael people, some of them Fianna Fáilers ... their whole lives could have been ruined if I'd been captured in their house.'[40]

McNally's recollections support other historical narratives regarding the sheltering of republicans. Louise Minihan, a former councillor in Dublin and current member of éirígí, has argued 'we have to clean the name of republicanism up because it has been dragged through the gutter by certain elements who claim to be republican.'[41] Radical republicans have argued that they have withstood imprisonment by the state, North and South, and state policies aimed at eradicating republicanism; however, republicanism could not withstand the loss of public support on a basis that it is viewed as mere 'criminality'.

Conclusion

Maurice Dowling, a member of RSF in Tralee, has argued that the public are confused regarding republicanism at present and has stated:

> The Free Staters, they'll get the publicity anyway. You see a lot of people don't realise, they don't know the difference. That's a lot of the problem as well. Even talking to them they'd be agreeing with you but they'd still be supporting the other crowd.[42]

Dowling has argued that a portion of the general public are confused about who the republicans are and the difference between the Provisionals and so-called 'dissidents'. Sinn Féin's journey from revolutionary movement to constitutional party has seen its absorption into the structures of the state of Northern Ireland, notably occupying roles on the policing boards – providing a significant interface between the Provisional and radical republican worlds. A central argument throughout the radical republican narrative is that Sinn Féin is no longer republican, nor is its electoral mandate a republican mandate. This was reflected by Francie McGuigan in Belfast: 'at least De Valera, when he left the Republican Movement, had the decency to change the name. He didn't try and take "Sinn Féin" with him.'[43]

Presently, radical republicanism can be characterised by a high level of individual movement between organisations, which is not conducive to the establishment and sustainable development of radical groups. During the course of this study, a number of individuals who had given an interview as a member of one organisation then moved to another organisation or became independent. Radical republicans are struggling to operate within a context in which Sinn Féin has largely held on to the republican 'brand' and the party has maintained a strong hold in local communities, particularly throughout the North of Ireland.[44] Martin Óg Meehan has argued 'Sinn Féin do not own republicanism no matter what they say and what they do.'[45] Radical republicans (both violent and non-violent) are aware of the lack of progress made towards advancing republican goals. At present, a significant aim of radical republicanism is simply to 'keep the flame burning' for the next generation, as illustrated by Kevin Hannaway in Belfast: 'mankind has only been able to move forward because the torch of freedom when [it] flickered lowest – there were those who at the cost to life itself stood forward and passed it on ablaze to the next generation. I would tend to replace mankind with republicanism.'[46]

Arguably, republicans are operating in a context of unprecedented hostility and public opposition where a war-weary public has failed to make a connection between republican ideology and their daily lives. However, a central premise of the radical republican campaign is the continued assertion of ideological republicanism coupled with disruption of the 'normalisation' process. Radical republicans are set to remain a permanent feature of the Irish political landscape. As stated in the (often quoted) graveside oration of O'Donovan Rossa in August 1915 by Patrick Pearse, 'Ireland unfree shall never be at peace'. In the current context, the words of Terence MacSwiney seem a particularly apt reflection on the position of radical republicanism: 'if we want full revenge for the past, the best way to get it is to remain as we are. As we are, Ireland is a menace to England.'[47]

Notes

1 Gerry McKerr, interview with the author, Lurgan, 22 August 2013.
2 *Ibid.*
3 *Ibid.*
4 *Ibid.*
5 Tommy McKearney, interview with the author, Belfast, 4 October 2012. Tommy McKearney is an independent republican who is a member of the Independent Workers' Union. McKearney departed the Provisional IRA (he was never a member of Sinn Féin) in 1986. He has stated that 'I had no problem with ending abstentionism. In '86 I was arguing that in the absence of an ideology there was an almost default position of ending up populist opportunistic, centre-right, pro-nationalist … I've seen nothing to change my mind.' *Ibid.*

6 *Ibid.*

7 *Ibid.*

8 *Ibid.*

9 Anthony McIntyre, interview with the author, Dublin, 3 April 2013.

10 Á. Fitzgerald, 'Limerick councillor resigns from "toxic and hostile" Sinn Féin', *Limerick Leader* (5 September 2017). www.limerickleader.ie. Accessed 24 July 2018.

11 See also Moloney, *Voices from the Grave.*

12 McIntyre, *Good Friday*, pp. 303–8.

13 Danny Morrison, interview with the author, Belfast, 7 May 2014.

14 Geraldine Taylor, interview with the author, Belfast, 14 October 2012.

15 Brian Leeson, interview with the author, Dublin, 1 February 2013.

16 *The Pensive Quill*, 'Saoradh – rebuilding the republican movement; Martin Galvin speaks to former Irish republican prisoner Packy Carty from Tyrone' (7 February 2017). http://thepensivequill.am/2017/02/saoradh-rebuilding-republican-movement.html. Accessed 24 July 2018.

17 McKearney, *The Provisional IRA*, p. 213.

18 Gerard Hodgins, interview with the author, Belfast, 13 September 2012.

19 Tommy McKearney, interview with the author, Belfast, 4 October 2012.

20 Gerard Hodgins, interview with the author, Belfast, 13 September 2012.

21 Martin Óg Meehan, interview with the author, Belfast, 12 December 2012.

22 Anthony McIntyre, interview with the author, Dublin, 3 April 2013.

23 Séamus Mallon, interview with the author, Newry, 19 January 2010.

24 Peig King, interview with the author, Dublin, 26 July 2016.

25 L. O'Neill, 'Dissident group Saoradh in pledge to "exploit" Brexit', *Belfast Telegraph* (20 November 2017). www.belfasttelegraph.co.uk. Accessed 21 November 2017.

26 Not to be confused with the 1916 Societies, the 1916 Clubs facilitate political debate around republicanism and are non-affiliated. The Clubs' Facebook page states 'the 1916 Clubs wish to ensure that the ideals of the leaders of 1916 are once more outlined, debated and expressed throughout the colleges of Ireland.' www.facebook.com/The-1916-Clubs-601754709952180/about/?ref=page_internal. Accessed 21 November 2017.

27 M. McGlinchey, 'North parties agree Brexit practicalities not strategy', *Village Magazine* (November–December 2016), pp. 30–2.

28 All quotations from this debate are taken from handwritten notes by the author, who has endeavoured to be as accurate as possible.

29 RSF assumed a pro-Brexit position.

30 The DUP, UUP and TUV were invited to partake in the debate but declined.

31 J. Manley, 'Morrison: little prospect of republicans returning to Stormont', *Irish News* (25 August 2017).

32 *Ibid.*

33 BBC, 'Martin McGuinness resigns as NI Deputy First Minister' (10 January 2017). www.bbc.co.uk/news/uk-northern-ireland-38561507. Accessed 24 July 2018.

34 For the full text of Martin McGuinness's resignation letter, see *Irish Times* (9 January 2017).

35 *Ibid.*

36 J. Gibney, 'Republicans will ask: is the north ungovernable?', *Irish News* (8 November 2017).

37 Manley, p. 8.

38 *Ibid.*

39 In 1977 McNally received a twenty-year jail sentence for causing explosions and other offences.

40 P. Deering, 'A sanctuary for Dermot', *Sligo Champion* (22 November 2017). This article details an interview with Dermot McNally regarding the recently released film on the Long Kesh escape. www.independent.ie/regionals/sligochampion/news/a-sanctuary-for-dermot-36189690.html. Accessed 22 November 2017.

41 Louise Minihan, interview with the author, Dublin, 1 February 2013.

42 Maurice Dowling, interview with the author, Tralee, 30 October 2013.

43 Francie McGuigan, interview with the author, Belfast, 24 July 2013.

44 See Cassidy, 'Organic Intellectuals", pp. 341–56.

45 Martin Óg Meehan, interview with the author, Belfast, 12 December 2012.

46 Kevin Hannaway, interview with the author, Belfast, 24 July 2013.

47 MacSwiney, *Principles of Freedom*, p. 4.

Appendix: methodology

Because of the conspiratorial, covert nature of the IRA, the regular collecting, ordering, and filing of documents has been out of the question. As little as possible was written and much was destroyed as soon as possible.

J. Bowyer Bell[1]

Accounts collected through intensive interviews and oral histories are an important source for understanding human behaviour.

Robert W. White[2]

Introduction

This book is a culmination of research into the ideology and motivations of Irish republicans who exist beyond the mainstream status quo. The aim of the research, which began in 2011, was to provide an analysis of the motivations, strategies and aspirations of what is commonly referred to as 'dissident republicanism'. With notable exceptions, including the work of Robert W. White and J. Bowyer Bell, literature in this field has been dominated by 'terrorism studies' or 'counter-terrorism studies'. This research was fundamentally different in nature from that approach, seeking to provide a theoretical and empirical understanding of non-mainstream republicans, drawing extensively on personal testimonies with republican activists (ninety in-depth qualitative interviews were conducted). While existing literature has detailed the various 'breaking points' at which the different 'dissident' organisations emerged, a significant aim of this book is to provide an insight into the experience of individuals within the Provisional Movement at these pivotal points (based on their testimonies) in order to produce a more nuanced analysis of the ideology and varied strands within radical republicanism.

Qualitative interviews

Interviews were conducted with all the 'dissident' organisations and were representative of gender and geographical location. The youngest interviewee was a nineteen-year-old Na Fianna Éireann member in Dublin and the oldest was ninety-three-year-old Billy McKee in Belfast. Interviews were conducted in the North and South of Ireland and interview locations included Belfast, Dublin, Galway, Tyrone, Armagh, Tralee, Cahersiveen, Mayo, Lurgan, Killarney, Kilkenny, Derry, Portadown, Strabane, Monaghan, Newry, Omagh, Skerries, Drogheda and Dungiven; as well as Nottingham, Birmingham and Stafford in England. Interviews were conducted with individuals at various levels in organisations, from those in leadership to local cumainn members; as well as prominent republicans and individuals who are less well known. Interviewees include individuals who are unemployed as well as those in a range of jobs, including the following: solicitors, a barrister, a taxi driver in Belfast, a retired psychiatric nurse, farmers in Galway and Tralee, elected councillors in the North and South, a teacher, a caretaker in the Catholic Church, a grave digger, construction workers, and graduates from Queen's University Belfast and Trinity College Dublin, among many others.

Significantly, the study included interviews with individuals who joined the Republican Movement at different points in time, reflecting a range of motivations and outlooks. Interviews were also conducted with a large body of 'independents', as it emerged throughout the research that independents form a significant section of the non-mainstream republican population. Interviews were also conducted with republican prisoners in Maghaberry prison, which is located outside Lisburn in the North of Ireland. In August 2013 the author undertook focus groups in Derry which included members of the 32CSM and independent republicans. The focus groups proved valuable to the research, demonstrating an exchange of views between members of different republican groups.

The study has undertaken numerous interviews with individuals who are currently labelled 'dissident republican' who have previously occupied senior leadership positions either in Sinn Féin or in the Provisional IRA; a notable example being the late Tony Catney, who occupied a position on the Northern Command of the Provisional IRA before departing the Provisional Movement and becoming a prominent member of the 1916 Societies. A further high-profile example is Kevin Hannaway, a former adjutant-general of the Provisional IRA; Hannaway's father Liam Hannaway was also a senior member of the Provisional IRA. Kevin Hannaway is now an independent republican in Belfast. Interviewees also include individuals who held leadership positions in Sinn Féin or the wider Republican Movement prior to 1986 such as Lita Campbell in RSF in Dublin (originally from Cork), Phil O'Donoghue, the honorary president of the 32CSM (who lives in Kilkenny), and Richard Behal, an independent republican in Killarney.

This book has benefited from the author's attendance at numerous republican meetings and events, which has provided insight into the organisational and social culture of radical republicanism. The author attended multiple republican commemorations, geographically spanning the North and South of Ireland; as well as the unveiling of a republican monument in Lurgan by RSF in May 2016. Additionally, the author attended seminars and Ard Fheiseanna of the various radical republican organisations. On 16 October 2013 the author attended the 'Burning of Long Kesh' seminar in Tyrone which was organised by the 1916 Societies and which included several prominent independent republican speakers. A further event which proved significant to the research was an internal mock debate which the 1916 Societies held in the Suffolk area of West Belfast in 2012. During the debate members of the Society assumed opposing sides regarding calls for a border poll, with Tony Catney arguing the Provisional Sinn Féin position. Finally, the author attended public events organised by éirígí in Belfast on the financial cuts in the North of Ireland as well as anti-internment marches in Belfast over a number of years which have encompassed members of all republican groups.

A key strength of this study is the range of interviews conducted. The large body of material amassed has enabled the extraction of themes which are of significance to radical republicanism. This work is based on the fundamental premise that the best way to understand the motivations and tactics of radical republicanism is to speak to the individuals and organisations involved. As documented by Robert W. White, 'accounts from activists offer rich, detailed information on the motives and social processes that promote recruitment and sustain activism'.[3] This research was conducted after the establishment of trust between the author and the interviewees for this book. The establishment of contacts, gatekeepers and potential interviewees took several years of trust-building; several interviews were gained through 'snowballing'.[4] Initial contacts were established through the author's attendance at republican events, as well as through the offices of radical republican groups in Belfast and Dublin.

Project problem

This research became a funded project titled 'A Theoretical and Empirical Assessment of the Membership, Strategies and Tactics of Dissident Irish Republicans' in 2012 when, subsequent to forming a research team (with Professor Jonathan Tonge at Liverpool University as the Principal Investigator; PI) the project gained funding from the Economic and Social Research Council. In August 2014 a serious problem arose concerning the research project and a book based on this research would not be complete without detailed comment. In August 2014 the author (also the researcher) first became aware of an impact statement which had been written by the PI as part of the funding application. In the impact statement the PI had written that 'the information yielded by this research project extends well beyond the academic community to [points 1–8]

… the Secretary of State for Northern Ireland, the PSNI (and security services), An Garda Síochána and MI5', among others listed. The PI subsequently stated 'The impacts listed at 1–8 will be achieved via the following: … d. Ongoing briefings as required to the organisations listed in 1–8 above.'[5] This issue came to light when the project's funding body posted the project's 'impact statement' on its website in a bid to showcase the projects which it was funding.

This impact statement was false and completely at odds with the nature and aims of the project. Until it appeared in the public domain, the author had not been aware of this impact statement which had been submitted by the PI to the ESRC. As is standard practice, such documentation does not come to the 'researcher', but is exchanged between the PI, co-investigators and the funding body. The application is also sent out for peer review. I find it imperative to state that, in my view, academic research should never be an information-gathering exercise for the security services or the state. As the researcher (and the person who initiated this research), it was distressing to learn of the contents of the impact statement, as this project was conducted to high ethical standards and in fact the project team had put in place multiple measures to protect interviewees, the research and the project team. The author was highly aware of the sensitivities associated with conducting research of this nature, particularly in the aftermath of the Boston College Project (Belfast Project).[6] As Robert W. White has commented, 'the Belfast project casts a long shadow over scholarship based on interviews with activists. Even if the questions asked are not controversial, respondents today are rightly concerned that their personal opinions might end up in the hands of the authorities. This may hinder scholarship for the foreseeable future but with time the controversy will fade.'[7]

Protections for interviewees

Highly aware of the hostile environment in which this research was being conducted, throughout the research the author did not allow any interviewee to disclose any information of an illegal nature. The author began each interview by advising the interviewee to refrain from discussing anything illegal in relation to themselves or to any other individual or organisation. From its inception, this research was not concerned with operational activities and each interviewee was informed of this fact. As interviewees can attest, the questions which were posed regarded ideology, motivations, aspirations and strategy.

Interviewees spoke about their ideology and activism without straying into illegal territory, often commenting that they would not discuss certain themes or periods, some even refusing to express an opinion on the contemporary utility of political violence. The late Brendan Madden, a member of RSF in Galway, concluded his interview with the author in 2013 by stating 'there's other things that I'm not going to go into no matter whether you ask them or not. I'm giving you the broad view. There's other things that I'm going to die with, that I don't discuss anywhere. But I think you're doing grand.'[8] Madden's strict adherence to discussing ideology and activism was the attitude adopted by all the interviewees. It became clear throughout the project that interviewees were internally weighting their concerns about giving an interview to a researcher, on the one hand, with what they often described as their 'duty' to promote the republican position and ideology, on the other hand. The author offered each interviewee a copy of their transcript to approve prior to its inclusion in this work; many requested their transcript, which they received.

As highlighted by J. Bowyer Bell, Richard English and Ed Moloney, among others, the Irish Republican Movement is authoritarian in nature, characterised by strict discipline. Stephen Hopkins has argued that 'a critical element of this perceived necessity for discipline was the requirement to maintain vigilance against the ever-present dangers of "informers" working on behalf of one or other branch of the British State's security forces (primarily either the Royal Ulster Constabulary Special Branch, or military intelligence).'[9] As demonstrated throughout this book, the Irish republican narrative and literature are littered with references to informers and agents, alongside stark warnings to remain vigilant about 'outsiders' and their motives for entering republican circles. Consequently, given the highly suspicious and insular nature of Irish republicanism, the author provided interviewees with full information about the project and transparent assurances about what information the author was collecting and how that information would be used for a book as well as articles in academic journals.

When the author became aware of the impact statement (it appeared online in August 2014 and the author's name was not on the statement), she immediately met with interviewees and explained face to face what had happened and clearly stated that Professor Tonge was no longer involved in the project. The author told interviewees that the research (which she began prior to formation of the research team) would continue but that interviewees had the right to withdraw unconditionally. A majority of the interviewees chose to remain involved, including prisoners in Maghaberry prison. Upon request, the author deleted interview recordings and destroyed transcripts, of individuals who withdrew from the project.

Why did this happen?

In July 2017 the author conducted an interview with Professor Jonathan Tonge regarding the impact statement which he had written, in an attempt to elicit an understanding of the reasons for the content of the statement. Academic work within the UK is assessed through the Research Excellence Framework (REF) which takes place approximately every seven years. The REF has put increasing emphasis on research with 'impact' and in the 2021 REF it is anticipated that impact will account for 25 per cent of the overall score attained by an institution.[10] Within a context where funding bodies seek 'research with real world impact', academics are striving to emphasise the impact of their research 'beyond academia'. Tonge has emphasised that no information was ever passed to the security services and has stated that there was never any aim to pass on information:

> My conscience is clear in terms of the intellectual design of the project in terms of what we were trying to seek research-wise. No information, no interviews were ever ever ever passed on to any other source … it's important that misunderstandings don't arise from the project. The impact statement shouldn't jeopardise the whole research area.[11]

Regarding his motivations for writing the impact statement Tonge has stated:

> I'd have been perfectly happy with this project just to have had a book at the end of it but the pressures of impact mean that you have to do more. Governments want value for money and they ultimately fund the research councils so you have to show that it's not just a book that will gather dust on the shelves. It has to have wider resonance. That's fine in a lot of cases but in more controversial ones you can see the dangers.[12]

Tonge has maintained that he was never approached by any state actors for information collected during the project and has stated that, had he been, he would not have handed over any material.

Conclusion

The impact statement, which was written by Tonge, is fundamentally at odds with the actual nature of the research project. At no point was any information passed to the security services. The author conducted all the interviews for this book and the recordings were securely stored in Belfast in the author's possession. Throughout the project, the author securely retained interviewee information in Belfast and transcripts were coded and anonymised. Tonge has stated 'I think I could name one person that was interviewed.'[13] The situation outlined above resulted in some individuals stating that the interviews should be deleted. However, the research which the author has gathered over several years provides a valuable archive of oral history regarding non-mainstream republicanism. For a number of interviewees, this project is the only time that they have ever given an interview, and three of the interviewees for this work are now deceased.

While attending a book launch in Belfast in 2015 an interviewee approached the author to inquire about the status of the book. This interviewee's two sons were killed in 1993 in Lurgan after gunmen entered his home and shot them while they were sitting on their sofa. The interviewee said to the author that he had 'poured his heart out' in the interview and that he would be angry if it was for nothing and if no book materialised. The author has also been approached by other interviewees who have stated that it would be unfair to them if the book did not proceed. This issue has illustrated the very real sensitivities associated with conducting research in this field. The author has conducted the research to the highest ethical standards and has maintained the protection of all interviewees for this study.

Notes

1   Bowyer Bell, *The Secret Army* (1990), p. 451.
2   White, 'From state terrorism to petty harassment', p. 53.
3   *Ibid.*, p. 51.
4   Snowball sampling is a research method in qualitative research where a research participant recommends a further research participant. This method is particularly valuable when researching groups or communities which are difficult to access.
5   J. Tonge, ESRC Funding Application, 2012.
6   Anthony McIntyre, 'The Belfast Project and the Boston College subpoena case', paper presented at the Oral History Network of Ireland (OHNI) Second Annual Conference in Ennis, Co. Clare, *The Pensive Quill*, 29 September 2012. http://thepensivequill.am/2012/10/the-belfast-project-and-boston-college.html. Accessed 25 July 2018.
7   White, 'From state terrorism to petty harassment', p. 53.
8   Brendan Madden, interview with the author, Galway, 4 June 2013.
9   Hopkins, 'The "informer"', p. 2.
10 See www.ref.ac.uk/about/whatref/. Accessed 25 July 2018.
11 Jonathan Tonge, interview with the author, Liverpool, 4 July 2017.
12 *Ibid.*
13 *Ibid.*

Select bibliography

Primary and internet sources

1916 Proclamation, 24 April 1916, http://cain.ulst.ac.uk/issues/politics/docs/pir24416.htm.

32CSM, 'Oration by Francie Mackey', Hunger Strike commemoration, Duleek, organised by the Duleek Hunger Strike Monument Committee, 17 September 2016, https://republican-news.org/current/news/2016/10/we_are_the_authors_of_this_str.html. 2018.

Aiken, Frank, *Éire; The Irish Nation*, Vol. 1, no. 33 (1 September 1923). Private collection.

An Phoblacht, 'North Kerry Sinn Féin condemns deceit and treachery' (February 1970).

An Phoblacht, 'Bodenstown oration by Martin McGuinness' (10 June 1973).

BBC, Speech by Martin McGuinness at Stormont after the murder of PSNI Constable Stephen Carroll in March 2009, http://news.bbc.co.uk/1/hi/northern_ireland/7934894.stm.

CAIN, text of the 162 resolution, http://cain.ulst.ac.uk/issues/politics/docs/sf/resolution162.htm.

CAIN, Ruairí Ó Brádaigh, full text of speech at 1986 Ard Fheis, http://cain.ulst.ac.uk/issues/politics/docs/sf/rob021186.htm.

CAIN, Martin McGuinness, full text of speech at 1986 Ard Fheis, http://cain.ulst.ac.uk/issues/politics/docs/sf/mmcg021186.htm.

CAIN, 'IRA statement on the ending of the Armed Campaign', 28 July 2005, www.cain.ulst.ac.uk.

CAIN, statement by church leaders on decommissioning, www.cain.ulst.ac.uk/events/peace/decommission/hgar260905.htm.

CAIN, 'The Patten report', www.cain.ulst.ac.uk.

Cairns, Eamon, *Our Sons – Our Brothers: An Account of the Murders of Gerard and Rory Cairns* (self-published).

Cairns, Eamon, *The Natives Solution: A Plan for a New Ireland For All* (self-published).

Continuity IRA, 'The voice of the republican movement', Easter Statement, *Saoirse: Irish Freedom* (April 2017).

Dáil Éireann, *Minutes of Proceedings of the First Parliament of the Republic of Ireland 1919–1921: Official Record* (Dublin, The Stationery Office, n. d. [1959]).

Faul, Denis and Murray, Raymond, 'The Hooded Men: British Torture in Ireland, August. October 1971' (Dungannon, Denis Faul, 1974).

Good Friday Agreement, www.gov.uk/government/publications/the-belfast-agreement.

IRPWA, 'August 2010 Agreement: a brief historical and political context', www.irpwa. com. For details on the Agreement see www.irsp.ie/news/?p=184.

Linenhall Library Belfast, Northern Irish Political Collection NIPC, P3394/ P3395, Hume–Adams Dialogue, 17 March 1988.

McIntyre, Anthony, 'The Belfast Project and the Boston College subpoena case', paper presented at the Oral History Network of Ireland (OHNI) Second Annual Conference in Ennis, Co. Clare, *The Pensive Quill*, 29 September 2012, www.thepensivequill. am/2012/10/the-belfast-project-and-boston-college.html.

National Library of Ireland, Sean O'Mahony papers, Brigadier James Glover, 'British Army Documents: Document 37', MS 44,296/1, November 1978.

Nolan, Paul, 'Northern Ireland Peace Monitoring Report: Number One', February 2012, http://cain.ulst.ac.uk/events/peace/docs/nipmr_2012-02.pdf. Accessed 4 July 2018.

Prevent Strategy, June 2011, www.gov.uk/government/uploads/system/uploads/attach-ment_data/file/97976/prevent-strategy-review.pdf.

PSNI, Annual PSNI chief constable's report, www.psni.police.uk/advice_information/ our-publications/chief-constables-annual-report/.

RSF, Éire Nua, https://republicansinnfein.org/rsf-policies-2/.

RSF, Saol Nua, https://republicansinnfein.org/rsf-policies-2/.

RSF archive, Des Dalton address to Ruairí Ó Brádaigh autumn school, Abbey Hotel, Co. Roscommon, 23 September 2017.

Saoradh Béal Feirste, Saoradh Facebook page, 'Lifelong republican and Saoradh Béal Feirste member Alex McCrory with an opinion piece regarding the promotion of the PSNI on West Belfast Taxi Association Vehicles', 10 February 2017. Text available at http://saoradh.ie/west-belfast-black-taxis-from-revolutionary-to-reformist-alex-mccrory-op-ed-saoradh-nuacht/. Accessed 4 July 2018.

Sinn Féin, Ard-Fheis: Clár (31 October–2 November 1986), pp. 83–5.

St Andrew's Agreement, 2006, www.legislation.gov.uk.

Terrorism Act 2000, www.legislation.gov.uk/ukpga/2000/11/contents.

The Northern Ireland (Offences) Bill, 9 November 2005, https://publications.parlia ment.uk/pa/pabills/200506/northern_ireland_offences.htm.

Secondary sources

Ambrose, Joe, *Dan Breen and the IRA* (Cork, Mercier Press, 2006).

Bean, Kevin, *The New Politics of Sinn Féin* (Liverpool, Liverpool University Press, 2007).

Beresford, David, *Ten Men Dead: The Story of the 1981 Irish Hunger Strike* (London, Hunter Publishing, 1987).

Beresford Ellis, Peter (ed.), *James Connolly: Selected Writings* (London, Pluto Press, 1997).

Bowyer Bell, J., *The Gun in Politics: An Analysis of Irish Political Conflict, 1916–1986* (New Brunswick, Transaction Publishers, 1987).

Bowyer Bell, J., *The Secret Army: The IRA 1916–1979* (Dublin, Poolbeg Press Ltd, 1990).

Bowyer Bell, J., *The Irish Troubles: A Generation of Violence, 1967–1992* (Dublin, Gill & Macmillan, 1993).

Bowyer Bell, J., *The Secret Army: The IRA 1916–1979* (Dublin, The Academy Press, 1997).

Bowyer Bell, J., *The IRA 1968–2000: Analysis of a Secret Army* (London, Frank Cass Publishers, 2000).

Bradley, Gerry and Feeney, Brian, *Insider: Gerry Bradley's Life in the IRA* (Dublin, O'Brien Press, 2009).

Carroll, Denis, *They Have Fooled You Again: Michael O'Flanagan (1876–1942): Priest, Republican, Social Critic* (Dublin, The Columba Press, 1993).

Cassidy, Kevin, 'Organic intellectuals and the committed community: Irish Republicanism and Sinn Féin in the North', *Irish Political Studies*, 20:3 (2007), pp. 341–56.

Clarke, Liam, *Broadening the Battlefield: The H Blocks and the Rise of Sinn Féin* (Dublin, Gill & Macmillan, 1987).

Collins, Eamon with McGovern, Mick, *Killing Rage* (London, Granta Books, 1998).

Connell, Joseph E.A. Jr, 'Founding of the Irish Volunteers', *History Ireland*, 21:6 (November/December 2013). www.historyireland.com/18th-19th-century-history/founding-irish-volunteers/.

Connell, Joseph E.A. Jr, 'Concessions be damned, England, we want our country!', *History Ireland*, 23:2 (March/April 2015). www.historyireland.com/volume-23/concessions-be-damned-england-we-want-our-country/.

Conway, Ciaran, *Southside Provisional: From Freedom Fighter to the Four Courts* (Dublin, Orpen Press, 2014).

Currie, P.M. and Taylor, Max, *Dissident Irish Republicanism* (London, The Continuum International Publishing Group, 2011).

De Bréadún, Deaglán, *The Far Side of Revenge: Making Peace in Northern Ireland* (Cork, The Collins Press, 2008).

Della Porta, Donatella, *Clandestine Political Violence* (New York, Cambridge University Press, 2013).

Dillon, Martin, *The Dirty War* (London, Arrow, 1991).

Doherty, Gabriel and Keogh, Dermot, *1916: The Long Revolution* (Cork, Mercier Press, 2007).

English, Richard, *Armed Struggle: The History of the IRA* (Oxford, Macmillan, 2003).

English, Richard, *Armed Struggle: The History of the IRA* (Oxford, Macmillan, 2012).

English, Richard, *Does Terrorism Work? A History* (Oxford, Oxford University Press, 2016).

Evans, Jocelyn and Tonge, Jonathan, 'Social class and party choice in Northern Ireland's ethnic blocs', *West European Politics*, 32:5 (2009), pp. 1012–30.

Fallon, Charlotte H., *Soul of Fire: A Biography of Mary MacSwiney* (Cork, Mercier Press, 1986).

Farren, Seán, *The SDLP: The Struggle for Agreement in Northern Ireland, 1970–2000* (Dublin, Four Courts Press, 2010).

Frampton, Martyn, *Legion of the Rearguard: Dissident Irish Republicanism* (Dublin, Irish Academic Press, 2011).

Gamson, William, *The Strategy of Social Protest* (Belmont, CA, Wadsworth Publishing, 1990).

Gaughan, J. Anthony, *Austin Stack: Portrait of a Separatist* (Dublin, Kingdom Books, 1977).

Gilmour, Raymond, *Infiltrating the IRA: Dead Ground: The Explosive True Story of a Special Branch Agent* (London, Little, Brown & Company, 1998).

Griffith, Kenneth and O'Grady, Timothy, *Curious Journey: An Oral History of Ireland's Unfinished Revolution* (Cork, Mercier Press, 1998).

Hanley, Brian, *The IRA: 1926–1936* (Dublin, Four Courts Press, 2002).

Hanley, Brian and Millar, Scott, *The Lost Revolution: The Story of the Official IRA and the Worker's Party* (Dublin, Penguin, 2009).

Hennessey, Thomas, *The Northern Ireland Peace Process: Ending the Troubles?* (Dublin, Gill & Macmillan, 2000).

Hickey, D.J. and Doherty, J.E., *A New Dictionary of Irish History From 1800* (Dublin, Gill & Macmillan, 2003).

Hopkins, Stephen, 'The "informer" and the political and organisational culture of the Irish republican movement: old and new interpretations', *Irish Studies Review,* 25:1 (2016) pp. 1–23.

Hopkinson, Michael, *Green Against Green: The Irish Civil War* (Dublin, Gill & Macmillan, 1988).

Hopkinson, Michael, *The Irish War of Independence* (Dublin, Gill & Macmillan, 2002).

Horgan, John, *Divided We Stand: The Strategy and Psychology of Ireland's Dissident Terrorists* (Oxford, Oxford University Press, 2013).

Ingram, Martin and Harkin, Greg, *Stakeknife: Britain's Secret Agents in Ireland* (Dublin, O'Brien Press, 2010).

Irish Political Review, 'Obituary: Ruairí Ó Brádiagh', Vol. 28, No. 7 (July 2013).

Irvin, Cynthia, *Militant Nationalism: Between Movement and Party in Ireland and the Basque Country* (Minneapolis, University of Minnesota Press, 1999).

Keane, Elizabeth, *Seán MacBride: A Life* (Dublin, Gill & Macmillan, 2007).

Khatchadourian, Haig, 'Terrorism and morality', *Journal of Applied Philosophy*, 5:2 (1988), 131–45.

Krutwig, Federico [pseud.], *Vasconia: Estudio Dialectico de una Nacionalidad* (Buenos Aires, Ediciones Norbati, 1973).

MacAtasney, Gerard, *Tom Clarke: Life, Liberty, Revolution* (Sallins, Co. Kildare, Merrion, 2013).

MacStiofáin, Seán, *Revolutionary in Ireland* (Edinburgh, Gordon Cremonesi, 1975).

MacSwiney, Terence, *Principles of Freedom* (Gloucester, Dodo Press, 2008).

Maillot, Agnés, *In the Shadow of History: Sinn Féin, 1926–70* (Manchester, Manchester University Press, 2015).

McArdle, Dorothy, *The Irish Republic* (Dublin, Irish Press Limited, 1951).

McCluskey, Fergal, *Fenians and Ribbonmen: The Development of Republican Politics in East Tyrone, 1898–1918* (Manchester, Manchester University Press, 2011).

McGartland, Martin, *Dead Man Running: The True Story of a Secret Agent's Escape from the IRA and MI5* (Edinburgh, Mainstream Publishing, 1999).

McGartland, Martin, *Fifty Dead Men Walking: The Heroic True Story of a British Secret Agent Inside the IRA* (London, John Blake Publishing Ltd, 2009).

McIntyre, Anthony, *Good Friday: The Death of Irish Republicanism* (New York, Ausubo Press, 2008).

McKearney, Tommy, *The Provisional IRA: From Insurrection to Parliament* (London, Pluto Press, 2011).

McLoughlin, Peter, *John Hume and the Revision of Irish Nationalism* (Manchester, Manchester University Press, 2010).

Moloney, Ed, *A Secret History of the IRA* (London, Penguin, 2007).

Moloney, Ed, *Voices from the Grave: Two Men's War in Ireland* (London, Faber & Faber, 2010).

Morrison, John F., *The Origins and Rise of Dissident Irish Republicanism: The Role and Impact of Organizational Splits* (London, Bloomsbury, 2013).

Murphy, Brian P., *Patrick Pearse and the Lost Republican Ideal* (Dublin, James Duffy & Co. Ltd, 1991).

Murphy, S., 'Easter ethics', in G. Doherty and D. Keogh (eds), *1916: The Long Revolution* (Cork, Mercier Press, 2007).

Murray, Gerard and Tonge, Jonathan, *Sinn Féin and the SDLP: From Alienation to Participation* (London, Palgrave Macmillan, 2005).

Nolan, Paul, 'The long, long war of dissident republicans', *Shared Space*, Issue 16 (November 2013). Published by the Community Relations Council.

Ó Brádaigh, Ruairí, *Dílseacht: The Story of Comdt. General Tom Maguire and the Second (All Ireland) Dáil* (Dublin, Irish Freedom Press, 1997).

O'Brien, Brendan, *The Long War: The IRA and Sinn Féin from Armed Struggle to Peace Talks* (Dublin, The O'Brien Press, 1995).

Ó Broin, Leon, *Revolutionary Underground: The Story of the Irish Republican Brotherhood 1858–1924* (Dublin, Gill & Macmillan, 1976).

O'Callaghan, Sean, *The Informer* (London, Bantam, 1998).

O'Doherty, Malachi, *Gerry Adams: An Unauthorised Life* (London, Bloomsbury House, 2017).

O'Farrell, Pádraic, *Who's Who in the Irish War of Independence and Civil War: 1916–1923* (Dublin, The Lilliput Press, 1997).

O'Malley, Ernie, *The Singing Flame* (Dublin, Anvil Books Ltd, 1978).

O'Rawe, Richard, *Blanketmen: An Untold Story of the H-Block Hunger-Strike* (Dublin, New Island, 2005).

O'Rawe, Richard, *Afterlives: The Hunger Strike and the Secret Offer that Changed History* (Dublin, Lilliput, 2010).

O'Sullivan, P. Michael, *Patriot Graves: Resistance in Ireland* (Chicago, Follett Publishing Company, 1972).

Powell, Jonathan, *Great Hatred, Little Room: Making Peace in Northern Ireland* (London, The Bodley Head, 2008).

Regan, John M., *The Irish Counter-revolution 1921–1936* (Dublin, Gill & Macmillan Ltd, 1999).

Shanahan, Timothy, *The Provisional Irish Republican Army and the Morality of Terrorism* (Edinburgh, Edinburgh University Press, 2009).

Sullivan, T.D., Sullivan, A.M. and Sullivan, D.B., *Speeches from the Dock* (Dublin, Gill &Macmillan, 1968).

The Earl of Longford and T.P. O'Neill, *Eamon De Valera* (London, Arrow Books, 1974).

Tonge, Jon, 'Dissidents, ultras, militarists or patriots? Analysing the strategies, tactics and support for 'dissident' republicanism'. PSA Conference, Dublin Institute of Technology (October 2010).

Tonge, Jonathan, '"No one likes us; we don't care": "dissident" Irish Republicans and mandates', *Political Quarterly*, 83:2 (April–June 2012), pp. 219–26.

White, Robert W., *Provisional Irish Republicans: An Oral and Interpretive History* (London, Greenwood Press, 1993).

White, Robert W., *Ruairí Ó Brádaigh: The Life and Politics of an Irish Revolutionary* (Bloomington, Indiana University Press, 2006).

White, Robert W., 'From state terrorism to petty harassment: a multi-method approach to understanding repression of Irish republicans', *Studi Irlandesi: A Journal of Irish Studies*, No. 7 (2017), pp. 45–64.

White, Robert W., *Out of the Ashes: An Oral History of the Provisional Irish Republican Movement* (Kildare, Merrion Press, 2017).

Whiting, Sophie, *Spoiling the Peace? The Threat of Dissident Republicans to Peace in Northern Ireland* (Manchester, Manchester University Press, 2015).

Newspapers and periodicals

An Phoblacht
Belfast Telegraph
Daily Mail
Derry Journal
Éire: The Irish Nation
History Ireland
Irish News
Irish Times
News Letter
Republican Bulletin: Iris Na Poblachta
Republican News
Saoirse: Irish Freedom
Sligo Champion
Sovereign Nation
The Guardian
United Irishman
Village Magazine

Blogs and websites

http://cain.ulst.ac.uk
http://thepensivequill.am/
https://republicansinnfein.org/
www.bbc.co.uk
www.derrynow.com

www.electionsireland.org
www.gov.uk
www.irishstatutebook.ie
www.irpwa.com
www.irsp.ie
www.legislation.gov.uk
www.politicalworld.org
www.psni.police.uk/advice_information/our-publications/chief-constables-annual-repo
    rt/ www.ref.ac.uk
www.saoradh.ie

Journals

Irish Political Review
Irish Political Studies
Irish Studies Review
Journal of Applied Philosophy
Political Quarterly
Shared Space
Studi Irlandesi: A Journal of Irish Studies
West European Politics

Index

Note: Page references in italic refer to figures.